Cruising the Mexican Riviera & Baja

A Guide to the Ships & the Ports of Call

Larry Ludmer

HUNTER

HUNTER PUBLISHING, INC.
130 Campus Drive, Edison, NJ 08818
732-225-1900; 800-255-0343; Fax 732-417-1744
www.hunterpublishing.xom

Ulysses Travel Publications
4176 Saint-Denis, Montréal, Québec
Canada H2W 2M5
514-843-9882, ext. 2232; Fax 514-843-9448

The Boundary, Wheatley Road, Garsington
Oxford, OX44 9EJ England
01865-361122; Fax 01865-361133

Printed in the United States

ISBN 1-58843-511-3

© 2005 Larry H. Ludmer

Cover & back cover images: Cabo San Lucas
(Bruce Herman, Mexico Tourism Board)
All other color images: Mexico Tourism Board
Maps by Kim André © 2005 Hunter Publishing

1   2   3

Acknowledgments

The seemingly simple task of compiling the facts about cruise lines, their ships, and destinations for presentation to the reader has become more and more difficult because of the sheer volume of choices. Any travel writer who wants to do the best for his readers must seek out the assistance of others to help amass this information. Ship facts and details on which ships have been assigned to cruising Mexican Riviera and Baja routes were provided by the media relations staff of the cruise lines. It is important to note, however, that their role in providing information and/or services to me in no way affects what I have to say about a particular cruise line or ship. Having said that, I am still especially grateful to and would like to acknowledge the special help and consideration that has been provided to me by Tori Benson and Susanne Ferrull of Princess Cruises; Susan Beresford of Holland America; Jaye Hilton of Royal Caribbean; Elizabeth Jakeway of Celebrity Cruises; Heather Krasnow of Norwegian Cruise Line; and Irene Lui of Carnival Cruises. All opinions expressed here are based on information gathered from a variety of objective sources and, most importantly, by firsthand experience.

Preface

This book is intended to serve as an information source for planning a cruise to Mexico's Pacific coast, as well as a companion to take with you on land while exploring this fascinating and beautiful country. It will enable both the first-time and experienced cruise traveler to select a cruise that's right for them and, once the trip has begun, to get the most enjoyment from their time both onboard ship and while ashore.

Experienced travelers rarely get their information from one source, and I wouldn't expect that you would so limit yourself. Because the port information offered in this book is geared to the general traveler with only a single day available, you should do further research for any port of call that is of particular or special interest to you. Obtaining a guidebook on that place would be the logical next step.

As you peruse this book you'll learn that there are many cruise lines offering service to the Mexican Riviera and Baja. I strongly encourage you to visit your local travel agent and grab a stack of cruise brochures. In combination with the information in this book, they will further help you to decide which ship and itinerary is right for you. Always remember, however, that those glossy brochures are carefully designed by slick marketing experts to get your business. Be a thoughtful consumer.

Enjoy your cruise vacation to sunny Mexico!

Contents

Contents

Maps

Introduction

Cruise Popularity

*I*t wasn't very long ago that cruising was an activity almost exclusively limited to people with lots of money to spend on their leisure time. While the number of people taking cruises has seen growth that is nothing short of spectacular over the past decade, it seems that a lot of people still think cruising is for the rich and famous. Studies done by the cruise industry indicate that only about three percent of Americans have ever taken a cruise. If, after reading this book, you become one of the travelers who starts working that figure toward four percent or higher, then my objective will have been fulfilled.

Cruising represents one of the fastest-growing segments of the travel industry, a trend that has continued to gain momentum in recent years. Preliminary figures show that during 2003 about 9½ million people worldwide took a cruise. By far the largest segment of the cruising public resides in the United States. Although the figures aren't yet available, the total number of cruisers was expected to take a huge leap – all the way to 10½ million – for 2004. In fact, annual increases in the range of 15 to 20% are anticipated over the next few years. Although the Caribbean market dwarfs all other cruise market segments (in 2003 it represented more than 40% of all North American cruise passengers), cruising to the west coast of Mexico has become a significant chunk of the market. During the same period a total of almost 650,000 people embarked on one of 356 cruises headed to the Mexican

Riviera and Baja. That figure does not count passengers on Panama Canal itineraries and the sizable number of Caribbean-cruise passengers who visited one or more of Mexico's east-coast ports of call. The western Mexico count represented an increase of 11% over the previous year. Given the continued increases in both the number and size of ships on Mexican routes planned, it wouldn't be surprising for double-digit increases, or even larger, to remain the norm over the next several years.

There are many reasons why cruising has become so popular. Certainly one of the biggest factors is that today's ships offer excellent value for whatever level of luxury your budget will bear. Cost factors will be explored in more detail later, but suffice it to say that a typical week-long cruise to Mexico will cost you considerably less than the same period of time at a good resort hotel, when all of the expenses are calculated. Other things that attract people to cruising are the variety of activities available on these floating resorts, the fact that it is a comprehensive all-in-one vacation, and the romance and luxury associated with the cruising experience. The ability to see several different and often exotic ports of call in a single vacation is also, no doubt, a draw. And, if you let the cruise line handle your shore activities, they present little of the hassle and uncertainty that can often accompany foreign travel.

What's Included

Mexico is a large country and almost all of its vast interior will be beyond the cruise passenger's reach. But the coastline is also too large to see for a single voyage of a week or even two. This book primarily describes the ports of call between the various California ports of embarkation and Acapulco, all of which are on Mexico's Pacific side. This encompasses the peninsula of **Baja California** and the stretch of mainland coast from Mazatlán south to Acapulco known as the **Mexican Riviera**. (Although there isn't any "official" designation of what the limits of the Riviera are, it is commonly considered to extend as far south as the Bahías de Huatulco, but only cruises through the Panama Canal call on this area so, for purposes of this book, Acapulco is the logical southern terminus.) Also included is a description of Catalina Island, a surprisingly exotic destination just off the coast of Los Angeles. See page 269 for additional information concerning cruises to other Mexican ports south of Acapulco, as well as the Panama Canal and ports in Central America. The Caribbean side of Mexico (on the Yucatán Peninsula) is also an important cruise market but, because of the distance between Mexico's Pacific and Caribbean coasts, there are no cruises that do both. If you are interested in visiting the Yucatán's many interesting destinations, then get a hold of one of my other books from Hunter Publishing, namely *Cruising the Caribbean: The Southern & Western Ports of Call*.

A Brief Survey of Mexico

*A*ny trip to a foreign country will be enhanced if you have some knowledge of that nation's history, land and people.

MEXICO FACTS

▶ **Official Name:** Estados Unidos Mexicanos (United Mexican States).

▶ **Area:** About 761,604 square miles, making it the 14th-largest country in the world.

▶ **Population:** 103 million (2004 estimate), the 11th-most-populous nation in the world.

▶ **Population Density:** 137 per square mile (US = 80 per square mile).

▶ **Highest Point:** Pico de Orizaba, an extinct volcanic peak, is 18,555 feet high.

▶ **Lowest Point:** 43 feet below sea level near Mexicali in Baja California.

▶ **Number of States:** 31, plus the Federal District.

▶ **Language:** Spanish is the official language, but many Indian languages are also spoken.

▶ **Major Industries:** Oil, mining, electronics, auto manufacturing textiles, and tourism.

▶ **Major Agricultural Crops:** Cotton, coffee, wheat, rice, beans and soybeans.

▶ **Tourism Industry:** Approximately $8 billion per year.

Geographically Speaking

Mexico covers an area roughly one-fourth the size of the Lower 48 United States. Although largely mountainous, the topography is extremely diverse, ranging from desert to rain forest and from swampy lowlands to soaring mountain peaks. Let's take a closer look at the regions of Mexico that are covered in this book.

Baja

The Baja California Peninsula, which on a map looks like the tail of a large animal, measures about 800 miles from north to south, but it is only between 30 and 120 miles wide. Because of its many indentations and bays, the jagged coastline is more than 2,000 miles long. The Pacific coast on the peninsula's western side and the Gulf of California coast on the east both have very narrow lowland areas. The Gulf of California separates the peninsula from the Mexican mainland and was originally known as the **Sea of Cortés**. Although Americans always refer to it as the Gulf of California, the other moniker is used more frequently while in Mexico and especially in Baja. Thus, I will call it the Sea of Cortés throughout this book. The northern border of the peninsula is contiguous with California from San Diego/Tijuana on the west to just across from Yuma, Arizona on the east at the Colorado River. The river empties into the Sea of Cortés. The approximately 50-mile stretch of land between the US border and the Colorado's mouth is the only part of Baja that actually abuts the mainland of Mexico.

The dominant features of Baja are its two mountain ranges. The **Sierra de San Pedro Mártir** is in the northern part of the peninsula and boasts 10,073-foot Picacho del Diablo (Devil's Peak), the highest point in Baja. The southern portion of Baja is comprised mostly of the **Sierra de la Giganta**. Both of these ranges are an extension of California's coastal mountain system.

Baja has a varied flora. Many varieties of cactus can be found throughout the peninsula. Because of Baja's relative geographic isolation, it is home to some plant species that are not found anywhere else in the world.

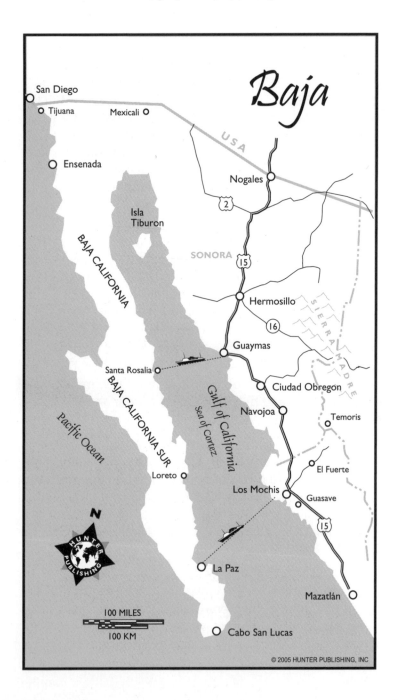

The most northerly section of Baja has a climate similar to that of Southern California – moderate temperatures and not a great deal of rain. The rain that does occur is almost entirely during the winter. The middle of Baja is extremely dry and hot. Summer temperatures in the lowlands in excess of 115° are not at all uncommon. The southern portion of the peninsula is semi-arid and not quite so hot as the central area. Much of its rain is associated with tropical storms. These same storms are sometimes also responsible for the rare drenching rains that occur in the drier central region.

Mexican Riviera

The Riviera doesn't have any "official" borders, but it is generally considered to extend from Mazatlán to the Bahías de Huatulco, a total distance of about 1,100 miles of coast, more than five times the length of the world-famous French Riviera. Most of the major resorts (and ports of call) are located in the 700-mile-long section between Mazatlán and Acapulco. There is almost no coastal plain to speak of along here because two massive mountain chains begin immediately behind the many bays that dot the Mexican Riviera. These are the **Sierra Madre Occidental** in the northern part of the Riviera and the **Sierra Madre del Sur**, beginning around Manzanillo. The mountains are generally farthest from the shore in the northern part of the Riviera.

Despite the impressive backdrop provided by the Sierras, it is the countless bays that have made the Mexican Riviera what it is today – one of the world's foremost resort destinations. The bays range from small and picturesque to large and beautiful. The sheltered bay waters provide good anchorage for boats and, thus, the development of port cities and towns. Recreation and tourism soon followed. The entire Riviera lies in tropical to semi-tropical climatic zones. Usually, cooler temperatures are limited to the higher elevations in this part of Mexico, but the Pacific Ocean breezes and currents make for generally more comfortable conditions. On the other hand, it is these same factors that bring the region's heavy summer and early autumn rainfall.

A Brief History

*T*here is no easy way to condense Mexico's history into a short space. It is a fascinating chronicle that is worth reading about. If this introduction whets your appetite to learn more, I suggest that you get a good Mexican history book from your local library. "Turbulent" is, perhaps, the best word to characterize the history of Mexico.

Well before the arrival of the Europeans (and at a time when Western civilization was not anything to boast about), the land we now call Mexico was the home of several advanced civilizations. The **Maya** occupied the Yucatán peninsula and had developed a complex society with impressive architecture and an advanced calendar. In central Mexico the previously powerful **Toltec** civilization had been superseded by the warlike **Aztecs**, who had arrived from the north (perhaps from what is now the United States). The Aztecs founded the great city of Tenochtitlan in 1325. It was eventually to become Mexico City.

The **Spanish** explorer and conquistador **Hernán Cortés** landed with a small force off the eastern coast of Mexico in 1519. Through diplomacy, wise use of an Indian interpreter who became his mistress, and alliances with Indian tribes who wished to be free of Aztec domination, Cortés managed to depose the Aztec emperor Moctezuma and bring down the mighty Aztec empire in less than three years. Part of this was due to the poor judgment of the emperor, who put too much faith in the Aztec legend of a light-skinned feathered god who was destined to return one day and rule Mexico.

Three centuries of oppressive Spanish rule eventually boiled over among the native population (which was reduced to virtual servitude and decimated by invader-borne illnesses). Almost as disenchanted with the situation were the Europeans and mixed-blood residents who were born in Mexico but were considered second-class to those who were born in Spain. The revolution known in Mexico as the **War of Independence** began in 1810 under the leadership of Father **Miguel Hidalgo y Costilla**. Hidalgo was eventually captured and executed by the Spaniards, but others took up the cause. In 1821 independence was declared and General Agustín Iturbide made himself emperor. However, this didn't go over well with the Mexican people and a republican form of government was instituted two years later. At that time Mexican territory covered a huge portion of what is now the southwestern United States, including Texas. The war for Texas independence was the beginning of a long period of hostile relations with America that culminated in the **Mexican War**, which lasted from 1846 through 1848 and ended with the fall of Mexico City. By terms of the peace agreement, Mexico ceded all of its land north of the Rio Grande (called the Rio Bravo by Mexicans) to the United States.

Mexico's class-dominated society continued to hold back the country's economic and social progress. Some reforms were instituted, mainly under the leadership of Benito Juárez, a Zapotec Indian of peasant origin. Well-educated, Juárez became an attorney and entered politics. He became president in 1858. To this day the memory of Juárez is celebrated in Mexico. Despite the work of Juárez and others, instability remained the hallmark of the Mexican government. This was of concern to the United States as well as numerous European powers who had financial interests in the country.

There was a brief interlude of **French** rule under **Maximillian**, who was designated by Napoleon III as Emperor of Mexico. He and his wife, Empress Carlota, were finally executed by Mexican patriots. Juárez was restored to the presidency but he died in 1872. This was followed by many years of dictatorial rule under **Porfirio Diaz**, who was in charge from 1876 through 1911, except for about four years. To his credit, Diaz did manage to usher in some reforms and instituted policies to modernize the country. However, his rule was extremely oppressive.

Opposition to Diaz by a number of his former allies and others began a new era of violence and civil war that included such popular figures as Pancho Villa, Francisco Madero, Venustiano Carranza and Alvaro Obregón. The violence did not end, despite the promulgation of a new constitution on February 5, 1917. Eventually, control of the government (a democracy, in theory) passed to the hands of the **Institutional Revolutionary Party (PRI)** who were at least able to achieve a degree of stability. They dominated all politics in the country from 1929 until the late 1990s. Demands for reform from the United States and within Mexico itself had been increasing dramatically through the '80s and '90s. This was accelerated by several economic and financial crises in the 1980s.

The PRI's dominance finally ended in 1994 when a non-PRI candidate became mayor of Mexico City, considered to be the second-most powerful position in the country after the president. Only a few years later, Vicente Fox, leader of the opposition **National Action Party (PAN)**, wrested the presidency from the PRI at the end of 2000. Fox has promised a great deal of reform but has had difficulty implementing his policies due to opposition in the legislature as well as the entrenched and all-too-often corrupt Mexican bureaucracy. He is not eligible to run for re-election in 2006 although it appears his wife may be a candidate.

Introduction

The 21st century has brought with it the hope of a new Mexico but one that still faces many economic, social and political challenges. Much progress has been made, but the wide disparity of income, pains of modernization and privatization, corruption and crime, and even limited insurgencies by native groups in isolated parts of the country are all long-term issues that need to be addressed. They will probably remain for some time to come.

People & Culture

*T*he population of Mexico is quite diverse, although it can be divided into three major groups. Direct ancestors of the original **Indian tribes** that inhabited pre-Colombian Mexico comprise a little less than 20% of the total. This covers a broad swath of cultures numbering more than 50 distinct tribes, including Maya, Tarhumara, Nahua and Zapotec. Most of these live in the interior. The only significant indigenous group found along the central Pacific coast is the Tarasco. Anthropologists and ethnologists refer to the indigenous (*Indigenas* in Spanish) as Amerindians. Descendants of Spaniards account for approximately 10% of the population and, for the most part, represent the upper classes, both economically and politically. The single largest group are the **Mestizos** (almost 70% of the population) who have mixed Amerindian and European backgrounds. Other groups comprise only about one percent of the population.

Beyond the numbers, categorizing a country's social and cultural characteristics is a task where too many travel guides are forced to generalize. I won't attempt to do that because it has the effect of stereotyping a hundred million people in order to make them fit into a neat little box. So, what can be accurately said about the people?

Language

First, the predominant language is Spanish (unlike the Castillian of Spain or the Puerto Rican dialect known to people from the eastern United States but understandable by all). However, there are about 50 native dialects in several major Amerindian language groups. For some this dialect is a second language, but the remote parts of the country house a substantial population that speaks little or no Spanish.

Religion

The country's cultural history and the Roman Catholic church (to which most of the population belongs) insure the importance of family and a degree of social conservatism. But this has been breaking down in recent years, especially in Mexico City and other large urban areas. Despite the influence of Roman Catholicism, native customs have worked their way into everything from the countless *fiestas* celebrated by the people to the reverence displayed towards deceased family members in the "Day of the Dead" ceremonies and practices.

Social Classes

Until recently Mexico's population was growing at an annual rate of more than 3%. This has now declined to about 1½%, a direct consequence of the rise of a larger middle class and a trend toward more women in the workplace. Mexico is a society with vast differences in wealth and, although there are many exceptions, wealth is directly related to which population group a person is part of. As previously indicated, the ethnic Spanish dominate the upper classes and have influential positions in government and private business. The Mestizos, being the largest group, do cut across all sectors, but they form most of Mexico's middle working class. The still mostly rural and sometimes isolated Amerindians are usually poor, sometimes to an extent seen only in the poorest nations of Africa or Asia. Still fiercely independent in many cases, they are largely a disenfranchised group prone to support their own leaders rather than the central Mexican government.

THE YANKS ARE STAYING

Everyone is aware of the millions of Mexicans who make the United States their home, either legally or otherwise. This is nothing new, of course, as people of Mexican ancestry occupied the greater portion of the American Southwest well before the arrival of settlers form the eastern United States. But many Americans have chosen to make Mexico their permanent residence. In fact, about 1.1 million Americans currently reside in Mexico, more than in any other foreign country. A significant number of these people are retirees who find their incomes go a lot further south of the border, making them part of the economic upper class, rather than middle class back home. A smaller group were already wealthy individuals who have found the climate and surroundings much to their liking.

The American expatriate community has, for the most part, not blended in with the Mexican population. Rather, they congregate in certain areas and have made their own "little America." Among the better-known areas of this type is the so-called *Gringo Gulch* in Puerto Vallarta.

The Cruise Lines & Ships

*W*hile there are fewer cruise lines and ships sailing the Pacific coast of Mexico than the Caribbean, the choice is still extensive and is growing each year. Until recently, the Mexican Riviera and Baja were step-children as far as the types of ships utilized on these itineraries were concerned. The newest, biggest and best ships were almost always sent to the Caribbean or even Alaska, but not to western Mexico. This began to change a couple of years ago and now several cruise operators have added top-of-the-line vessels on these routes. The number of ships has also increased, as has the average size of the vessels. This increased capacity is likely to mean heavy competition and good prices for the consumer for several years to come. In addition, those lines that haven't up-graded their Mexican fleet will likely have to do so in or-der to compete, since many cruise travelers want to sail on the latest and greatest ships. Still smaller and more traditional vessels can still be found on Mexican routes, for those who prefer them.

Types of Cruises

*C*ruises to Baja and the Mexican Riviera can be classi-fied in two major ways – by their destination or their duration.

Destination

*T*he typical cruise from southern California includes one port on the Baja Peninsula (almost invariably Cabo San Lucas) and usually two on the Riviera. There are also cruises that concentrate solely on one or the other. Cruises that sail only along the Mexican Riviera are usually one-way trips, either embarking or disembarking at Acapulco at one end, with the other gateway port in California. Some one-way itineraries begin from farther away than southern California – in San Francisco for example. However, most of the cruises are round-trips from either Los Angeles or San Diego. Many cruises that originate in Florida or Puerto Rico traverse the Panama Canal and then cruise up along the entire Pacific coast of Mexico before typically ending in California. Some of these are year-round but the majority are "repositioning" cruises that are designed to eventually get ships to Alaska for the summer season. Repositioning cruises can often be had at much lower rates for cruises of comparable length in seasonal or year-round markets.

Duration

*W*hile the typical Baja-Mexican Riviera "combination" cruise is one week long (seven nights) and runs from Saturday to Saturday or Sunday to Sunday, there are other cruises both longer and shorter. There are both three-day and four-day cruises from Los Angeles or San Diego that go only as far south as Baja's Ensenada. The four-day cruises include a port call at Catalina Island, while the three-day versions do not. Cruises of anywhere from eight to 14 nights are also available and these typically stop at a greater number of ports along the Mexican Riviera and Baja. Itineraries originating in San Francisco or other ports farther from southern California can be anywhere from seven to 11 nights. Panama Canal cruises with Mexican ports of call can run from 11 to 16 nights.

Style

A third possible means of classification is by the *style* of cruise. This involves the degree of luxury and the degree of formality. The mass market lines don't vary a great deal in this regard. It's only when you get into the upscale lines such as Crystal that there is a significant difference. Read more about this on page 66ff.

Cruise Lines with Baja & Mexican Riviera Itineraries

T he primary cruise lines operating in Baja and the Mexican Riviera are Carnival, Celebrity, Holland America, Norwegian, Princess and Royal Caribbean. This list includes the biggest cruise lines in the industry, names almost all American travelers are familiar with. Carnival and Royal Caribbean are the only lines that offer three- and four-night Baja cruises year-round. They, along with the four other lines, also offer itineraries covering the Mexican Riviera from the fall through the spring and lasting a minimum of one week. All six lines have trans-Panama Canal cruises. Sometimes these are offered on a regular basis, but in many cases they are repositioning cruises, with one departure per ship in each direction annually. Complete details on these lines and their ships, along with some information on other operators, is given in the section that follows. For other cruise lines serving Mexico, see page 66.

The Mass Market Lines & Their Ships

The term "mass market" isn't meant to be derogatory in any sense. It simply means that these cruise lines appeal to the broadest section of the traveling public because they offer choice and luxury at an affordable price. They are also the lines that have the most ships in service on Mexican routes. The largest lines are innovative in terms of onboard activities and services and are also known for having many new ships, including some of the largest that can be found operating in any part of the world. Each of the major lines will be profiled in depth prior to a ship-by-ship description of their vessels. Only those ships serving the Mexican Riviera and Baja will be fully described. Vessels visiting Mexico via trans-Panama Canal itineraries only will have more limited descriptions.

Some things apply to all ships of a given cruise line. For example, cuisine and entertainment policy won't vary much at all from one ship to another on the same line. Thus, general information that is given in the cruise line profile won't be repeated in the individual ship descriptions unless it significantly differs in some way.

Statistical information for the cruise lines and individual ships is mostly self-explanatory. However, a few items should be clarified. The number of ships shown under the *Fleet* heading is the total vessels in service as of January,

2005. This includes all of the ships of that line and isn't limited to the number serving the Mexican Riviera and Baja. The figure for *Under Construction* includes projects currently in the shipyards and firm order commitments. Individual ship description details are listed below.

Year Built: The year of the ship's maiden voyage. The year of any major refurbishment will be indicated in brackets for any ship built in 1995 or earlier.

Passengers: Indicates the number of passengers the ship will carry based on double occupancy of all staterooms. I use this basis because it is the most commonly accepted method in the cruise industry. You might well see other numbers given in various sources of information on any particular ship. These may include additional persons in the rooms. A ship that is fully booked will almost certainly be carrying far more people than the double occupancy figure.

Passenger/Crew Ratio: The number of passengers divided by the number of crew members, expressed as a ratio, such as 2.4:1. In theory, the lower the number, the better the service. While the luxury lines are the only ones that have ratios of less than 2:1, I have yet to find any reliable correlation to minor variances in the ratio. I have been on ships with a 2.7:1 ratio where the service was better than on a ship with a 2.2:1 ratio. The ratio is a general indication of service only.

Stateroom Size: Rooms on ships are a lot smaller than what you will find in a hotel, or even in most inexpensive motels for that matter. This is important to keep in mind if you have never sailed before. The measurements are in square feet and the range shows the smallest to the largest accommodation, including suites. Measurements are for the room only – that is, they do not include the balcony in cases where one exists.

Cruise Lines & Ships

Space Ratio: A measure of how "roomy" the ship is. It is calculated by dividing the Gross Registered Tonnage by the number of passengers. The higher the number, the more space you have per passenger, at least in theory. Some cruise experts consider this figure almost as gospel. While I agree that it does provide some indication of available space, there is no way to mathematically account for the "feel" the ship has. The design layout (including traffic flow) is a more important indicator of how much space you have than a simple number. Take this figure with a grain of salt. Extremely low space ratios, however, should be a warning.

One fact that I've deliberately omitted for each ship or line is the nationality of the crew (that is, non-officers). Although in the past it was the norm for each line to draw its crew from mainly one national or ethnic group, this is no longer the standard practice. It is not uncommon for crew members who directly serve passengers to encompass 40 or more different nationalities. In effect, every ship is a United Nations and that adds a lot of flavor to your experience. A few lines still emphasize one or two nationalities. Holland America crews, for instance, are dominated by Indonesian or Filipino men and women.

CARNIVAL CRUISE LINES
☎ (800) 227-6482
www.carnival.com
Officers: Bridge officers are Italian, but others may be international.
Ships' Registry: The Bahamas for most of the fleet, but a few ships are registered in Panama.
Fleet: 21 ships; 1 under construction.

The world's largest cruise line has played a major role in making cruising affordable. While Princess' "Love Boats" caught the imagination of the public on television back in the 1960s, it was the newly established Carnival line that introduced more new ships and more ideas back then. Then and now they offer excellent value and a casual, mostly informal experience on their self-proclaimed "fun ships." The entire Carnival fleet features a striking all-white exterior, except for the mostly red-and-blue Carnival logo and their distinctive funnel – which is shaped like the tail of a jet airplane. This feature adds a graceful flair to all of their ships. One of the most notable features of any Carnival cruise ship is its large main showroom, which puts an emphasis on lavish Vegas-style entertainment. Glitz is evident in more than just the production shows. Interior décor places an emphasis on eye-popping features and tries to dazzle you with the "wow" factor. This is especially true in Carnival's famous large atriums and the public areas surrounding them. Those who prefer a more refined atmosphere may need sunglasses! Activities are geared much more toward the fun side than to cultural enrichment. In fact, entertainment is so important at Carnival that toward the end of dinner in the main dining room your waitstaff will put on a brief song and dance act that differs each night of the cruise – it's a lot of fun and many passengers get involved.

Speaking of dinner, Carnival vessels offer a wide variety of dining choices and their newest ships even have elegant supper clubs. Although Carnival doesn't break much culinary ground, they always provide excellent meals that are colorfully presented by a friendly waitstaff and that get high marks from most passengers. You won't, however, get the white glove treatment. The buffets are excellent and feature many stations, including an excellent deli on their larger and newer vessels. Midnight buffets are big at Carnival but their once-per-cruise Midnight Gala Buffet is an experience to remember. Concentrating on sweets, it's such a visual spectacle that guests are invited to view it an hour before it opens just for picture-taking! Carnival's handling of the Captain's cocktail reception is

Cruise Lines & Ships

also something special, as practically an entire deck becomes a walk-through feast of hors d'oeuvres and colorful exotic drinks. A 24-hour pizzeria and ice-cream bar are other popular features with ever-hungry cruise passengers. Children's activities and facilities are always extensive but the bigger the ship, the more it has.

In general, Carnival provides a cruising experience that is equally good for couples and families with children. Carnival is one of the great innovators and was a pioneer in the mega-ship category for contemporary cruising.

⚓ *Carnival Pride/Carnival Spirit*

Year Built: 2002/2001
Gross Tonnage: 88,500
Length: 963 feet
Beam: 106 feet
Passengers: 2,124
Passenger Decks: 12
Crew Size: 930
Passenger/Crew Ratio: 2.3:1
Stateroom Size: 160-388 sq ft
Space Ratio: 41.7

Carnival Pride

The *Spirit*-class vessels are no longer Carnival's largest, but I still give them the nod as the most beautiful ships in what is a fabulous fleet. (The larger *Conquest*-class is not represented in Carnival's Mexican itineraries.) The public facilities and layout of these two ships are the same, although the décor varies. The description that follows applies to the even more gorgeous interior details found on the *Pride* because the *Spirit* visits Mexico somewhat less frequently. The *Pride* features one of the most spectacular décors of any ship on the high seas. Ornate and opulent, even by Carnival standards, the primary theme is the art of the Renaissance and nowhere is this more in evidence than in the eight-deck-high atrium with its fabulous murals. The main showroom is a three-deck affair with the look and feel of an elegant European opera house. There are many other lounges and entertainment facilities of varying sizes.

The two-level main dining room is simply gorgeous. However, because of its size some people might feel that the noise level is too high. Aside from the buffet, alternative dining takes the form

Carnival Spirit-class stateroom

of the extra-fee **David's Supper Club.** Located high atop the ship and connected to the Lido deck by a glass staircase suspended above the atrium (those prone to vertigo might wish to take the elevator or inside stairs to get there), the centerpiece is a full-sized replica of Michaelangelo's masterpiece. The angled and rose-colored glass ceiling over the club lends a special atmosphere during the day. The glass dome, by the way, appears to be part of the funnel from the outside. If you go up to the very top of the ship on the outside, you can look down into the club!

A two-level disco, wedding chapel and a gently curving "shopping street" are other important public areas. Although the promenade doesn't wrap around the entire outside of the ship (at the bow end), it is wrap-around if you go inside and walk through the exotically decorated **Sunset Garden**. This beautiful spot isn't used by a lot of people so it provides a nice place to get away from it all for a drink or just to relax. The *Pride* has plenty of recreational facilities, including its two large main pools, water slide, gymnasium and full-service spa.

Accommodations are also excellent as even the smallest rooms are fairly spacious by cruise ship standards. The décor is pleasant and the functionality is just fine. If you've been on other Carnival ships, you'll notice a similarity in style, with the probable major difference being that these rooms are larger than on older Carnival vessels. Except for a few somewhat smaller cabins, the interior rooms are generally the same size as outside rooms minus the balcony. This makes them an especially good value. The majority of outside rooms do have private balconies.

David's Supper Club, Carnival Pride

⚓ *Paradise*

Year Built: 1998
Gross Tonnage: 70,367
Length: 855 feet
Beam: 103 feet
Passengers: 2,052
Passenger Decks: 10
Crew Size: 920
Passenger/Crew Ratio: 2.2:1
Stateroom Size: 173-410 sq ft
Space Ratio: 34.3

Paradise is one of eight sisters in the Fantasy class, making it the largest class of ships regardless of line. This class, along with the original "Love Boat" from Princess, is responsible to a large degree for the popularity of cruising. The Fantasy-class ships ushered in a new era of both size (i.e., more facilities) and glitzy luxury that appeals to so many people. *Paradise* was the last ship of its class that was built so it's quite a bit younger than many other Fantasy-class vessels. Some readers with past cruise experience may remember that it was once a totally non-smoking ship, the only one if its kind in the world of cruising. However, that practice has ended and it now has the same smoking restrictions as any other ship in the fleet. Serving the three- and four-day runs, *Paradise* traded places with the *Ecstasy*, which had been on this route for many years.

The ship generally has an easy-to-navigate layout of public rooms, which begins four decks above the lowest deck with cabins. An attractive and glitzy atrium rises five decks and provides a focal point for most public areas. There are two dining rooms separated from one another by the galley. This arrangement means each room is somewhat more intimate than if they had been combined into a single room. The dining room at the stern can be the most confusing part of the ship to get to since you have to use the stern elevators or stairs – no access is available from the front section of the deck it's on. *Paradise* has a very attractive two-level main theater, as well as many col-

Carnival Paradise

orful bars and lounges concentrated on the Promenade Deck. The piano bar adjacent to the aft lounge is a beautiful spot to relax. As far as other facilities go, *Paradise* has all of the usual things one would expect on a large ship, but sometimes on a smaller scale. The sports deck has excellent gym and spa facilities, along with a jogging track on the very top public deck.

Normandie show lounge on Carnival Paradise

Accommodations are quite spacious (a common strength on most Carnival vessels). While standard staterooms aren't luxurious, you'll find pleasant color schemes and a well-planned layout. Corridors on stateroom decks tend to be long and straight, which means you shouldn't have much trouble locating your room when you come back late at night!

CELEBRITY CRUISES

☎ (800) 437-3111
www.celebritycruises.com
Officers: Greek
Ships' Registry: Liberia, except for *Mercury*, which is registered in Panama
Fleet: 9 ships

Celebrity's ships, like most other cruise line fleets, have certain distinguishing exterior characteristics that make them easily recognizable. Their vessels feature a mostly white upper superstructure with large broad bands of dark blue across the bottom section of the hull and additional blue trim on the superstructure. Their hallmark funnels are marked with a slanted huge white letter "X." The overall effect may not be as beautiful as the more common all-white exterior, but there is no denying that Celebrity vessels are both striking and sleek.

Celebrity is perhaps best known for its outstanding level of service. It is consistently rated as one of the best cruise lines in the world by experienced cruisers. This shouldn't come as a surprise when you consider that Celebrity ships have 300 to 600 fewer passengers than ships of equal size on many other mass market lines. The cruise experience on Celebrity is refined. There are sommeliers to help you choose the right wine, wine classes, cooking workshops, lectures on many interesting topics, as well as educational programs concerning the area of the world you're visiting. Beautiful works of art from the masters to modern grace all Celebrity vessels.

Excellent cuisine is certainly another Celebrity hallmark, and the sophistication of the food preparation, presentation and service is higher than most of the mass-market lines. Dining flexibility is not as great as on some lines because many of the ships aren't as large, although it varies quite a bit from one ship to another. Their larger ships offer plenty of choices, while the smaller ones do not. The **Cova Café Milano** is a wonderful feature of all their vessels. Here you can select from a wide variety of specialty coffees while treating yourself to a delectable European pastry. All Celebrity ships have the usual array of amenities and facilities, but their **AquaSpa by Elemis** is a Celebrity feature that warrants special attention. Their spa facilities may well be the best anywhere on the sea and, in addition to the usual exercise equipment and beauty treatments, they have sauna, steam, aroma-therapy and other goodies for those who appreciate the finer things. Gymnasium patrons can even avail themselves of a certified personal trainer.

Celebrity caters to adults, but they have incorporated additional facilities for children in order to extend the appeal of Celebrity beyond just couples. These facilities are sometimes divided into four age groups (during peak sailing periods) but most of the time all children are grouped together regardless of age. Celebrity offers "adults only" (minimum age of 21) cruises to most of its destinations, including Mexico. There are limited sailing dates for these trips.

Celebrity's Infinity Grand Foyer

You'll find first-rate accommodations throughout the fleet, featuring tastefully appointed rooms that are generally larger than industry averages. Finer quality towels, robes and linens are standard. "Concierge Class" is an upgraded status where you get little extras. However, the added cost isn't justified, in my opinion, since the room size is the same. Once you get into the suite category on Celebrity, the extra luxuries offered really start to pile up.

⚓ *Infinity/Summit*

Year Built: 2000/2001
Gross Tonnage: 91,000
Length: 965 feet
Beam: 106 feet
Passengers: 1,950
Passenger Decks: 11
Crew Size: 1,000
Passenger/Crew Ratio: 1.9:1
Stateroom Size: 170-1,432 sq ft
Space Ratio: 46.7

Infinity Aquaspa

Trans-Panama Canal itineraries only. Along with its sister ships of the Millennium class, these are the largest vessels in the Celebrity fleet and it shows that a mega-sized ship and top-notch quality are not conflicting concepts. While Celebrity has always been known for its fine and elegant facilities, it takes a ship of this size to offer the full range of activities that today's cruise traveler has come to expect. The three-level **Grand Foyer** is gorgeous, yet understated. There's more drama in the outside glass elevators that ascend 10 decks above the sea. Despite the large size of the ship, the main dining room is not so overwhelming as to be distracting and it is simply beautiful. *Infinity* and *Summit* have a wide range of shopping options, bars and lounges, plus fabulous recreational facilities. The **Constellation Lounge** at the bow near the top of the ship is a wonderful multi-purpose venue for entertainment, dancing, lectures, or just taking in the view. When it comes to big shows, this class of ship provides more extravagance since the large stage in its beautiful three-level theater is of Broadway quality. All staterooms include bathrobes of Egyptian cotton, mini-bar, safe and a host of other amenities in spacious and attractive surroundings.

Infinity main dining room

⚓ *Mercury*

Year Built: 1997
Gross Tonnage: 77,713
Length: 866 feet
Beam: 106 feet
Passengers: 1,870
Passenger Decks: 10
Crew Size: 909
Passenger/Crew Ratio: 2.1:1
Stateroom Size: 171-1,514 sq ft
Space Ratio: 41.6

From the beautiful two-level **Manhattan Restaurant** and its adjoining foyer and champagne bar to the showroom with its European-style opera house balcony boxes, the interior décor is delightful. The four-deck **Grand Foyer** is visually appealing with its understated elegance. Especially worthy of note is the **Navigator Club**, a multi-purpose facility with wrap-around windows and seating at different levels that makes this an ideal spot for gazing at the sea or the passing scenery. The colorful and cheerful décor maintains a mostly informal look despite its feel of luxury and elegance.

The buffet is called the **Palm Springs Café** and is especially nice. Besides having a great selection of excellent food (much better than most buffet food), the eight bay-type windows provide a degree of privacy and views that are not usually part of shipboard buffet dining. Even though *Mercury* isn't nearly as large as many of the ships now being put into service in Mexico, it has just about all the features and facilities of its bigger competition. It even boasts the latest in onboard recreation – a golf course simulator. The shopping arcade is surprisingly large and varied.

Staterooms are exceptionally spacious and well furnished. They're among the most comfortable of any ship. Little amenities are numerous, even in the lower-priced categories, and include things like private mini-bar, hair dryer, personal safe and interactive television. Choosing a room on *Mercury* can be somewhat easier than on many other ships because the number of room categories isn't as great. The lowest-priced suite category (Sky Suites) are mostly located on upper decks. There are even some inside rooms on these levels. This is an option that is not available on many of the newest ships where the top two or three decks are often devoted exclusively to public facilities.

I should also re-emphasize that the service onboard *Mercury* is consistent with the high standards that have been established on all Celebrity ships.

HOLLAND AMERICA LINE
☎ (800) 426-0327
www.hollandamerica.com
Officers: Dutch
Ships' Registry: The Netherlands. One ship (not sailing in Mexico) is Bahama registered
Fleet: 12 ships; 1 under construction

With almost 140 years of sailing experience, it's little wonder that traditions are very important at Holland America. Although they've adapted to the modern world of cruising, HAL is still, in many ways, an old-fashioned and traditional cruise line that appeals to a large segment of the sailing public. It starts with the basic exterior design and features such as their conservative midnight blue hull, as well as the color trim on the white superstructure. All of the public areas (including those ships with atriums) tend toward a classy styling that features understated elegance rather than a deliberate attempt to "wow" you. The result is a fine setting for a sophisticated cruise experience.

Works of art, including paintings and sculpture, are a big part of HAL ships, and sometimes these vessels seem like floating art galleries. The art work is mainly themed to Dutch nautical traditions. There is always a wrap-around promenade deck; you can walk around the entire ship without going inside. This is another way that all Holland America vessels keep older cruising traditions alive. Not that the new world of cruising hasn't had an affect on HAL ship design and décor. Their new and fabulous *Vista*-class vessels have some of the splashiness and eye-catching glitz that is so popular elsewhere. However, even these ships do it in Holland American style. Fortunately, beginning with the 2004-2005 Mexican season, HAL has assigned this class of vessel to their Mexican routes. Ships of this size allow for better shows, produced by top figures in the entertainment industry.

Holland America has a well-deserved reputation for fine food, outstanding personalized service and a host of onboard activities. Like Celebrity, it is always one of the highest-rated lines. They do a good job of combining fun with culturally enriching activities. Informative lectures and discussions on the ports of call are one of HAL's strong points. Also in this vein, HAL is one of the most active lines when it comes to "theme" cruises. The themes can be on just about anything but might, for example, concentrate on a particular type of music during the course of a cruise.

Accommodations are quite varied, especially when it comes to size. This depends largely on whether it's a newer ship since HAL's older vessels have some room categories where the square-footage is very low. Many amenities are a feature of HAL staterooms but this is especially true when you enter the upgraded suite categories. These include personal concierge service and an invitation to the *Rijstaffel* (literal translation is "rice table"), a traditional and extravagant Dutch-Indonesian buffet lunch hosted by the Captain. Unfortunately, it is no longer HAL's practice to have the *Rijstaffel* as a feature for all guests.

A few final notes about Holland America. Note that tipping is no longer included in the basic cruise fare. Social hosts, that is dancing or dining partners for unescorted female guests, are available. This is something that used to be a common practice in the cruise industry. HAL and Celebrity are the only mainstream cruise lines that offer this feature. HAL is also the only line that offers cruises concentrating on the Sea of Cortés.

THE VIEW FROM THE CROW'S NEST

One of the pleasures of cruising has always been to enjoy the view from a special interior spot where you could sit and gaze out upon the water or the passing scenery without getting blown away by the wind. Fortunately, Holland America has retained one of the most enduring institutions in the cruise industry and that is the Crow's Nest – their observation lounge. The name comes from an even older nautical tradition: a lookout high up on the ship's tallest mast. But on HAL you don't have to climb a rope or ladder to get there. An elevator will whisk you to a beautiful lounge on the top or next-to-the-top deck, with unobstructed views on three sides. The Crow's Nest also has a small dance floor, so there is often entertainment. It is a common venue for lectures and other shipboard events. If you sail on Holland America, be sure to spend some time at the top.

⚓ *Oosterdam*

Year Built: 2003
Gross Tonnage: 85,000
Length: 951 feet
Beam: 106 feet
Passengers: 1,848
Passenger Decks: 11
Crew Size: 842
Passenger/Crew Ratio: 2.2:1
Stateroom Size: 154-1,343 sq ft
Space Ratio: 46.0

Not that HAL would ever say so, but the debut of this vessel on the Mexican Riviera for the 2004-2005 season was, in my opinion, a response to the introduction of ever-more extravagant ships on this run by other lines, especially by Carnival and Princess.

The second of Holland America's four magnificent new Vista-class vessels, the *Oosterdam* (pronounced OH-STER-DAHM) represents a dramatic departure from HAL's typical ship. Not only is it significantly larger than most of the other ships of this line, but it has a dazzling, colorful and often extravagant style. In fact, the change was so great that they toned down the décor on the three subsequent ships in this class because some of HAL's more tradition-oriented guests found the *Oosterdam* a bit too much! I have to say that I like the lively appearance and feel of this ship. Moreover, despite the unusual degree of glitz, the décor doesn't detract from the fine service and overall classy experience that a Holland America cruise always offers.

Perhaps it is just as important to emphasize how this ship follows the traditions of HAL. That begins with the full wrap-around promenade deck, the three-level atrium and the **Crow's Nest Lounge**. The latter has an open observation area above it. The *Oosterdam* features extensive use of glass and curved, flowing lines to create a dramatic and airy atmosphere. This is most evident in the two-level main dining room and the magnificent tri-level main showroom called the **Vista Lounge**. There's also an alternative theater and more dining options than on other Holland America ships. The recreational facilities are

Oosterdam

Cruise Lines & Ships

Oosterdam Atrium

larger and more extensive than on any other class of ship in the fleet. Among the options are a golf simulator and tennis and basketball courts. Spa facilities are among the largest and most sophisticated at sea. There are separate facilities for small children and teens, respectively called the **Kid Zone** and **Wave Runner**. While these will be welcomed by parents, HAL still is not the best choice for families.

When it comes to accommodations the *Oosterdam* raises the bar a few notches compared to this line's more traditional ships. This begins with the higher percentage of outside rooms that have private balconies. Spaciousness is generally also the order of the day, with most rooms being larger than cruise industry norms. However, be careful when booking inside rooms. HAL's brochures shows 185 square feet but this refers to **large** inside rooms. Those that are standard measure in at 154

Standard outside stateroom on the Oosterdam

square feet, which isn't bad but is a far cry from what you would be led to believe. While the décor isn't much different from other ships of the HAL fleet, there is a generally more cheerful color scheme that gives the rooms an airier look. The *Oosterdam* offers bathtubs in all but the lowest-priced stateroom categories.

⚓ *Ryndam/Veendam*

Year Built: 1994 [refurbished in 1998]/1996
Gross Tonnage: 55,451
Length: 720 feet
Beam: 101 feet
Passengers: 1,258
Passenger Decks: 10
Crew Size: 602
Passenger/Crew Ratio: 2.1:1
Stateroom Size: 156-1,126 sq ft
Space Ratio: 44.0

Although these are identical vessels from a deck-plan point of view and are quite similar as to the interior details, this description applies to the *Ryndam* since the *Veendam* visits Mexico only as part of its trans-Panama Canal itineraries. One of HAL's smaller "S"-class ships, the *Ryndam* definitely fits the more typical description of what most people expect from this line. As one of the finest cruise lines in the world, with a well deserved reputation for excellence in all categories, you can't say that the *Ryndam* is bad in any important way. However, if you're looking for a mega-ship, this one isn't it. It offers a distinguished and refined cruising experience in keeping with the older traditions of this line.

The *Ryndam* is exclusively sailing Holland America's "Sea of Cortés" itinerary (round the tip of Baja and then north to La Paz, Loreto and Santa Rosalia) so it provides quite a different experience than most other ships that visit Baja. In fact, HAL is the only major cruise line offering this kind of itinerary and that by itself may be an important factor for some travelers, especially those who have already taken the standard Mexican Riviera run.

The stern reflects the traditional raked design, with terraced levels affording lots of outdoor space and great views. The **Lido** buffet is unusually large given the overall size of the ship and passenger count. The interior is beautifully designed and exudes the luxury that is associated with Holland America. Public areas display a generous use of teak wood, many works of art, and beautiful fresh flowers. Interior architectural highlights include a multistory atrium, and both the main dining room and showroom also span two decks. There's also a cinema. As always, the **Crow's Nest Lounge** is a great place to watch the passing scenery.

This was one of the first ships to have a retractable glass dome over one of its pools so any unexpected bad weather won't spoil your time in the water. All of the

Ryndam, looking aft

staterooms feature easy-on-the-eyes pastel tones and comfortable, tasteful furnishings. While most ships require significant upgrading to go from shower to bathtub, the *Ryndam* offers tubs in all categories except inside state-

Lido buffet

rooms. Almost all rooms (including the majority of inside cabins) are at least 182 square feet, making them exceptionally spacious. However, the two lowest-priced inside categories are the smallest rooms on the ship and a tad too small for most people's tastes.

⚓ *Volendam/Zaandam*

Year Built: 1999/2000
Gross Tonnage: 63,000
Length: 780 feet
Beam: 106 feet
Passengers: 1,440
Passenger Decks: 10
Crew Size: 561
Passenger/Crew Ratio: 2.6:1
Stateroom Size: 113-1,125 sq ft
Space Ratio: 43.8

Trans-Panama Canal itineraries only. These very attractive sister ships are similar in size, layout and facilities to HAL's more famous *Amsterdam* and *Rotterdam*. Both are tradition-

Volendam

Volendam stateroom

ally designed vessels with an older look, although the public areas show the influence of more recent trends in ship design. The attractive three-deck atrium serves as a focal point for many public facilities and that's a plus because some areas of these ships are not as easy to navigate as they could be. However, you'll quickly get used to the peculiarities of the layout. The main two-level dining room is an elaborate and luxurious facility. In fact, just about everything on theses vessels has the rich feel that makes Holland America so popular with a large segment of the cruising population. There is one potential problem that you should be careful to avoid. While the overwhelming majority of staterooms on these ships are comparable in size to HAL's usual larger standards (i.e., beginning at around 180 square feet), the lowest price category is so small and cramped that it is likely to spoil your cruise. Fortunately, there are only a few rooms in this category.

NORWEGIAN CRUISE LINE

☎ (800) 327-7030
www.ncl.com
Officers: Norwegian
Ships' Registry: The Bahamas or Panama, except for some American registered ships. See the discussion below.
Fleet: 12 ships; 2 under construction

The 2004-2005 sailing season was the first time that Norwegian offered a round-trip Mexican Riviera itinerary from southern California. Previously, if you wanted to go by NCL to Mexico it had to be via a trans-Canal cruise. This

Above: Acapulco Bay (Nadine Markova)

Below: Beach in Mazatlan (Guillermo Aldana)

Above: **Mazatlan** *(Guillermo Aldana)*
Below: Las Altas beach in Mazatlan

Above: Panoramic view of Mazatlan (Guillermo Aldana)
Below: Puerto Vallarta (Bruce Herman)

addition is good news for the cruising public, since it adds even more options.

The beautiful ships of NCL mostly feature an all-white exterior, except for the graceful dark blue trademark funnel that is placed far to the stern. A few of their newest and biggest ships have introduced a flashy and unique design on the fore section of the hull – colorfully painted "ribbons" that lend a festive atmosphere. The response from the public seems to be positive and I wouldn't be surprised if this becomes standard throughout their fleet. In general, the ships of NCL have a nice combination of both traditional and modern styling that is pleasing to the eye. Norwegian has a reputation for efficient and friendly service that is not particularly fancy or intruding. Their food hasn't earned special honors but it would have to take a very fussy gourmet to find anything significant to complain about. Norwegian is justly popular with both young couples and families as much for their casual and fun approach to cruising as for their relatively low prices.

If I have one complaint about NCL (and this even applies to their newest and best ships) it is that many staterooms are smaller than those on most competing lines. It is not uncommon for cabins to be only about 135 square feet. Make sure you upgrade enough to a somewhat larger room if size matters to you. When it comes to other facilities, Norwegian's vessels have everything that big ships can offer, including extensive children's programs (divided into three age groups), top-notch entertainment that varies from Broadway- to Las Vegas-style, and full-service spas.

It's also the degree of flexibility offered by NCL that attracts many passengers. A trend that began in earnest perhaps five or six years ago and continues unabated today is to offer much greater freedom of choice when it comes to where and when you dine, how you dress, and other things. NCL has been a pioneer in this with their *Freestyle* cruising. Although other lines have followed suit, Norwegian's *Freestyle* offers passengers the greatest degree of flexibility.

Depending upon the ship, there can be up to 10 restaurants representing a wide variety of cuisines and styles. There is a fee for some of the specialty restaurants. Dining times and seating arrangements are completely flexible (open seating from about 5:30 pm to as late as 10 pm). This even applies in the more traditional "main" dining room. Regardless of where you eat, you can dress as you wish (within reason – beachwear, for example, is taboo in dining establishments). Even in the most formal restaurant you can go casual if you wish. Of course, you can dress up as much as you want and many people still do. Formal nights are designated in various restaurants, but that just means it's dress-up time if *you* want it to be. *Freestyle* is also applied to activities, although every cruise line allows you a big choice in this area. NCL also has flexible disembarkation procedures that allow you to spend more time on board. But be warned that this feature might cost you some extra money.

Norwegian has heavily promoted its "Homeland" cruising program and cruises to the Mexican Riviera are part of this. The line is the first to embark on a program of renovating and building vessels all or mostly in the United States. As a result, they will soon have three ships that are US-flagged, something that hasn't been seen in this country for a long time. Because of legal and financial considerations, these ships will operate under the label of "NCL America," but there will be little difference of significance to guests except that the crews will be largely American. There doesn't seem to be any rush by other lines to copy this strategy. For the time being, ships of NCL going to Mexico are not part of the NCL America program. This could change in the future, especially on repositioning cruises through the Panama Canal.

⚓ *Norwegian Star*

Year Built: 2001
Gross Tonnage: 91,000
Length: 965 feet
Beam: 105 feet
Passengers: 2,240
Passenger Decks: 11
Crew Size: 1,100
Passenger/Crew Ratio: 2.0:1
Stateroom Size: 142-5,350 sq ft
Space Ratio: 40.6

Norwegian Star

Originally assigned to cruising the islands of Hawaii, *Norwegian Star* has been chosen to be NCL's first ship regularly on a Mexican Riviera run. Lucky for would-be Mexico cruise passengers because this beautiful ship is one of the best in their fleet. It was the first NCL vessel that was truly designed around their *Freestyle* cruising program. As such, it offers an extraordinary array of dining options. In fact, there are no fewer than 10 different dining choices, including **Soho** (fusion cuisine); **Ginza** (Asian); **Aqua** (contemporary); and **Le Bistro** (French and Mediterranean). There are many other more casual options – you'll even find a beer garden! If you want to opt for a more traditional "main" dining room, then the beautiful **Versailles Room** fits the bill. Speaking of décor, there are a variety of styles in the dining venues commensurate with the variety of cuisines, but thoughtful attention to detail is a hallmark throughout. Both the food and the service are just fine. NCL has been improving their staff ratios in recent years and the result is a level of service that is considerably better than what would have been expected from a budget-oriented line just a few years ago.

The ship's other public facilities are no less varied or beautiful, beginning with a host of bars and lounges of all sizes, from intimate places to the large **Spinnaker Lounge** high up on Deck 12 and affording great views from three sides. The tri-level **Stardust Theater** handles production shows that are among the most elaborate at sea. A nightclub and cinema are some of the other entertainment options. The tapas bar is an unusual feature and provides a more grown-up alternative to burgers and hot dogs when the urge for a snack arises.

There are extensive recreational facilities, including a large spa with accompanying full-service fitness center. You'll find plenty of deck space for lying in the sun, although the ship could use some more swimming pools given its size. The *Norwegian Star* offers a full children's program separated by age group.

Norwegian Star, standard room

Turning now to the accommodations, *Norwegian Star* is generally above the level you'll find on most ships of this line. Even the smallest of the outside rooms are of a nice size with or without a balcony. The décor is colorful and attractive and the design is functional. My major complaint concerns inside accommodations which, at only 142 square feet, are quite small for today's biggest ships. At the other end of the scale, most suites are in the 300-800-square-foot range, but the two huge 5,350-square-foot Garden Villas are a surprise since NCL isn't usually considered by travelers looking for that kind of luxury. The villas, which are the biggest suites at sea, have five rooms plus a private garden with hot tub and come with a butler and concierge service. The tab of roughly $12,000 per week isn't likely to appeal to most travelers but, if you have a few couples sharing it, the cost per person does come down quite a bit.

Norwegian Star received a minor makeover in 2004 that changed some of the interior décor. But perhaps the most notable change is outside where the hull now features large and colorful flowing "ribbons" painted on the otherwise snow-white ship. NCL began this with some of their ships in Hawaii and the reaction from the public seems to be mostly favorable. Of course, I don't think anyone will select their cruise ship based on whether or not it has ribbons!

⚓ *Norwegian Sun*

Year Built: 2001
Gross Tonnage: 78,309
Length: 848 feet
Beam: 108 feet
Passengers: 1,936
Passenger Decks: 10
Crew Size: 950
Passenger/Crew Ratio: 2.0:1
Stateroom Size: 121-459 sq ft
Space Ratio: 40.4

Trans-Panama Canal itineraries only. The *Norwegian Sun* is typical of many ships of this line with similar statistics. For a short time it was the biggest ship in the fleet, but it

Norwegian Sun, Garden Café

has been surpassed by a number of other vessels in the past three years. The ship has a rather broad beam for its length, but still it has graceful lines. The *Sun* has been configured for *Freestyle* cruising and has nine restaurants. There is a rounded three-deck atrium and a two-level showroom at the stern, a somewhat unusual location for modern ships. (Not that it makes any difference if you watch a show at the front or rear of the vessel.) The main drawback is that if you want to save money by going for lower-priced accommodations, then you will have to accept rooms that are far too small to be comfortable. Oceanview staterooms on the two highest decks have private balconies and are much larger.

⚓ *Norwegian Wind*

Year Built: 1993 [refurbished 1998]
Gross Tonnage: 50,760
Length: 754 feet
Beam: 94 feet
Passengers: 2,183
Passenger Decks: 10
Crew Size: 614
Passenger/Crew Ratio: 3.5:1
Stateroom Size: 140-350 sq ft
Space Ratio: 23.3

Trans-Panama Canal itineraries only. The best features of this sleek-looking ship are its beautiful and spacious public areas, including wide decks. *Freestyle* options aren't as extensive on the *Wind* as they are on other Norwegian vessels for two reasons. First, as a somewhat older ship, it was designed before the advent of this policy (although modifications have increased the choices to include, for instance, a bistro café). Second, the ship isn't one of the bigger ones in the fleet and that limits design flexibility. However, the main dining room (**The Terraces Restaurant**) is a gorgeous facility with Norwegian's usual competent service and good food. On the entertainment side, the **Stardust Lounge** is an excellent showroom, while the **Observatory Lounge** is used for less formal productions. It's also a good place to go during the daytime when you want to have a drink while watching the scenery. A higher percentage of the thoughtfully designed and pleasantly decorated staterooms are pleasantly sized compared to many other ships in the NCL fleet, although you still have to watch for a tight fit in the lowest price categories.

PRINCESS CRUISES
☎ (800) 774-6237
www.princess.com
Officers: British or Italian
Ships' Registry: Britain or Bermuda
Fleet: 13 ships; 1 under construction

Princess, of *Love Boat* fame, can be said to have started the current popularity of cruising as a result of the television series that featured a Princess vessel. While the original *Love Boat* is no longer in service, the tradition continues with newer and better vessels. When the mega-ship *Grand Princess* was introduced in 1998 it began a revolution in cruise ship-building that opened up a whole new world to the cruising public. It was called "Grand Class" and meant not only that you were on a ship with grand proportions, but you had a grand variety of onboard options. The public response was so positive that Princess extended the concept of Grand Class in one form or another to the entire fleet. Ships that were too small to accommodate the changes were phased out. "Grand Class" as a style of cruising has been renamed by the Madison Avenue ad executives and now goes under the moniker of *Personal Choice* cruising, obviously meant to compete with Norwegian's freestyle. One thing it encompasses is their so-called "anytime dining," which allows you to choose between specialty restaurants without fixed seating arrangements and traditional fixed dining in the main restaurant. The buffet becomes a late-night bistro so you can have a light or even a full meal at two in the morning if you want. This feature has replaced the traditional midnight buffet on Princess vessels. The newer and bigger the ship, the more "personal choice" there is to select from.

The modern and rapidly growing Princess fleet features all-white exteriors with generally graceful lines and gentle curves. The cuisine is excellent, falling somewhere between Carnival and Celebrity in sophistication. The same applies to the service. Entertainment is some of the most lavish and spectacular at sea and ranges from Broadway to Vegas. There are numerous lounges in addition to the showroom where all types of entertainment take place – even karaoke.

Princess' vessels have become increasingly popular with families and programs for children are extensive. They are grouped by ages (three or four groups depending upon the ship). Other features are the Asian-style **Lotus Spa**, varied recreational opportunities, including a putting green, and extensive personal enrichment programs. The latter is known as the **Scholarship@Sea** program and it is safe to say that Princess has developed this more than any other cruise line. Also on the cultural side is the art gallery that is part of every ship in the fleet. This is in addition to works of art that are displayed throughout the ship. A dedicated concierge staff is available to all guests and provides a convenient way of making reservations for dining and other "personal choice" services.

Stateroom facilities on Princess are uniformly excellent with very few cabins that I would consider sub-par (these are limited to the very lowest categories on some of their older vessels). When it comes to accommodations, Princess boasts balconies, balconies, and more balconies. They were among the first to promote this as a feature and their ships are designed to have a majority of rooms with balconies. This is all very nice, no doubt, but do keep in mind that such rooms do cost more. Don't fall into the trap of cruise line advertising (certainly not limited to Princess) – you can have just as wonderful a trip without a balcony!

Princess has, and continues to introduce, wonderful new ships on their Mexican routes.

⚓ Coral Princess

Year Built: 2003
Gross Tonnage: 88,000
Length: 965
Beam: 106 feet
Passengers: 1,970
Passenger Decks: 11
Crew Size: 900
Passenger/Crew Ratio: 2.2:1
Stateroom Size: 156-470 sq ft
Space Ratio: 44.7

Trans-Panama Canal itineraries only. The *Coral Princess* and a sister-ship form a new sub-class of Princess vessels designed to have the amenities and facilities of the largest Grand-class ships but carrying considerably fewer passengers. The result is a fabulous ship that has everything you could want but isn't so big that it might scare away people who are turned off by the thought of sharing their cruise with between 2,500 and 3,000 other people! Except for the missing nightclub on the upper aft-section, *Coral Princess'* exterior profile is similar to the gem-class vessels, including the "jet engines" (see the *Diamond/Sapphire* descriptions below). Somewhat unusual is the arrangement of the ship's "Lido" deck – the **Horizon Court** (buffet and 24-hour bistro) is at the bow-

Coral Princess

end, rather than amidships. This gives passengers views on three sides while dining. The stern section has the fabulous **Lotus Spa** and accompanying fitness center. These facilities are very extensive on all of the newer and bigger Princess ships but, given *Coral's* overall size, they are even larger, practically making this a "spa" ship. Accommodations are first-rate and feature plenty of room, comfort and lovely décor in all categories, with top-notch luxury in the highest categories.

⚓ *Dawn Princess*

Year Built: 1995
Gross Tonnage: 77,000
Length: 856 feet
Beam: 106 feet
Passengers: 1,950
Passenger Decks: 10
Crew Size: 900
Passenger/Crew Ratio: 2.2:1
Stateroom Size: 135-695 sq ft
Space Ratio: 39.5

When this ship hit the waves in 1995 a lot of people thought it was the ultimate in cruising for a long time to come. How wrong they were. It's still a beautiful ship that should please just about everyone, but it already seems somewhat dated compared to the upgraded part of the Princess fleet that the line is currently sending to Mexico. There's little doubt that this was the ship that set the stage for all of Princess' Grand-class vessels and the whole concept of "Grand" cruising that has evolved into their "Personal Choice" program.

The beautiful exterior was one of the first to feature the more modern design with the superstructure moved toward the bow. However, it retains a degree of traditional grace by having this section gently raked. On the other hand, the stern is less raked, with the result that there is little terracing effect.

The main interior feature is the lovely **Atrium Court**, spanning four decks and featuring graceful curving staircases, lots of rich woods offset by brass, towering palm trees and glass elevators, all topped by a colorful Tiffany stained-glass ceiling. Numerous shops surround one level of the atrium. The one-deck main theater is not particularly impressive in itself, but it's a good facility that is capable of hosting Princess' most extravagant shows. At the opposite end of the ship is the almost-as-large **Vista Lounge**. This multi-purpose entertainment venue is eye-catching and a great place to watch more informal shows or to go dancing. There's also a rather large **casino** with a spiral staircase in the middle that connects it with the deck below where you'll find the ship's lovely wrap-around promenade.

The *Dawn Princess* has two main dining rooms. They are exactly on top of one another and are of the same size and layout but somewhat different decoration. The two rooms are not connected by a staircase within the rooms, so each is a single deck high and is more to the liking of those who prefer smaller dining rooms. On the other hand, this makes them somewhat less visually impressive. Other dining op-

Dawn Princess

tions include the forward-facing **buffet/bistro** and a **patisserie**, where you can purchase mouth-watering cakes and pastries to go with your specialty coffee.

The *Dawn Princess* has an exceptional amount of open deck space so you should never feel crowded when trying to soak up the sun. There aren't that many pools but it does have lots of hot tubs. This was one of the first ships to feature **Princess Links** – a mini-golf facility. When it comes to children's facilities this ship doesn't come close to what's available on the newer and larger vessels in the fleet. However, this isn't necessarily a reason not to take children on the ship. There is a good childcare staff. Like-

Outside cabin, Dawn Princess

wise, while the spa and fitness facilities are more than adequate, they are a notch or two below what Princess guests have come to expect on their newer ships.

All of this ship's staterooms boast beautiful décor and warm color schemes that are typically Princess. Where they fall somewhat short is in size. All interior rooms are less than 150 square feet and even the lower-priced outside categories can be between 135 and 155 square feet. So, if having a lot of space is important to you and you don't want to upgrade to much more expensive accommodations, be sure to verify how big the room is at the time you book and don't hesitate to ask for a larger room. Some may be available at little difference in price.

⚓ *Diamond Princess/Sapphire Princess*

Year Built: 2004/2004
Gross Tonnage: 113,000
Length: 952 feet
Beam: 123 feet
Passengers: 2,670
Passenger Decks: 13
Crew Size: 1,133
Passenger/Crew Ratio: 2.3:1
Stateroom Size: 168-1,329 sq ft
Space Ratio: 42.3

These ships are a newer and slightly altered version of Princess' unbelievable Grand-class ships. Their introduction into Mexican Riviera service (along with one of Carnival's Spirit-class ships) definitely raised the bar on mega-sized luxury vessels in this market. Ship competition being extremely fierce, it's likely that these ships will result in other lines improving the quality of their fleet assigned to Mexican runs. Although these are Grand-class ships, they have been tweaked quite a bit and Princess refers to them as their "Gem"-class. Indeed, they are beautiful gems that have just enough differences from the original class of ships to make them a distinct entity.

The *Diamond* and *Sapphire Princess* are virtually identical. Their exterior presents an impressive and beautiful all-white profile. If you have ever traveled on one of the original Grand-class vessels, you are familiar with the rather bulky looking stern section of the ship resulting from the Skywalkers nightclub being perched atop the highest part of the aft. On Gem-class ships the club is located slightly forward of that point, resulting in a much more pleasant appearance. In fact, despite the ship's immense size, it is the epitome of grace. (Do go into Skywalkers during the day for a wonderful view of the ship looking forward. An opposite view is available from the open deck above the bridge.) An unusual exterior feature are the "jet engines" perched above the decorative grillwork that surrounds the funnels. Well, many people are convinced that they're jet engines. In reality, they are also just decorative features that have become something of a conversation piece in the Princess fleet.

Dining on Gem-class ships is a wonderful experience. Passengers choose from traditional dining or alternative dining options. The "traditional" means you have fixed seating in the so-called main dining room. I refer to it that way because this attractive restaurant is rather small and intimate compared to what you see on most ships of this size. That's because a large number of guests opt for the alternative dining program. Each evening you can select from one of four specialty restaurants – Oriental, Italian, Southwestern or a steak house. They feature the full main dining room menu plus a number of specialty items from the cuisine that is each restaurant's specialty. It is best to make reservations so you don't have a long wait. If you choose the tradi-

Diamond Princess

tional dining it is still possible to sample the specialty restaurants on a space-available basis. In addition to these wonderful dinner choices there is **Sabatini's**, a popular upscale Italian trattoria, at an additional charge. The fine service is a seemingly endless parade of well-prepared favorites, along with unusual items. The buffet option is also available for dinner, as well as for breakfast and lunch. After-hours, the buffet turns into a late-night bistro where you can choose from a variety of delectable treats. There is table service.

Dining room on the Diamond Princess

Public areas are spacious and appealing, beginning with the three-level atrium. It isn't the biggest at sea, but is certainly one of the most beautiful with its abundance of white marble and exquisite detailing. Those seeking recreation will find an abundance of activities, including tennis and basketball courts, mini-golf at Princess Links and cybergolf simulators where you can select from dozens of famous courses throughout the world. The **Lotus Spa** and its adjacent aerobics room and gymnasium is one of the largest and most beautiful facilities of its type at sea. There are plenty of pools and hot tubs, including the fabulous **Conservatory**, with its retractable roof. It features beautiful tile work with colorful fish. The balcony surrounding the **Calypso Reef** pool hosts many activities and events.

The variety of entertainment is equally astounding. Among the larger lounges are the wild, Egyptian-themed **Explorers Lounge** (a popular feature on many new Prin-

Cruise Lines & Ships

cess ships) and the multi-purpose **Club Fusion**. The more traditional **Wheelhouse Bar** is another great place, but **Skywalkers** late-night disco (14 decks above the sea) is the undisputed hot spot. There are also several smaller and more intimate places to have a drink or chat. The main theater is rather plain and disappointing visually, but you still get those elaborate Broadway-style shows for which Princess is known. There is an extensive children's program with three separate facilities catering to separate age groups.

Staterooms occupy five consecutive decks that have no public facilities. A large percentage have balconies. There are also a large number of mini-suites that provide an opportunity to upgrade to a more luxurious level without getting into stratospheric prices. But you may not care to upgrade much at all since even the smallest rooms on these *Princesses* are a nice size and feature easy-on-the-eyes pastel shades with rich wood trim and beautiful fabrics.

ROYAL CARIBBEAN INTERNATIONAL

☎ (800) 327-6700
www.royalcaribbean.com
Officers: Primarily Scandinavian or Italian with some international for non-bridge positions
Ships' Registry: The Bahamas or Norway
Fleet: 19 ships; 1 under construction

This is the second-biggest cruise line in terms of the number of ships, trailing only Carnival by a small margin. That gives you an idea of how successful they are and what a good product they deliver at affordable prices. Although Royal Caribbean has a good number of ships serving Pacific Mexico in one way or another, the selection is not as great as it could be considering what they have in their inventory. The Radiance-class ships (the first two listed below) are just dandy and are among the stars of the cruising world. Unfortunately, they sail to Mexico only as part of repositioning trans-Panama Canal cruises. The ships that ply both the Riviera and Baja (the *Monarch of the Seas* and *Vision of the Seas*) are not among their top ships, although *Monarch* has been nicely refurbished, while the somewhat newer *Vision* didn't need to be. Unfortunately, the almost unbelievable Voyager-class ships aren't likely to enter the Mexican market because they're too big to get through the Panama Canal and Royal Caribbean isn't likely to send them around Cape Horn at South America's tip. On the other hand, competition being what it is, you never know. (Do see the sidebar on Voyager-class ships.) However, with both Carnival and Princess having upgraded the ships going to Mexico, one has to believe that Royal Caribbean won't be far behind.

The almost all-white exteriors of Royal Caribbean's vessels are an appealing part of this line's impressive fleet. The easily recognizable Royal Caribbean funnel with its dark blue crowned anchor symbol is generally placed fairly far back on the vessel. All of their newer ships (those built since 1995) are definitely in the mega-liner category. Royal Caribbean has been an innovator in ship design and it is reflected in their exceptional size and varied facilities as well as in the brilliance of their architecture. Among their innovations were new recreational ideas such as a rock climbing wall. This feature first appeared on their giant new ships and proved so popular that it has been extended to almost the entire fleet.

They also realized that a ship's eye-appeal is part of the cruise experience. They were among the first to incorporate an atrium into their ship designs. They call it the **Centrum** and it is always something spectacular. Royal Caribbean ships also feature the **Viking Crown** lounge high atop the vessel. Similar to Holland America's Crow's

Nest, this makes for a great place to socialize while enjoying the passing view.

Royal Caribbean offers excellent food and friendly service. They are on the same level as Carnival in terms of formality and quality. While the majority of Royal Caribbean ships feature numerous alternative dining options, many do impose an additional fee. The entertainment and onboard activities are extremely varied and cater to those seeking a fun time, as opposed to the more culturally oriented programs found on the sophisticated luxury lines. This line also boasts one of the most extensive children's programs at sea. Called **Adventure Ocean**, it features five different age groups. For parents who want a romantic evening by themselves now and then, the children's activities include dining separately with their friends at least one evening per cruise. They also have a kids' menu in the main dining room, which should delight them and make parents a whole lot more comfortable.

⚓ *Brilliance of the Seas/Radiance of the Seas*

Year Built: 2002/2003
Gross Tonnage: 90,000
Length: 962 feet
Beam: 106 feet
Passengers: 2,501
Passenger Decks: 12
Crew Size: 859
Passenger/Crew Ratio: 2.9:1
Stateroom Size: 166-584 sq ft
Space Ratio: 36.0

Trans-Panama Canal itineraries only. The Radiance-class vessels are second only in size in the Royal Caribbean fleet to the Voyager-class (which aren't used on any Mexican itinerary). Second-biggest, yes; but definitely not second-class because these are gorgeous ships with a host of wonderful features and facilities. The ships are identical

Dining room on Brilliance of the Seas

except for the names of some public areas. Extensive use of glass and open spaces give these ships an even more spacious feel. In addition to the usual recreational facilities, you'll find a golf simulator, separate swimming pool for teens (thank you!), and a rock-climbing wall. The fitness center and spa facilities are first-rate. The **Viking Crown Club**, a Royal Caribbean feature, goes well beyond what this facility usually offers in terms of both size and eye appeal. There's also a spectacular central atrium with glass-enclosed elevators running almost the entire vertical span of the ship. Called the **Centrum**, this visually stunning area provides convenient access to most public facilities. There are a good variety of entertainment venues, including a first-rate three-level main theater. The two-tiered main dining room has a gorgeous grand staircase, exquisite color schemes and graceful tall columns to go with a huge central chandelier. There are also alternative

The Centrum on Brilliance of the Seas

Cruise Lines & Ships

dining options in addition to the buffet. There aren't any bad accommodations on Radiance-class vessels either.

⚓ *Legend of the Seas*

Year Built: 1995 [refurbished 1997]
Gross Tonnage: 70,000
Length: 867 feet
Beam: 105 feet
Passengers: 2,076
Passenger Decks: 10
Crew Size: 720
Passenger/Crew Ratio: 2.9:1
Stateroom Size: 138-1,148 sq ft
Space Ratio: 33.7

A big ship, but not huge by Royal Caribbean standards, *Legend* was one of the first vessels to introduce many features that are now considered standard and are almost taken for granted. These include the miniature golf course called "**Legend of the Links**", the canopy-covered **Solarium** and pool area, and an extensive children's activity area. They even have a video arcade and you know how those electronic baby-sitters can come in quite handy. *Legend* maintains Royal Caribbean's **Centrum** atrium. It's quite attractive but isn't as large (and, therefore, somewhat less impressive) than on many other ships of the fleet.

The two-level main dining room is very appealing and the food and service are both just fine. Where *Legend* does lack something is in its limited alternative dining options. There's the buffet (which isn't one of Royal Caribbean's better buffets), but little else. One thing you certainly won't have trouble finding is a cocktail, as there is an abundance of attractive bars. The **That's Entertainment Theater** is only on one deck so the sight-lines aren't as good as on most newer ships, but the shows themselves certainly live up to the name. The **Anchors Aweigh**

Legend of the Seas

Lounge is the primary venue for less formal entertainment and it's a good facility where something is always happening. The ship has plenty of recreational facilities and lots of open deck space on the upper decks. There's a forward observatory area in addition to the standard **Viking Crown Lounge**.

The layout is simple and the ship doesn't feel crowded despite the relatively large number of passengers for its size. Some decks are devoted solely to accommodations, or nearly so. *Legend* avoids having a seemingly endless maze of corridors with inside rooms tucked into every nook and cranny, a somewhat unpleasant reality on some of this line's ships built before the new millennium. Stateroom sizes are generally adequate, although beneath the junior suite level you won't find anything especially noteworthy. Only the lowest two classes are likely to have you wishing that you had more room. The arrangement of the rooms is highly functional and the décor is pleasant. A large number of outside staterooms have private balconies, another feature of this ship that paved the way for what was to come afterward in the world of cruise-ship design.

⚓ *Monarch of the Seas*

Year Built: 1991 [refurbished 1997]
Gross Tonnage: 73,941
Length: 880 feet
Beam: 106 feet
Passengers: 2,744
Passenger Decks: 11
Crew Size: 822
Passenger/Crew Ratio: 3.3:1
Stateroom Size: 120-441 sq ft
Space Ratio: 26.9

Atrium on Monarch of the Seas

Monarch has a mostly traditional profile featuring clean lines. This was among the first ships to have a large atrium design. The **Centrum** on *Monarch* spans four decks and is quite attractive. The great majority of interior public facilities are located off the Centrum, which makes finding things easy. In fact, the layout of this particular ship is among the simplest that you are likely to find on ships of similar size.

All but the top two decks contain staterooms. Likewise, there are only two decks that don't have public areas. This tends to eliminate overly long corridors and provides a cozy feel but, depending upon your sleep habits, you might do well to avoid rooms that are near some of the lounges.

The ship has two main dining rooms stacked one on top of the other. However, because there are no connecting stairways within them, they are completely separate rather than being like a two-tiered facility. The

Outside stateroom on Monarch of the Seas

buffet provides the major alternative dining option on this ship. The primary showrooms are fairly big for a vessel of this size and both span two levels. There are also two other major lounge facilities so you have a great variety of entertainment to choose from and should never feel crowded.

When it comes to recreational facilities you'll find much to choose from, including two pools and a complete fitness center. Children's areas are somewhat more limited compared to most of the newest ships but are still adequate. There's also a cinema.

Staterooms are attractive and generally comfortable, although you have to select carefully because of the large number of tiny rooms. Most outside rooms have portholes rather than large windows and there are no balconies unless you choose the highest non-suite category or above. Perhaps the only real negative on this vessel is that the lower-priced staterooms are simply too small. This applies to all interior rooms and even the first four categories of outside staterooms. Thus, if you want a decent-sized room you won't find any bargain prices on *Monarch of the Seas*. Overall, although this ship isn't the best in the fleet, it provides an enjoyable cruising experience.

⚓ *Vision of the Seas*

Year Built: 1998
Gross Tonnage: 78,491
Length: 915 feet
Beam: 106 feet
Passengers: 2,435
Passenger Decks: 10
Crew Size: 775
Passenger/Crew Ratio: 3.1:1
Stateroom Size: 149-1,059 sq ft
Space Ratio: 32.2

Vision of the Seas is the third sister in its class and it brought with it a new standard of size and luxury to the world of cruising. Regarding that, it's almost unimaginable what has followed in only a few years since this ship made its debut! It's clear that the popularity of many features on this and similar ships was translated into the *Radiance*-class that followed *Vision*. Perhaps because of its impressive size, *Vision* avoids having a cramped feeling, despite a space ratio that is lower than most of the competition. Another reason for this is the extensive use of glass throughout the ship. Entire walls are made of glass and it almost always seems that you're actually out on the open seas while on board. Views are best from Royal Caribbean's trademark **Viking Crown Lounge** and the more quiet observatory directly beneath it. Many other public areas also provide great viewing and this even extends to the large and well-equipped gym. The latter is on the sports- and view-oriented **Compass Deck**, which features a large retractable canopy. *Vision* has an excellent art collection and you'll encounter paintings in just about every nook and cranny of the ship.

The extensive public areas are designed to dazzle you from top to bottom and from bow to stern, but especially impressive is the stunning décor of the two-tiered **Masquerade Theater**. Not only is this a first-rate facility, but

Centrum on Vision of the Seas

the shows are top-notch. For other entertainment options the **Some Enchanted Evening** lounge at the ship's stern is another good spot. The ship boasts many facilities that are almost mandatory in today's cruise vessels, including an excellent spa/fitness center and separate programs and areas for teens and younger children. This was one of the first ships to do that.

Although you can't go wrong in the highly decorative two-level **Aquarius Dining Room** or the **Windjammer Café** buffet, *Vision of the Seas* did come out before the trend toward a wider choice in alternative dining. Consequently, there isn't much else available. Some of the older ships in the Royal Caribbean fleet are being done over to expand dining choices. This ship isn't quite ready for a major retrofit but, if it does get one, more restaurants are sure to be at the top of the agenda.

Inside stateroom on Vision of the Seas

Cruise Lines & Ships

In general, nicely sized staterooms are a hallmark of this class of ship. The most common type of cabin has 153 square feet, which barely exceeds what I consider to be a minimum requirement for comfort. But it is nicely decorated and well-equipped. Colorful curtains add an informal touch of home and are also used to separate the sleeping area from the living area. The majority of outside rooms have private balconies. I do suggest avoiding the small number of staterooms that measure less than 150 square feet.

NOW THAT'S A BIG SHIP!

When Cunard's *Queen Mary II* made its maiden voyage in early 2004 it created a stir in the cruise world that I've never seen. Certainly a part of this was because it was the world's largest cruise ship in terms of length, height and some other measures. Yet, it isn't that much bigger than Royal Caribbean's *Voyager*-class vessels, which were first introduced in 1999 and now number five sisters, with the final ship in the class having been delivered in 2004. In fact, they each hold more passengers than the *Queen Mary II* and are the biggest ships in the world in that regard.

Other Lines

These lines mostly serve Mexico through their trans-Panama Canal itineraries, although some have a few Pacific Mexican-only itineraries. Perhaps an even more important distinction for the average traveler is that all are more luxury-oriented than the lines previously described. They feature smaller ships with more intimate and personalized service. Of course, they are considerably more expensive than any of the mass market lines, often as much as three times the price or greater. I am not trying to discourage people who have the financial means or a strong desire to travel in this style from doing so. However, because most people won't want to spend the money for this type of experience, I haven't included ship-by-ship descriptions for any of these lines.

The roster of such lines in Mexico includes:

Crystal Cruises: ☎ *(800) 446-6620; www.crystalcruises. com.* Crystal is one of the most honored of all cruise lines and people looking for luxury will certainly not go wrong by traveling with them. What makes Crystal different from the other stratosphere-priced lines is their ships. While the high-budget lines such as Radisson, Silversea and Seabourn are almost exclusively small-ship operators (generally under 500 passengers and sometimes considerably fewer than that), Crystal's ships have a capacity of about 1,000. As such, their ships have the amenities of the large mass-market vessels, such as a big showroom. This is attractive to many people and gives Crystal a niche in the market. Its passengers have the best of both worlds. That's if you can handle the fare. In addition to trans-Canal itineraries, Crystal's Mexican cruises last anywhere from 10 to 14 days and are roundtrip from Los Angeles. There are limited departure dates. Because of the longer cruise length these itineraries include more ports of call than the typical week-long Mexican Riviera trip.

Oceania Cruises: ☎ *(800) 531-5658; www.oceaniacruises. com.* Oceania is the new kid on the block, having begun operations in the latter part of 2003. They acquired two very nice "R" ships from the former Renaissance Cruise Line that went bankrupt. (Apparently this type of midsized ship was quite in demand since almost all of the Renaissance fleet was bought by other cruise lines, includ-

Cruise Lines & Ships

ing Princess.) They are not as high-priced as Crystal or Radisson but definitely more than the mass-market lines. Their Pacific Mexican itinerary is limited as to number of sailings but has an interesting route from Puerto Caldera in Costa Rica to Los Angeles or the reverse.

Radisson Seven Seas Cruses: ☎ *(866) 314-3212; www.rssc.com*. This upscale line is considered one of the best in the world if you are a member of the *Condé Naste* set. Their fleet has about a half-dozen ships – all quite small and personalized service is the name of the game. All of their staterooms are suites so you'll always have plenty of room to spread out. Their Mexican itineraries are quite limited as to the number of departures, but they do have a good selection of ports, including some of the less-visited places.

Royal Olympia Cruises: ☎ *(800) 872-6400; www. royalolympia.com*. This old Greek line has, historically, sent a couple of ships over to the Caribbean during the winter and they've made a few trans-Canal runs with stops along the Mexican Riviera and Baja. However, ROC is in bankruptcy and, although they are still operating a limited schedule in Europe with some of their oldest ships, it doesn't appear that they will be a factor in the Mexican market. Their telephone number is included for reference purposes should the current situation change. Unfortunately, their newest and best ships, which were used in North America, were reclaimed by the finance company.

If you look quickly at cruise line brochures you will probably find some other upscale cruise lines that might say they go to Mexico. However, these serve only Mexico's Caribbean-side ports of call. On occasion they may also offer an itinerary or two that covers the Pacific side of Mexico, but not on a regular scheduled basis. At most they would be repositioning cruises. On the other hand, if you are interested in traveling in a more upscale mode, it always pays to get brochures when you're ready to go because schedules do change frequently and a line may decide to add an itinerary where you want to go. In this category are **Seabourn, Silversea** and **Cunard**. The latter isn't in the "yacht" class but is somewhere between the Holland Americas of the cruise-line world and Crystal.

WHO'S WHO IN THE CRUISE BUSINESS

There are literally dozens of cruise lines throughout the world, many of them completely unknown to the American traveler because they don't cater to this market. But even if you limit yourself to North America there are more than a dozen major lines. At least in name. Consolidation, so common in every industry, is also a trend in this business. There are relatively few cruise companies if you consolidate brands by their corporate banner. Here's the lineup:

Carnival: Besides Carnival, this industry behemoth owns Holland America and Princess, as well as world-famous Cunard, Costa Cruises, Windstar and Seabourn.

Royal Caribbean: The Royal Caribbean brand is, by itself, the second-largest cruise line after Carnival. That goes for the group as well because RC also owns Celebrity Cruises.

It is the practice of Carnival and Royal Caribbean to let each line operate independently, thereby allowing for more variation in cruise style. Despite the consolidation there has yet to be any upward trend in prices although now that Carnival has acquired Princess (in 2003) there is some concern that this could happen. On the positive side, the cruise lines will (with lots of restrictions) give you credit for traveling on a sister line. For instance, you can get past-guest treatment and prices on a Carnival Cruise if you sailed in Europe on Costa or Cunard. As far as the rest of the industry is concerned, most of the remaining lines are independent. Norwegian Cruise Line is owned by a large Asian-based cruise company called Star Cruises. But NCL also largely operates according to its own style on a day-to-day basis.

Setting Priorities

Selecting Your Dream Cruise

With so many options for cruising the Mexican Riviera and Baja in terms of different cruise lines, different ships and even different itineraries, it can be a somewhat difficult (although fun) task to select the right cruise for *you*. So, how do you go about selecting the best cruise? Begin by defining "best" – what is best for one person will not be the best for another. People have different priorities. Let's take a look at some of the major factors that will determine which cruise is going to be your dream cruise come true.

The Cruise Line

As you have just read, each line has a distinctive style or personality that is reflected throughout its fleet. Do you want a sophisticated luxury experience or a more fun-oriented cruise? Do you like refined elegance in the ship's public areas or is glitz more your style? Is this a romantic getaway for two or a family affair? Formal or informal? More or fewer dining choices? These and many other questions can help narrow down which cruise lines are in the running for your dollars. To a large degree, your available budget will also help determine what line or lines to consider. Crystal is, for example, a lot more expensive than Carnival. You have to judge how much certain features of a cruise line (and the ship) are worth to you.

The Ship

Many ship features are determined by the line that owns them. However, even within specific cruise lines, there can be a great variation in the age, size, and facilities of different ships. The newer and larger ships are likely to have the most diverse facilities, dining choices and activities. But larger doesn't always mean better since a lot of experienced travelers prefer a somewhat smaller vessel. Within the major lines there is often a big difference in the size of their largest ship compared to their smallest. Even when limiting the list just to ships with Mexican itineraries, as I did in the preceding section, the choices still reveal many differing types of ships.

The Ports of Call

Look for an itinerary that hits more of the places you want to see. There will be more information on this in the next section, which will serve as your guide to evaluating itineraries.

Wrapping it all up and weighing the relative merits of these and other factors isn't always easy. Keep in mind that cruising to Mexico is different than cruising to, for example, Alaska. There, people usually take a cruise because you can't get to many of the places of interest by any other means. European cruising, on the other hand, has some of the great cities of the world as a draw in addition to the cruise experience. Mexican cruises have much similarity to Caribbean cruises. While the ports undoubtedly have their own unique charms and have plenty that is worth seeing, a large percentage of cruise ship visitors come for the cruising experience itself. Therefore, when choosing a Mexican Riviera cruise, the ship itself will be a more important factor.

Information Sources

*T*here are many sources for general information on the cruise lines and on cruising itself. The cruise line brochures are a necessary piece of literature before you make any decision, but I cannot emphasize enough that these are marketing tools for the cruise lines. As a result, they're often far from objective. The same, of course, can be said about the extensive websites that each and every cruise line has. There are also more general sites about cruise ships but, here too, many are run by travel agencies looking for business or feature only certain cruise lines. The **Cruise Lines International Association** (CLIA) is an industry organization composed of all the major cruise lines and many smaller ones. Their website, www.cruising.org, also paints the experience in a purely positive light, as you might expect. Despite this, it is a useful site because it contains a wealth of information, both statistical and otherwise. You can also call CLIA at ☎ (212) 921-0066.

In addition to CLIA, I recommend that web surfers check out the following sites before making any final decision on their cruise:

www.cruise2.com
www.cruisecritic.com
www.cruisemates.com
www.cruiseopinion.com
www.cruisereviews.com
www.sealetter.com

The primary feature of most of these sites is unbiased reviews submitted by travelers like you. In fact, *you* can send in a review of any ship you've cruised on and it will be added to their database. Because the people sending in the reviews are not affiliated with the cruise industry, they are generally more objective. Of course, you have to read the reviews carefully. Some people can get ticked off at one little thing and then decide to knock everything else about their cruise experience. **Cruise2.com** is a little different in that it offers a wealth of statistical and other information for all cruise lines and ships. **Sealetter.com**, too, is a more comprehensive site and is one of the best sources of information. It is similar in some ways to the website that is described below in the sidebar.

Cruise Lines & Ships

A CRUISE FANATIC'S ULTIMATE WEBSITE

For people who just can't learn enough and read enough about what's going on in the world of cruising, there's *Cruise News Daily*, which can be accessed on the Internet at **www.cruisenewsdaily.com**. It is written in newspaper fashion with timely reports on everything from new ships to itineraries that are being altered because of current weather conditions. Their staff has inside access to what is going on at the cruise lines and you can often find out things at *Cruise News Daily* well before they become generally known. I look at it every day. That's the good part. The bad part is that what you get on their free website is just a synopsis of the full articles. You can see the full article only if you subscribe to their service. Subscription rates begin at about $20 for a month although there are discounted rates for longer subscriptions and new subscribers. You receive the full text via e-mail either on a daily or weekly basis – the option is yours. The free site does offer access to some of their other features, including photos of ships under construction and a complete rundown on what ships are being built in the yards. It's a fascinating site but only for the dedicated cruise-aholic!

Evaluating Ship Itineraries

In some of my previous cruising guides I listed the actual itineraries for each ship and evaluated them on a case-by-case basis. I find that I can no longer do that because the cruise lines seem to change itineraries so often that it's impossible to keep the information timely in a book that comes out only occasionally. Moreover, Mexican itineraries tend to be much more similar in nature than in the Caribbean or the Mediterranean where the number of ports is much higher and the combination of possible ports of call is almost endless. The greater similarities in Mexican cruising do make things easier to discuss in general terms. You should always check itineraries in the most current cruise line brochures. However, in the last year or so I've seen an increasing number of instances where the cruise lines will change itineraries (or ships) prior to the printed expiration date of the brochure. Often you can find more up-to-date itineraries on the cruise lines' websites. Regardless, you should always check at the time you book to make sure that you're getting the itinerary you want.

Baja Itineraries

These are three- or four-night trips from either Los Angeles or San Diego. The shorter version inevitably calls on Ensenada, while the longer one adds Catalina Island. One day is always spent at sea. Both Carnival and Royal Caribbean offer these two itineraries in exactly the same form so there is no edge that either line has in the itinerary itself. If you opt for this trip, then it should be based solely on the line and/or ship that you prefer. **Cabo San Lucas** is also in Baja but it's much farther and, hence, isn't a part of any of these short Baja itineraries. The other ports in Baja are **La Paz**, **Loreto** and **Santa Rosalía** (all on the Sea of Cortés), all offered only by Holland America on nine- or 10-night cruises. They also include a couple of Mexican Riviera ports.

One-Week Roundtrip Mexican Riviera Itineraries

Whether they leave from Los Angeles or San Diego, the typical seven-night Mexican Riviera cruise will stop at **Cabo San Lucas** in Baja and **Puerto Vallarta** and **Mazátlan** on the Riviera. In fact, this itinerary is so standardized (except for the order of ports and small variations in the number of hours spent at each) that it is quite difficult to find *any* other one-week Mexican Riviera cruise from southern California. A few lines are now offering an eight-night trip that adds **Acapulco**. Some of these run on a regular basis while others are scheduled only on a few dates, mostly around holiday periods.

Other Itineraries

Except for the trans-Panama Canal itineraries – which can vary quite a bit in point of embarkation/disembarkation, duration and ports of call – other itineraries are usually longer versions of the Mexican Riviera. They may be longer because they originate at a more distant port (such as San Francisco) or because they add one or more ports of call. These would most likely be **Manzanillo** and/or **Acapulco**, depending upon just how long the cruise is. There are also cruises that originate or end in Acapulco at one end and a southern California port at the other end. Because these one-way cruises have less time at sea than a round-trip cruise, you can usually count on a minimum of four ports on such trips. You might even get five but this means a cruise of longer than a week except for a few of the fastest ships.

If the ports of call are a very important part of your selection process then the right itinerary for you will be the one that visits the most ports that are of interest. However, that is not *always* the full story. So, as you peruse itineraries in the brochures, keep in mind the following when making a decision:

▶ Does the itinerary visit the ports that you are *most* interested in? While no cruise is likely to include every port that you want to visit (since you are not designing a custom itinerary), if it stops at most of what you consider the desirable ports then that is a good first step.

▶ How much time is allotted in each port? Is it enough for you to see most of the sights that are important to you? The answer to the last question should be easy enough because the port descriptions that follow later in this book will give you a good idea of what can be done in one day. Of course, if you are going to be taking organized shore excursions, you will know in advance exactly what you will be seeing.

▶ Even if the number of hours allowed is sufficient, what about the hours of the visit? Some ships may spend a significant number of hours in a port but arrive late in the day, leaving little time for sightseeing before attractions close. This is alright if the types of activities you are most interested in aren't restricted to certain hours or if they fit into the time the ship will be in port. Just be sure that you factor this into your evaluation.

▶ Compare the amount of time at sea versus that spent in port. Depending upon the itinerary, a one-week cruise may have anywhere from one day at sea to four and stop at as few as two ports or as many as four or five. Typically, week-long cruises spend two full days at sea. The relative importance of this will depend upon the primary purpose of your cruise. Many days at sea are fine if you are most interested in the cruise experience. However, if you want a port-intensive vacation you will not be well served by an itinerary that spends three or more days at sea.

▶ If other activities such as shopping and watersports are as important or more important than sightseeing, then look to visit ports where those activities are considered best. Again, the port descriptions will help you with this aspect of itinerary selection. In general, all of the Mexican Riviera ports are great for watersports. Although there are a couple of

Cruise Lines & Ships

ports where such activities are the main event, none of the cruise lines have recreation-oriented "private islands" such as in the Caribbean.

Options in Port

*U*nless you have sailed all the way to Mexico *only* for the undeniable pleasures of the cruise experience, the ports you visit will certainly be one of the most important aspects of your trip. Selecting the itinerary was only the first step in planning your land activities. Now it is time to decide how you are going to see what you have traveled so far to reach.

There are two basic choices: either you use the cruise line's shore excursion program of guided or escorted tours, or you head out on your own. As with everything else, there are advantages and disadvantages to each approach depending upon your interests, planning capabilities and spirit of adventure to go it alone. Of course, you might want to take an organized shore excursion in one port and to go on your own in the next port. Some places are more suited to individual exploration than others.

Organized Shore Excursions

A long list of shore excursion options will usually be provided to you in advance for each port that your ship calls on. When it comes to sightseeing, I don't normally recommend a shore excursion, except in those places where it may be better to go on a tour due to local conditions. This generally isn't the case in either Baja or the Mexican Riviera unless you plan to head away from the port cities and into more rural areas where traveling conditions might be much more difficult. Unlike some areas of Mexico, the Pacific ports of call and nearby regions are reasonably safe, so security is less of a factor. These considerations aside, shore excursions are very popular for two reasons. The first is convenience. You will be picked up at the ship, taken to all of the places listed in the itinerary with a knowledgeable local guide to explain things, and then be transported back to the ship. You don't have to do any real planning, worry about getting lost, or getting back late and missing the ship's departure. On the other hand, the shore excursions do have definite limitations. Group travel is slower than individual travel, so you will see less. This becomes even more pronounced if a lengthy lunch stop is made or if time is allowed for shopping and you don't want to do that. Also, and perhaps most important, the excursions available may not even cover most of the places that *you* want to see. Finally, shore excursions are no bargain. Two people using public transportation, renting a car, or even using some taxis can expect to pay less for a day of sightseeing than they would on a shore excursion, even if all of the activities are the same.

The list of available excursions in each port will be almost identical regardless of which cruise line you take. The only exception of note is that some very long excursions may be omitted for those ships spending a limited time in a given port. The reason for the sameness is that the cruise lines aren't running the tours. All the lines make arrangements with local tour operators and these are usually the same for all the lines coming to a particular port. Although the cruise lines obviously get group rates and claim that they don't get anything out of the independently run excursions, I have some difficulty swallowing that as the cost of just about every excursion I've examined is virtually identical to the price you would pay if you

Cruise Lines & Ships

went on your own to a local tour operator and booked the exact same trip.

Shore excursions generally take one of two forms. The first is the **sightseeing** variety, which is usually a highlight tour of the port city, although more detailed visits to specific points of interest are also common. Many full-day excursions leave the city and explore the surrounding countryside. These trips frequently allow at least some time for shopping, whether or not you're interested in doing so.

The other type of excursion is **recreation-related**. These essentially provide transportation to a site to partake in whatever sport or activity you choose and you can do so with the camaraderie of your fellow passengers. Some excursions allow time for both sightseeing and recreation.

As indicated before, I generally prefer seeing the sights on my own where possible. However, for recreational and sporting activities the organized excursion is much more convenient. Often, as in the case of golf or tennis, it is the only way for day-trippers to partake in these activities because the local resorts sometimes make their facilities available only to hotel guests. Whether on a sightseeing or recreational excursion, lunch may or may not be included, so do check the itinerary. Also make certain how long the excursion is. You may be able to do a guided shore excursion in the morning, for example, and explore the town on your own in the afternoon. Sometimes you will find it's possible to book two half-day excursions in the same port.

BOOKING SHORE EXCURSIONS

You can find out about available shore excursions for whatever cruise itinerary you've selected in advance. Sometimes, the cruise line will send you a brochure on the excursion options with your sailing documents. However, the increasingly widespread use of the Internet has had a huge impact on the process. Every cruise line will have detailed information about *all* of their available excursions on their website.

All of the major lines have now implemented a system where you can book your shore excursions on-line prior to your cruise. If you don't have access to the Internet, then you'll have to wait until you board the ship to make reservations. Do so as soon as possible after boarding so that you won't be closed out of an excursion you really want to take. This can be done either at the shore excursion desk or, in most cases, via the ship's interactive closed-circuit TV system. Regardless of whether you book on-line or onboard the ship, tickets will be delivered to your stateroom. All charges for shore excursions will be put on your onboard account.

On Your Own

Travel on your own in port is best done where most of the sights are close by or where transportation is readily available. It allows you to see exactly what you want to see, to spend more or less time in a given place depending upon how much you are enjoying it, and also often allows you to have a better feel for the local people and customs. In those cases where you have many hours in port and it includes lunch time, you have the option of returning to the ship to eat or trying some of the local cuisine on shore. Either of those options has a greater appeal to me than being herded as a group to a restaurant chosen by the tour operator (not that they'll take you to a bad place).

One possible disadvantage of going on your own is that if you get lost, or lose track of time, the ship isn't going to wait for you. It will, however, always wait for the rare late-returning excursion. Whenever you venture out on your own (except in those tiny ports where you'll always be within a few minutes walk of the ship), take the telephone number of the ship's port agent. If you are going to be a little late or have any other problem, you can phone ahead and let them know. *Do not*, however, use this as a means of getting more time in port. It should be used only in a genuine emergency. The telephone numbers will be provided to you, usually in the daily program. If not, be sure to ask for them.

ANOTHER TOURING OPTION

The cruise lines are always looking for ways to enhance their passengers' experiences in the ports of call. Holland America has come up with an interesting concept. They realize that a car provides the greatest flexibility but that many people are hesitant about driving in foreign countries. HAL's answer is the *Signature Collection* of shore excursions. It's a fancy name but a simple program – you sightsee in a private car with your own personal driver, along with an English-speaking guide. The program was first introduced in Europe but Holland America has announced that they will be expanding it to cover all foreign ports of call. The major drawback is the expense because this option does not come cheap – it starts at $300 in Europe and one can expect that Mexico would have similar prices.

Tours can accommodate two to eight people and are for either four or eight hours. This will be tailored to fit various ports. Although there is a "standard" itinerary for each port, if it's only your party in the car you can ask that they change the itinerary a little or a lot. Similar private touring is sometimes available in various ports from other cruise lines, especially Princess. However, to date, Holland America is the only line that has firmly committed to making this a standard option in all ports.

Complete Cruise Tours

Cruise tours are package plans that combine land travel either before or after the cruise – or perhaps both. These types of packages are popular in Alaska and in Europe and are offered in an amazing variety. The nature of cruising Mexico's Pacific coast, however, with its common round-trips to California ports, doesn't lend itself nearly as much to complete packages. Extended stays in your embarkation or debarkation city are available from the cruse lines and these are usually the closest thing you'll find to cruise tours when it comes to Mexico. But check those brochures because you just never know when one or more cruise lines will put such a package together. Remember to always compare the cost of extended stays and cruise packages with the cost of doing it on your own. In general, you will find that the cruise lines aren't offering any bargains. In fact, they are most often overpriced, especially when you compare the charges for these plans to the good value provided by the cruise itself.

A NAUTICAL PRIMER

Those who live and work on the sea have always had a language of their own. This continues today whether it applies to the navy, commercial shipping or the cruise industry. Although the staff of most cruise ships will usually speak in terms that land-lubbers understand, nautical terms will be heard frequently during the course of your journey. Here's a quick rundown on some of the ones you'll be most likely to encounter either during the planning of your trip or while onboard.

Beam: The width of the ship measured at its widest point (generally mid-ship).

Bow: The front of the ship. (*Fore* indicates toward the bow or near the bow.)

Class: A grouping of ships of the same type. Two or more ships in the same class can also be said to be *sister* ships. It is customary in the cruise industry to name the class after the first ship built of a particular type. The only major line not following this practice is Holland America. They make up a name for each class of ship in their fleet. Ships in the same class have identical or nearly identical deck plans and facilities. However, the décor can be and usually is quite different. Sometimes ships of a particular class that were built several years after the original one can wind up having some significant differences as the cruise lines are always trying to improve things.

Gross Registered Tonnage (GRT): This has nothing to do with the weight of the ship. Rather, it's a useful measure of just how big a ship is. The GRT, although listed in tons or tonnes, is the available internal space of the ship.

Knot: A measure of speed equal to about 1.15 miles per hour.

Nautical mile: The equivalent of 1.15 miles on land.

Port: The direction to the right of the ship, when facing the bow. Also refers to that side of the ship.

Starboard: The opposite of port; that is the direction to the left when facing the bow. Also refers to the left side of the ship.

Stern: The rear of the ship. (*Aft* is toward the stern or near the stern.)

Cruise Lines & Ships

A Practical Guide to Your Cruise

*W*hether you are a first-timer or an experienced sea voyager, this A to Z directory of practical information should help to answer many of your questions and make your cruise a more enjoyable experience.

Accommodations on Land

Certainly one of the best parts of cruising is that, once you unpack your bags in your stateroom, there is no living out of a suitcase. The ship is your hotel, whether it's a three-night mini-cruise to Ensenada or a two-week or longer extravaganza through the Panama Canal. In some cruise markets (most notably Europe and Alaska) many passengers decide to spend extra time on land either before or after the cruise. This is not generally the case with Mexican cruises. For the most part, the only hotel night you are likely to need is in the embarkation city and perhaps the disembarkation city if that is different from your point of origination and you want to spend more time there. If you are arriving at your embarkation point via air, then it is very possible that it would be difficult to arrive early enough on the day your cruise starts. In such cases the cruise lines will often arrange a hotel night for you as part of your transportation option. Or they may offer multi-night stays before or after the cruise as a way to extend your vacation. Be forewarned that they always pick out fancy places with fancy prices. Moreover, you could probably book the same hotel as they do at a lower rate.

The US cities where you are most likely to need accommodations are, of course, the gateways of Los Angeles, San Diego and San Francisco. Moreover, those passengers beginning their cruise in Acapulco will almost certainly have to spend a night in that city (although some cruises do schedule a night onboard ship prior to departure). In the California cities accommodations are ubiquitous and range in price and quality from budget motels to the most luxurious upscale resorts and city-center hotels. All of the national chains are well-represented in every price category. If you are simply spending the night to ensure that you get to your ship on time and don't plan on sightseeing or other activities in California, then it makes sense to pick out a location that is reasonably close to the cruise ship terminal. Some hotels will even have shuttle service to the port. For **Los Angeles**, the most convenient places to stay are in San Pedro and Long Beach, where the terminals are located. They are close to one another so you could even stay in San Pedro for a Long Beach departure or vice-versa without spending a fortune on getting to the dock. Other close-by locations (especially for Long Beach) are Newport Beach and Anaheim. In **San Diego** and San **Francisco**, downtown locations are closest to the port, but more expensive. You might consider staying by the airport instead.

Acapulco presents much more of a problem for those just trying to make connections. While there is no shortage of hotels, you will find that reasonably priced accommodations are hard to come by, especially if you want standards that are up to those expected by American travelers. Prices in excess of $200 per night are not uncommon. Try to avoid the most expensive areas such as Acapulco Diamante or Puerto Marqués. There are hotels along the waterfront Costera that are relatively close to the cruise ship dock and are somewhat less expensive.

Snorkeling in Puerto Vallarta (Bruce Herman)

Above: Beach at Santa Maria. Cabo San Lucas (Bruce Herman)

Below: Kayaking in Los Cabos (Bruce Herman)

Climate & When to Go

When to cruise to Mexico can be influenced by two main factors in addition to your own availability. These are the dates on which the cruise you're interested in is offered and the weather. To some extent, these two are related. Scan the table below and you'll see that the summer months in Baja and the Mexican Riviera are very hot. As a result (and because many ships that sail the Riviera transfer to Alaska for the summer), even though some ships travel this route all-year long, many Mexican Riviera cruises are offered only from around September through early May. The shorter Baja cruises are given throughout the year. Prices are highest in the middle of winter and around holiday times such as Thanksgiving, Christmas through New Year's, and Easter; they drop as you get close to summer.

	Acapulco	Cabo San Lucas	Ensenada	La Paz	Manzanillo	Mazatlán	Puerto Vallarta
Monthly Average High & Low Temperatures (°F) & Rainfall *(inches)*							
Jan	88/72/.3	79/60/0	66/45/2.6	73/54/.6	83/68/.9	75/63/.6	80/62/1.1
Feb	88/72/.1	75/60/.3	68/45/2.5	77/54/.1	83/68/0.5	73/63/0.2	80/62/.7
Mar	88/72/.1	77/60/.3	68/46/2.4	89/55/.1	81/67/0	74/63/.1	81/63/.3
Apr	89/73/.1	84/63/0	69/48/.9	86/58/0	82/69/0	77/66/.1	82/65/.3
May	90/75/1.1	85/65/0	70/52/.2	90/61/0	83/72/.1	81/71/0	85/70/.5
June	90/77/10.4	85/67/.3	73/54/0	94/65/.1	87/77/4	85/77/1.2	88/76/8.1
July	91/77/8.9	92/73/.3	77/61/0	97/74/.5	88/78/4	86/78/6	89/76/13.2
Aug	91/77/10.4	95/74/.3	79/61/0	96/74/1.4	89/78/5.4	87/78/8	90/76/12.9
Sept	90/76/15	95/76/1.5	79/59/.2	94/74/2.5	88/78/15	86/78/8.9	90/76/13.8
Oct	90/75/6.3	91/74/.8	75/54/.8	91/66/.5	88/77/5	85/76/2.9	89/74/4.8
Nov	90/74/1.9	85/65/.8	72/48/.9	84/61/.2	86/73/.7	80/70/.5	85/68/.7
Dec	88/72/.3	80/65/.3	68/45/1.7	77/55/.8	84/70/2.1	75/65/.6	81/65/.8

I suggest avoiding the Mexican Riviera during the summer months, not because of the temperature (which doesn't vary all that much from one part of the year to another) but because of the often excessive amount of rain that the distinct summer wet season brings with it. Baja is, indeed, hot in the summer, but it is a dry heat and isn't as bad as you might expect. On the other hand, a place like Ensenada is quite cool in the middle of winter and isn't ideal for swimming or sitting on the beach. Elsewhere, you can count on good temperatures for bathing at any time of the year.

When it comes to stormy weather (most of those huge rainfall amounts in the chart come in the form of brief but torrential downpours), it is the late summer and early fall season that has the most chance of Pacific **hurricanes**. These occur anywhere from the southern part of Baja all the way down to the end of the Mexican Riviera. There are also **Pacific storms** in the winter that become somewhat more frequent the farther north you head. However, these are not reasons in themselves not to go at these times since it is relatively rare for a cruise ship to have to alter its itinerary due to the weather. Still, sometimes a port might have to be skipped due to sea conditions that would make it unsafe to dock. This almost never happens where the ship ties up at the pier but can be the case in ports where tenders are required. It is the captain's call whether using the tenders, which lack the stability of large ships, would be too risky.

Costs

A logical question to ask is "how much is this cruise going to cost me?" This section will explore *all* of your potential costs, except airfare, something the brochures sometimes tend to bypass. A few things should be kept in mind before you scan the prices. Cruise fares are always quoted on a per person basis and this assumes double-occupancy in a stateroom. Persons traveling alone will have to pay what two people traveling together would pay, or close to it – outrageous by any standard. On the other hand, a third person in a room (either child or adult) pays a much reduced rate. The costs below represent the list price or so-called **brochure** rate, which is equivalent to the rack rate in a hotel. However, before you fall out of your chair, remember that significant discounts are almost always available off the brochure rate.

The fares shown below are for a seven-night cruise, because that is what the majority of cruise lines offer. Cruises of less than a week are often higher-priced on a per-night basis. Accordingly, a four-night Baja cruise, for instance, is usually only slightly more than the three-night version. Conversely, cruises of more than a week are frequently less expensive on a per-night basis than the standard cruise of one week. Within each cruise line the rates from one ship to another usually vary only by a small amount, if at all. Now let's take a look at typical average brochure prices for various classes of staterooms on the major lines, rounded off to the nearest hundred:

	Inside Room	Outside Room	Outside Room (with balcony)	Suite (minimum)
Carnival	$1,500	$1,800	$2,000	$2,500
Celebrity	$1,800	$2,200	$2,600	$2,900
Holland America	$1,900	$2,400	$2,800	$2,900
Norwegian	$1,400	$1,600	$1,800	$2,100
Princess	$1,700	$2,100	$2,400	$2,800
Royal Caribbean	$1,300	$1,500	$1,800	$2,100

The actual list price in each non-suite category can be anywhere from a few hundred dollars less to a few hundred dollars more depending upon season. The price

Practical Information

range between lines reflects the level of "luxury" for each line. In reality, if you were to rearrange the prices from most expensive to least expensive, they would roughly reflect the approximate order in which most cruise experts rank the lines. (The even more upscale lines that were briefly mentioned earlier would almost always be much more expensive, often two or even three times as much.)

Average prices are affected to a great extent by two important factors. The first, as already alluded to, is the variation in prices between low and high seasons. The difference of a week can sometimes mean a large drop in price. For example, although the winter is the high season, there are often much-reduced prices in the week or two following New Year's.

The second reason for a range in costs is that there are so many different classes of staterooms within each general category. There are almost always a very limited number of staterooms in the lowest price category. Suites have the greatest possible range in price because of the wide variation in size and level of luxury. On some ships aren't that many suites and the price range might be more limited. So, while the minimum suite prices shown don't vary by a wide amount, the maximum suite prices can be as low as $5,000 or possibly a little less on some lines and go up to as much as $15,000.

You should also be aware that, depending upon which ships are serving Mexican routes, not all categories may be available on every line. Which type of accommodation to choose is discussed further in the *Selecting the Right Stateroom For You* section, page 134. The cruise prices shown above also include port charges assessed on each passenger, which are often quite significant. It does not include various other taxes and fees imposed by different governments. However, compared to port charges, these are not that significant, typically running from about

$20-$50 per person for the entire cruise. While cruise lines are now in the practice of quoting rates *with* port charges, many discount travel agencies and websites give you a low-ball figure by *excluding* the port charges. Always be sure what you are dealing with before you pronounce a price as good or bad.

The only other mandatory (or almost mandatory) expense that you will incur is for **tips**. Although there is no law that states you must leave a gratuity, it is common practice; rare, indeed, is the individual who will not do so. You can expect to spend about $100 per person for a week-long cruise. More guidelines on this topic will be given in the *Gratuities* section.

Other onboard expenses of an optional nature that you may incur are as follows:

▶ **Drinks and snacks:** Both alcoholic beverages and soft drinks are (with rare exceptions) on a fee basis. Since the cruise staff will constantly be offering you drinks, this can become quite expensive if you don't keep watch on it. Most cruise lines offer pre-paid packages for children that include unlimited sodas. My suggestion is that when you get thirsty during the day head up to the buffet. The majority of major cruise lines offer free self-service fruit juices all day long. There's always plenty of free food to be found as well, but some lines may charge for things like premium ice cream; likewise for pastries at the patisseries.

▶ **Dining:** While all of your on-board meals are included in the cruise fare, almost all of the larger new ships (and an increasing number of remodeled older and smaller ones) have one or more upscale alternative restaurants for which an additional fee is usually imposed. More will be said about this in the next section on dining.

Practical Information

93

▶ **Personal Expenditures:** This includes a wide variety of items, such as the spa, beauty salon, the onboard shopping facilities, laundry service and so forth. The amount you spend on this category can run from practically nothing to hundreds of dollars. Prices are always available in advance, so when you receive the bill at the end of your cruise, the balance shouldn't come as a shock to you.

▶ **Shore Excursions:** This is the only other significant cost factor that you should encounter, either on your own or for guided excursions. Here, again, the cost will be highly variable, depending upon the number and nature of the tours you take. In general, you should know the cost of available shore excursions prior to your cruise even if you wait to book them until you're onboard. Some websites list the cost of excursions. If not, you'll almost certainly be provided with a descriptive price list with your cruise documents. Those touring on their own will have to figure on the cost of a car rental, taxi or public transportation, admissions, and so forth. Lunch might also be an added expense. The practice of cruise lines offering a box lunch seems to have gone the way of the dinosaur, but you might ask about it. If you plan your day so that you can be back at the ship for lunch it will save a lot of money and maybe even time. Of course, this is not always possible without wasting too much time.

Discounts

Seeing is not believing when it comes to prices listed in the cruise brochures. Every line offers a price reduction for booking early. Some form of discounted pricing is always shown in the brochure as well. Most lines offer a straight cash discount, which may begin at around $400 for lower-priced staterooms and rise to well over $1,000 for more expensive accommodations. A smaller number of lines give a percentage off the regular fare, as much as 40% in some instances but typically more in the range of 10% to 20%. Additionally, your discount will vary within the same cruise line, depending upon how far in advance you book. In general, the earlier you do it, the greater the discount. Refer to the individual cruise line brochures or your travel agent for specific cruise line-sponsored discounts.

If there's room available, you can also sometimes get aboard at a greatly reduced rate if you wait until the last minute. Cruise lines hate to sail with less than a full ship and they will offer ridiculously low prices if space is available. However, I don't recommend this as a regular practice if your heart is set on a particular cruise. If sales are brisk, a last-minute discount may never be offered and you might not get on the ship at all.

Another way to cut costs is to book through a discount cruise travel agent who buys large blocks of staterooms at sharply reduced prices. Newspaper travel sections are filled with advertisements for such agents. To ensure that you are dealing with a reputable company, make sure they are a member of at least one of the following: **CLIA** (Cruise Lines International Association, www.cruising.org), **NACOA** (National Association of Cruise Oriented Agencies, www.nacoaonline.com), or **ASTA** (American Society of Travel Agents, www.astanet.com). There are other reputable travel organizations, but the preceding three are the standards. Consult your local phone directory to find the cruise-only travel agents in your area. There are dozens of nationwide firms, including many that operate via the Internet. Among the larger national cruise agencies of this type are:

Practical Information

▶ **Cruises of Distinction**, www.cruisesof-distinction.com, ☎ (800) 434-5544

▶ **Cruise.com**, www.cruise.com

▶ **CruisesOnly.com**, www.cruisesonly.com, ☎ (800) 278-4737

▶ **National Discount Cruise Co.**, www.nationaldiscountcruise.com, ☎ (800) 788-8108

▶ **White Travel Service**, www.whitetravel.com, ☎ (800) 547-4790

Package deals that include air sometimes work out to be less expensive than booking the air and cruise sections separately (see the upcoming section on *Flight Arrangements* for further details). But no pricing system is ever static in the travel world. Do some research. Price things separately and as part of a package deal and see which is the best price at the time. And don't hesitate to tell a travel agent or supplier of a good price you were quoted elsewhere. They may just come back and beat it.

Since all of the cruise lines are anxious to have your repeat business, it's standard practice for them to offer discounts to travelers who have sailed with them before. These discounts can sometimes be substantial. They usually start at 10% (on top of any other discounts that may apply) but sometimes can be much more, especially on those lines that increase the benefit based on the number of cruises you have taken with them. Another way to take advantage of past cruising is to request such discounts when you book on an affiliated line – that is, a different line than you've cruised in the past but which is owned by the same company. See page 107 for a list of who's who in the cruising world. All of the industry works this way and the ultimate example is the **"Vacation Interchange**

Privileges" offered by seven lines, all of which are part of Carnival Corporation. For past guests the news seems quite good. But here's the bad news. Popular cruise destinations, especially during peak travel periods, are often excluded from discount-eligible departure dates.

The essential point of all this is quite clear: with the variety of discounts available being so great, you should never have to pay the full fare!

Gratuities

Except for a few lines (mostly the top-dollar luxury lines), gratuities for ship personnel are *not* included in the base cruise fare. And, as is the case throughout the travel and leisure industry, tipping is a way of life. Most ship personnel that will be directly serving you (dining room staff, cabin attendants, etc.) do not earn a great salary and tips provide a substantial portion of their income. The question of how much to tip involves your evaluation of the service provided and your own personal preferences and beliefs regarding gratuities.

Cruise line management will always provide written guidelines as to what is the suggested amount to tip. But it is important to remember that these are only guidelines and that you – the customer – have the final say. Don't be intimidated into giving more than you think is warranted or more than you can afford. On the other hand, exceptional service is always a good reason to consider tipping above the suggested amounts. Here are some commonly accepted guidelines:

Dining Room Staff: $3-3.50 per day per person for your waiter and about half that for his or her assistant. Your dining room area head waiter (or captain) should also be given about $1-2 per day, but in my opinion this can be reduced or omitted unless he does something spe-

Practical Information

cial for you. Likewise, most cruise lines also suggest tipping the restaurant manager (i.e., the maitre d'), but I don't see the need for that unless he also has performed some special service for you. If you frequently ask advice from the wine steward (where a separate individual handles this chore), then he should receive a tip of a dollar per day.

Cabin Attendant: $3-3.50 per person per day is acceptable. Some sources recommend a small amount for the chief housekeeper but, as above, I don't see the need for that unless he or she has handled a particular problem well for you.

Other Staff: The only other people you will likely have to consider tipping are bartenders, cocktail waiters and waitresses, as well as deckhands who help out with the lounge chairs. These individuals are tipped each time you use their services However, all cruise lines have already included a mandatory gratuity (usually 15%) for those who serve you drinks so you should not feel obligated to give anything additional. If you wish, you may give a buck to deckhands when they help you but, again, this is not required.

No tipping of dining room staff and cabin attendants takes place during the course of the cruise. All gratuities are given at the very end. Now we get to the tricky part – the actual procedure for handing over the tips. In the old days of cruising (three or four years ago), it was still common for gratuities to be given in cash. Marked envelopes for each staff member were left in your stateroom and you gave the envelope with the cash tips to the appropriate person on the last night of the cruise. This is now becoming an obsolete method and that's good because few people felt very comfortable with the procedure.

The most common method in use today is for all gratuities to be charged to your shipboard account automatically in the amount recommended by the cruise line. If that is the amount you want to give then you don't have to do anything at all. However, even though your account is charged automatically, the amount can be changed. You have complete freedom to raise or lower the amount to all personnel or to one or more specific people who have served you. Procedures to do so may vary slightly from one line to another but the basic way is to go to the information desk (purser) and fill out a form that indicates how you want gratuities to be distributed. Do this on or before the last night of the cruise.

There are other methods of gratuity-giving on a few lines, such as pooled tips. These won't be encountered on any line serving Mexico. Norwegian, however, has introduced a new policy to comply with regulations for its US-flagged ships. Essentially, it's a compulsory $10 per day service charge.

As mentioned before, there are relatively few lines that include gratuities in the cost of the cruise. And don't fall for the advertisements of "free" tips on some of these lines. It simply isn't true. The price has been raised to reflect this cost – it just relieves you of the burden of having to do it on your own. If you're traveling with a line that does this, there's no need to tip any more. On the other hand, if you feel that a particular crew member's service has been outstanding, show your appreciation by providing a small additional gratuity.

Practical Information

Dining

Dining is one of the most important and obvious pleasures of this form of travel. Even if you have never cruised before, I'm sure you've met someone returning from a cruise who can't stop boasting not only about how great the food was, but how much of it there was. If you're on a diet there's no doubt that a cruise isn't the best place to be. But, heck – you only live once. Forget about your diet and enjoy! You can lose the pounds when you come back or maybe even try to shed a few pounds before the cruise in preparation for it. (If a special diet is essential, this should be arranged at the time you book your cruise. Most cruise lines can accommodate various dietary needs.) You'll savor wonderfully prepared cuisine, often from renowned chefs, and try delicacies from a wide variety of destinations, including the area in which you're cruising. In the case of a Mexican cruise that's a plus because food from south of the border is both colorful and flavorful.

In the old days of cruising, shipboard dining was pretty straightforward. You had dinner every night in the main dining room while breakfast and lunch could be there or in the buffet. The latter was often somewhat limited in selection. And, of course, there was afternoon tea and the midnight buffet. How things have changed! In addition to the main dining room, almost all of today's ships have at least one alternative restaurant. This can take the form of a bistro, café or other type of specialty restaurant. It is usually open only for dinner, although you will find that the choice for lunch has also expanded greatly. The buffet has been spruced up, too, with more choices. Many buffets are supplemented by specialty areas that feature a particular type of cuisine. There may even be a deli. Buffets are especially popular for breakfast when you want to make a quick exit to get on shore. Likewise, if you return from shore for lunch, the buffet will take less of your activity time away from you. Most cruise lines also have a pizzeria (often open 24 hours or close to it).

▶ **Note:** You will not receive any credit for meals that you miss when you eat ashore.

In general, the larger the ship, the more alternative restaurants there will be. Although some of them may always be casual, some are the opposite – they can be the most formal of the ship's dining venues. It is becoming increasingly common for some new ships (such as Princess' Gem-class or the newer Norwegian Cruise Lines ships) not to even have a "main" dining room in the traditional sense. Rather, there is a selection of several restaurants included in the basic cruise fare. Unfortunately, along with the increase in choice, it has become almost a universal practice among the cruise lines to charge a fee for at least one alternative restaurant and sometimes more. Should you choose this dining option, plan on paying anywhere from $10 to $30 extra per person for dinner. This may seem like a high amount for an "all-inclusive" vacation but remember that a dinner like the one you get in these alternative eateries would most likely cost you around $100 per person in a fine land-based restaurant.

On some lines there may be one or more nights when a particular alternative restaurant may not operate. Typically this will be on the night of the Captain's dinner when they want everyone in the main dining room. However, even this seems to be becoming a thing of the past. Choice every night is definitely the wave of the future. Make sure you familiarize yourself with alternative restaurant policies regarding reservations.

Practical Information

The main dining room is always a beautiful place where the cruise line shows off. These days it is extremely rare (outside of the luxury cruise lines) to offer a single-seating dinner – that is, everyone is served at the same time. Ships generally have early and late seatings. The early seating commonly begins around 6 pm, although it can be adjusted slightly to fit in with port calls. Late seatings usually commence about 2½ hours after the early seating starts. Some people avoid the early seating for fear that it will be rushed, but I haven't found this to be a significant problem. You will be given a choice of which seating you want at the time you book your cruise and every effort will be made to accommodate your wishes. Don't be afraid to complain if you don't like the table you have been given. It is often possible for the dining room staff to make adjustments. If you have a preference, such as sitting at a small table as opposed to a large one with many people, make this known at the time you book.

Dinner in the main room is always a multi-course affair and, although the portions in each course aren't overly large, nobody walks away hungry. In fact, the dining room staff will gladly accommodate requests for additional servings or even two different selections if you can't make up your mind what you want to eat! Don't be shy about asking. If you don't see anything on the menu that you like, make it known. There are usually a couple of items available that aren't listed.

While a few lines (i.e., the more exclusive and expensive ones) may offer complimentary wine or other alcoholic beverages a few times during the cruise, drinks (including soft drinks) are always at additional cost. Your cruise ship will have a good selection of wines and champagnes and your wine steward (or headwaiter if wine stewards are not utilized on the line you select) will be happy to assist you in making the right choice to accompany your dinner. The more upscale the line, the better the selection of wines. Spirits of all types are available throughout the day at numerous bars and lounges and, of course, during evening entertainment performances.

Three meals a day doesn't seem to be enough for hungry cruise passengers. Two other standard features that you'll encounter are the **afternoon tea** (usually around 4 pm) and the **midnight buffet**. The former is generally comprised of small sandwiches, pastries and fruits, in addition to a variety of coffees and teas. As is the case with meals, however, there is often a charge for other drinks. The midnight affair is usually heavy on sweets, often sinfully so. Even if a late-night cheesecake isn't for you, do at least look at one of these often beautiful and bountiful displays. See if you can resist taking something. Although the midnight buffet is usually offered every night of the trip, on a week-long cruise there will normally be one night where this becomes an extra-special affair. The chefs show off not only their cooking artistry, but their flair for the showy and dramatic with exquisite food and ice carvings. At least a few lines are so proud of this feature that they invite passengers in before serving begins just to take pictures! It's that impressive. But not every line offers the midnight buffet. Princess, for example, uses the buffet as a late-night bistro with waiter service. But don't fret about not being able to see all the exquisite food carvings and other visual delights. These will be featured at other times throughout the cruise.

Regardless of whether the ship you select has a midnight buffet or whether you choose to partake, there's no doubt that there are plenty of other opportunities to eat. Sweets, such as ice cream, are often served out on deck in the afternoon, sometimes even 24 hours a day. And, as alluded to earlier, pizza, hamburgers and hot dogs are another choice. Charging for ice cream isn't common but

Practical Information

I'm aware of at least one line that does impose a fee for "premium" ice cream.

Finally, if you decide that you don't want to go to the dining room or elsewhere to eat, **room service** is a standard feature on all ships. Hours of operation are always long and 24-hour service is available more often than not.

Disabled Travelers

There has been some controversy in recent years about just how far the cruise lines have to go in order to meet the needs of handicapped travelers. The public relations staff working for the cruise lines will be quick to point out that amenities for the handicapped are provided "voluntarily" (since there are few handicapped access laws required of cruise ships), but the fact of the matter is that the nature of cruising does present some difficulties for the disabled traveler.

Almost all major cruise lines can offer rooms that are suitable for handicapped guests. This is especially true on the larger, more modern vessels. Also, crew members will often go out of their way to assist those with physical limitations. That's the good news. The bad news is that, by their very nature, ships impose limitations for the disabled traveler. Even though you can get from one deck to another by elevator, corridors are often narrow and negotiating some areas can be difficult. Because physically challenged persons, to their credit, are traveling more these days, the number of people bringing motorized scooters onboard to help get around has increased. Because this can present safety problems, some lines do impose size and other restrictions on their use. If you require oxygen, this must be made known to the cruise line in advance. You are required to bring your own oxygen. In general, despite the helpful nature of ship person-nel, cruise lines require that disabled persons be accompanied by someone who can tend to their needs.

Shipboard limitations are not a big problem. The greater potential problem is actually in port, when it's time to get on and off the ship. Almost all of the most important Mexican Riviera and Baja ports allow most ships to tie up at the dock, thereby eliminating the need to use tenders, which would definitely present a degree of difficulty for almost all physically challenged individuals. However, airport-style walkways where you directly enter a termi-nal are rare, except at the largest gateway ports. Else-where it is far more common to have to negotiate a gangplank or stairway. Depending upon the nature of the pier, these can often be at fairly steep angles and could be next to impossible for those with more severe disabilities. As a safety precaution, the cruise lines and their captains reserve the option to prohibit physically handicapped passengers from disembarking at certain ports if they deem the individual would be at risk of in-jury.

If you have any questions concerning this subject, con-tact the cruise line directly and ask specific questions about facilities, including access at ports of call on the cruise you're interested in. Be prepared to explain your level of handicap as this will help cruise line staff to assess your personal situation. Places requiring use of tenders will be so indicated in the ports of call chapter.

Practical Information

Dress (On & Off Ship)

On Board

Attire during the daytime is highly casual and comfortable. How you dress after dinner depends upon what you are doing. If you're going to take in a show or dance the night away, the general practice is to remain dressed as you were for dinner. Otherwise, you can return to your cabin and change back into more casual attire. The dress codes for dinner don't vary that much from one line to another. In the past it was customary to divide dinner dress into three categories – formal, informal and casual. But the past few years have seen a blending of the last two and more lines are now listing only two categories in their brochures. Regardless, the distinction between informal and casual has become so blurred that for practical purposes there are now only two categories. Let's take a closer look at what each one means.

Formal attire technically means a tuxedo or dark suit for men and a gown for women. However, on all but the most formal ships there is a big range in what people actually wear on the so-called formal evenings. While a lot of men do wear tuxedos, they aren't necessarily in the majority, especially on the less expensive lines. The dark-suit crowd is always well represented. You will also certainly see quite a few men in suits whose color is definitely not dark, along with some in sport jackets. So, it all comes down to how comfortable you will feel if most other men are more dressed up. If that doesn't bother you, then you needn't be concerned about how spiffy you look. If you want to wear a tuxedo but don't have one, the cheapest option is to rent one through the cruise line. Each cruise line works with a tuxedo rental place and they will take care of everything and have your tuxedo waiting in your stateroom upon arrival.

Now for the ladies. Gowns of varying style and elegance are predominant but, again, there are quite a few women who choose not to be so fancy. Cocktail dresses and fashionable pants suits are becoming more and more common on formal evenings. Although women may tend to feel more obligated to dress to the level of the occasion than men do, it does seem that the level of formality has been decreasing. Gowns, as well as other attire for women, can be rented from the same places that provide men's tuxedos.

There are typically two formal nights per week of cruising. These are the Captain's dinner (often the second night of the cruise) and the farewell dinner, which is usually the next-to-the-last night. The Captain's dinner is usually where people dress the best. Keep in mind that there are only two such nights because, even if you intend to follow all the dress guidelines, it will not pay for most people to go out and buy a whole new fancy wardrobe.

Alternative restaurants are often a means of avoiding formal and even informal dress. But do keep in mind that they may not always be open on formal evenings and some of these specialty eateries have formal dress codes all of the time. On some ships you may be limited to the buffet if you want to avoid getting dressed up. Some lines will always have at least one alternative restaurant here you can dress casually.

Casual attire has two meanings, depending upon the time of day. In the afternoon, anything goes, from cut-off jeans to polo shirts to tank tops and halters. Pool attire is generally frowned upon in all indoor public areas of the ship. When evening arrives, casual attire translates into

Practical Information

what most people would call business casual and what the chic-conscious cruise lines often refer to as "smart casual" or "resort casual." Not quite anything goes. Specifically, jeans (even "dress" jeans), shorts, halter tops and any kind of beachwear are definite no-nos in the dining room. Sandals and sneakers are likewise looked down upon, although you can get away with nice walking shoes that are in good condition.

Dress in Port

How you dress when in port depends not only on the weather, but also on your activities. Casual and comfortable is generally the best way to dress. Since a lot of people will be going to the beach or partaking in other outdoor activities, even "sloppy" is usually an acceptable way to go. However, one should keep in mind that Mexican culture is basically conservative. Although the residents of the major ports are used to tourist attire and don't pay much attention to how visitors dress in tourist zones, beachwear or skimpy attire will be frowned upon in downtown areas and especially outside of the cities in small towns and rural areas. If you are doing a lot of sightseeing, it's likely that part of your touring will include a church or cathedral and there, especially, showing a lot of skin is not acceptable. Proprietors of small retail establishments will also likely frown on a lack of proper dress.

You should be prepared to dress for the nature of your activities. If you are going exploring, sandals or open-toed shoes could make walking on uneven or rough surfaces difficult and expose you to minor foot injuries. Sneakers or walking shoes are more advisable for sightseeing. If you are taking a tour into the lush jungle-like terrain that is often very close to the port cities of the Mexican Riviera, it is far better to cover up with a long-sleeve shirt or blouse and long pants than expose your skin to biting insects and sometimes sharp flora.

Packing

A few words are in order about how much to pack for your cruise. Wise packing can save you time, effort and aggravation. While I usually recommend packing light for a vacation, cruising does represent the one possible exception to this fundamental rule of smart travel. There are two reasons. First, you will be in one room for a length of time, so you don't have to worry about constantly packing and unpacking. Also, even though the trend has been toward more casual dress, there is still a great deal of dressing up and many people, especially women, will want to make sure that they have a different outfit for each night of the cruise. Heaven forbid that your table-mate might see you in the same outfit more than once!

Wise packing extends beyond what clothes you are going to take on the cruise. So don't forget to pack the following:

- ☐ **Sunscreen**
- ☐ **Insect repellent.** Brands containing DEET have long been considered the best, but recent studies show that brands with picaridin or oil of lemon eucalyptus are just as good. The latter are considered safer, especially for children.
- ☐ **Sunglasses**
- ☐ **Hat**
- ☐ **Collapsible umbrella**
- ☐ **Sweater or light jacket.** Depending upon when you go, this can come in handy on land. But even if traveling during the summer you should bring along some light outerwear because many public areas of cruise ships are kept quite cool.

Practical Information

☐ **Binoculars**

☐ **Camera and/or camcorder.** And plenty of extra film, tapes and battery packs. Although you will be able to purchase film and other needs in port (as well as on board ship), the prices are much higher than at home. Do price film developing on your ship, as it is less expensive than you might think. All ships now have full digital services as well. Sometimes this can be a relative bargain. If you are going to be snorkeling, scuba diving or otherwise going beneath the surface of the water, you should bring along an underwater camera as well. Disposables will do quite nicely.

☐ **Medications.** Making sure that you have all of your medicines with you goes without saying. However, you should also be sure to bring along a copy of your prescription because you might lose your medication. In addition, this will assist in the Customs process. Although it is rare to be challenged by Customs officials about this, a prescription will help clear things up rapidly.

☐ **Documents.** This is another thing that should go without saying but you won't believe how many people forget about bringing the necessary documentation, including tickets! This includes copies of your identification papers (especially the information page of your passport). Keep the copies in a safe place separate from the originals.

Driving/Rental Cars

There is little doubt that driving offers the maximum flexibility when in port, especially if you intend to get away from the immediate area near the cruise ship dock. I often recommend driving yourself rather than going the shore excursion route in most places, including Alaska, the Caribbean and even some ports in Europe. However,

Mexico is a different story because driving here presents a number of special problems that you may not want to deal with.

In the port cities most attractions are relatively close to the cruise ship dock or easily accessible via some form of public transportation. In addition to heavy traffic, visiting drivers can expect to encounter confusing street patterns with streets that often change names, a lack of signs indicating what street you're on and often unpredictable local drivers who use signals that are different than we're accustomed to. These things can be a problem for pedestrians too, but are more manageable on foot. In addition there are often giant potholes that are difficult to negotiate.

On the edges of cities and towns there are killer **speed bumps** known as *topes* or *vibradores*. Although usually signed in advance, this is not always the case. Even if you know they're coming you will need to come to a virtual stop to avoid doing serious damage to the vehicle. These speed bumps can sometimes be encountered within cities as well.

While driving has a definite advantage when heading out of town, there are other problems that you'll have to deal with. Roads are not well marked and it's easy to get lost. The state of repair ranges from excellent (at least on the very expensive toll roads) to extremely poor, especially after bad weather. Lanes are narrow (again, except on toll roads) and you'll often encounter very winding and mountainous roads. Mexican drivers tend to be aggressive when it comes to lane changing and passing; you are not likely to be thrilled with the way the locals drive. There are also many narrow one-way bridges. In general, Mexico uses international picture signing on roads, but wording is in Spanish.

Practical Information

If you do drive and your ship will be in port until the late evening, **never** drive at night. In addition to all of the above potential problems being more difficult to cope with, nighttime brings even more hazards. These include few, if any, lights on the roads, the tendency of many drivers not to use their headlights (especially truckers), animals and pedestrians on the road, and the possibility of encountering road crime.

A few general guidelines are in order to summarize the situation.

▶ Always drive cautiously and be sure to heed speed limit signs.

▶ Verify before you leave home exactly what coverage your insurance policy will provide if you rent a car in Mexico.

▶ If there's a problem with the car, contact the rental agency.

Mexico's famous "Green Angels" highway patrol probably won't be of use to you on drives from the port cities because they don't cover most of these areas and, if they do, their services are usually limited to the main highways.

Should you choose to rent a car in one or more ports of call, it is best to go with one of the major international companies. Car rental rates aren't cheap in Mexico. In fact, you will probably wind up paying a daily rate that equals or exceeds what it costs to rent a car in most major American resort areas. Although local or regional Mexican firms are generally cheaper, the reliability of their cars (and, indeed, their promised prices) are less so. In addition, it's best to have reservations before you leave and it may be difficult to accomplish that unless you can communicate well in Spanish over the telephone. Consequently, I haven't included any of these companies' names or contact numbers. To make a reservation with one of the majors, call the toll-free reservation number of the company of your choice well in advance of your trip (at least a month). Alternatively, you can use the Internet. In either case you won't have a communication problem and you can be certain that the car you selected will be waiting for you. Make sure that you know the location of the rental agency (in some cases they'll be at the airport rather than near the cruise ship dock). If it is not within walking distance of the port, find out what arrangements can be made to pick you up.

The major companies represented in Mexico have at least one location in all of the main ports of call (Acapulco, Cabo San Lucas, Ensenada, Ixtapa/Zihuatanejo, La Paz, Manzanillo, Mazatlán, and Puerto Vallarta) – *except* for the towns indicated below:

Car Rental Companies			
Alamo	☎ (800) 327-9633	www.alamo.com	All except Ensenada and Manzanillo
Avis	☎ (800) 831-2847	www.avis.com	All except Ensenada, Ixtapa/Zihuataneo, Manzanillo, and Mazatlán
Budget	☎ (800) 527-0700	www.budget.com	All except Ensenada
Hertz	☎ (800) 654-3131	www.hertz.com	All except Cabo San Lucas
National	☎ (800) 227-7368	www.nationalcar.com	All except Acapulco and Ensenada
Thrifty	☎ (800) 847-4389	www.thrifty.com	Only Cabo San Lucas and Puerto Vallarta

Practical Information

Electrical Appliances & Other Technical Tidbits

Virtually all cruise ships serving the Mexican Riviera have the same 110-volt system found in the United States and their outlets accept the two-pin plug (including those with a third grounding prong) found on all of your appliances. Some European lines have 220-volt electrical systems and use the two-round-pin plug that is found throughout most of Europe, but even they may have dual voltage systems. Find out before you leave if the ship you're traveling on has only a 220-volt system, which means that you will need a transformer and, probably, an adapter for the plug. Although they may have some of the latter on board, it is best to bring your own.

You should also be aware that some electrical appliances are not permitted on board the ship. These are usually appliances that heat, such as irons and hair dryers, because of the risk of fire. Many cruise ship staterooms supply these items because their safety condition is frequently monitored. If you are the type of traveler who always brings along a host of electronic goodies (other than electric shavers and the like) then, once again, it is always a wise idea to check in advance concerning the cruise line's regulations.

Financial Matters

Since shipboard life is "cashless," you don't have to worry about carrying a lot of money with you while you're at sea. Once in port, however, it's another matter, as your cruise line-issued card won't be recognized on land! Most major credit cards (with the exception of Discover) are accepted at the more heavily visited tourist shops and attractions, while small privately owned stores may not accept them. This is especially true once you get away from the main visitor pathways. The same rules apply to travelers checks. When in port, you should carry with you only the amount of cash that you think you might need for the day. Leave the rest on board in your stateroom safe if there is one, or in the safe deposit facilities provided by the purser's office.

The unit of currency in Mexico is the **peso**. Exchange rates can vary but at press time it took roughly 10 pesos to equal one US dollar. The good news is that Yankee dollars are readily accepted in the resort ports of the Mexican Riviera and Baja. As a rule of thumb, the more popular the destination is with Americans, the more accepted US currency will be. However, once again, this may not be the case in smaller shops, out-of-the-way places and some small towns. It's also useful to have pesos for small expenditures such as local bus transportation and telephone calls (or buying a local calling card). If you plan on doing a lot of local shopping, it may be helpful to have some pesos for cash purchases.

Foreign exchange facilities on cruise ships are either limited or non-existent. Although you can exchange dollars for pesos in the United States, a better idea is to wait until you get to Mexico and then use your ATM card to make cash withdrawals in pesos. Even though you will pay fees for using an ATM that is not part of your bank, the exchange rate on ATM use is far better than you will get anywhere else. ATMs are becoming quite ubiquitous in Mexico and there is always one at or near major ports. Actually, most cruise ships these days also have an ATM on board but be aware that the cash dispensed will be US dollars, which may or not be of much help to you while in Mexico. In addition, the fees charged at these ATMs are very high – generally about $5 per transaction, plus whatever your bank may tack on.

Flight Arrangements

It's nice to be able to take a short ride to the cruise ship terminal, leave your car and get on board. But, despite the increase in availability of American ports of embarkation, many passengers will have to fly to their gateway port. Every airline offers you the option of including round-trip air transportation with your cruise package. In fact, there are even a few lines that price the cruise with an air-inclusive rate and you then have to subtract an "air credit" if you intend to book your own transportation. This type of pricing is rare for Mexico cruises.

Using the cruise line's air program will certainly be your easiest option. Everything will be taken care of for you and transfers between the airport and your ship at both ends of the cruise will also be included. If you make your own air arrangements, you will almost certainly have to make your way to the ship on your own. Also, if several guests are arriving via a cruise-sponsored air program and the plane is late, the ship's departure will be delayed in order to accommodate those passengers or they will make arrangements for you to catch up with the ship if sailing can't be held up any longer. Don't expect that courtesy if you're traveling on your own. (The possibility of that kind of disaster can be avoided by planning to arrive in the embarkation port a day early.)

So far it sounds like a really good deal to go with the cruise air program. But there are some disadvantages that need to be considered. The air fares offered by the cruise lines range from average to very high. For domestic flights I've never seen a cruise line offering a fare lower than what you can get on your own. Comparison is the key; you'll probably find it relatively easy to get a lower fare for individual travel even after adding in the cost of transferring from the airport to the ship.

What makes your task more difficult in comparing prices is that the cruise lines don't usually give you detailed information, such as the airline, departure times, and number of connections, until final documents are issued (usually two to four weeks before your departure). You'll probably want to book your flight long before that if you're going to be doing it on your own. Furthermore, cruise line-sponsored flights are sometimes inconvenient as to both routing and times. Carefully weigh the advantages and disadvantages of the air program and don't be bullied into something that you would prefer not to do. These days all of the cruise lines offer "custom" air arrangements. That is, you can pick the flight and airline that you want to take. Unfortunately, the extra charge for doing so is exorbitant.

Making your own air arrangements for a cruise to Mexico is a simple task since there is such a great variety of airlines and flights from Los Angeles, San Diego and San Francisco. It becomes a little more complex if your ship either begins or ends its voyage in Mexico. The airport would almost inevitably be Acapulco, but this city has fairly poor direct service to the United States. Almost every flight will involve a stop or change of plane, usually in Mexico City.

Practical Information

Major Airlines Serving Mexico		
Aeromexico	☎ (800) 237-6639	www.aeromexico.com
Alaska Airlines	☎ (800) 252-7522	www.alaskaair.com
America West	☎ (800) 235-9292	www.amricawest.com
American Airlines	☎ (800) 433-7300	www.aa.com
Continental	☎ (800) 523-3273	www.continental.com
Delta	☎ (800) 241-4141	www.delta.com
Mexicana	☎ (800) 531-7921	*www.mexicana.com*
Northwest	☎ (800) 447-4747	www.nwa.com
United	☎ (800) 241-6522	www.united.com
USAirways	☎ (800) 428-4322	www.usairways.com

Gaming

Other than the Disney Cruise Line, there isn't a cruise ship afloat that doesn't have a casino, and with good reason – passengers enjoy the games and the cruise line enjoys the profit! Depending upon the ship, the onboard casino can range from a very small room to a rather large and elaborate affair that is more reminiscent of Las Vegas. Today's biggest ships largely reflect the latter. There are both slot machines and table games. Small denomination slot machines are easy to find but minimums at the tables will probably be higher than you are used to from Stateside gaming. The majority of casinos are operated for the cruise lines by a well-known gaming company. For example, "Caesars Palace at Sea" is the name given to some ship-board casinos as the facilities are operated by the same company. Regulations prohibit ship casinos from operating when they are docked in port. Once a ship enters international waters, however, the casino comes alive. Minors are not allowed to play but the minimum age is sometimes as low as 18 on a cruise ship, as compared to 21 in the United States.

Don't expect good odds on slot machines – they're tighter than any you would find in Las Vegas, Atlantic City, or any other domestic gaming destination. On the other hand, table game odds are more akin to their land-based brethren in terms of your chances of winning, so you would be well advised to stick to them if you're serious about winning.

What about "comp" cruises (i.e., free or heavily discounted cruises) for people who gamble a lot? Yes, many cruise lines do offer this. But you would have to guarantee putting down a very large amount of money. If you are interested, contact the cruise line of your choice for details.

Getting to Your Ship

I've already touched on the subject of transfers from the airport to your ship. It's easy if the cruise line will be providing the transfers (that is, you book through their air program). Otherwise, the best bet in most places is to take a taxi, which can cost a considerable amount. Public transportation between the airport and cruise ship terminal in all of the gateway cities for Mexican Riviera and Baja cruises is – to put it mildly – very limited and can't be considered as a practical solution. In other words, do you really want to lug around four pieces of luggage on a train or bus?

If you chose to take part in a pre-cruise tour of the gateway city, all transportation to the ship will be included. Independent travelers will once again have to make their own way but can minimize inconvenience by choosing a

Practical Information

hotel that is relatively close to the cruise ship terminal. Some hotels in these locations will provide complimentary shuttle service. Alternatively, if you had been renting a car in the gateway city you should be able to return it close to the cruise ship terminal.

Many cruise lines offer passengers who make their own flight arrangements the option to add ground transfers to and from the ship. The fee for this service is very high and it will almost always be less expensive to take a taxi. Inquire at the time of your booking if this is available and what the cost will be. Your first priority as an independent traveler is to make sure that you allow enough time to make the transfer without missing your cruise ship's departure time. I cannot emphasize enough that the safest way to do this (and the most relaxing) is to arrive in your embarkation city on the day before your sailing date.

In the section on gateway cities, page 153, there will be directions to the cruise ship terminal for those of you who plan to drive to the port. Again, make sure you allow enough time for the drive, traffic, parking your car and checking in. The aforementioned section will also provide details on things like charges for parking and how much time to allow between the airport and the cruise ship port.

Health

No one likes to think about the possibility of becoming ill while on vacation. However, a little advance planning and precaution is necessary because such things do, unfortunately, occur. The things to know about helping to ensure a healthy cruise can be divided into two separate issues: health on the ship and health on shore.

Onboard

Despite big-time press attention to outbreaks of minor viruses on cruise ships that occur from time to time, cruising is a healthy way to travel. As with any place that serves food, there can be occasional instances of food poisoning, but they are usually mild. A greater risk are the annoyances of over-indulging in food and alcohol. This doesn't mean that you won't or shouldn't eat more than you normally would at home or even take an extra drink or two. But don't overdo it. Know your limits.

In Port

Health on shore is an entirely different matter. Standards of health and cleanliness are generally lower in Mexico than they are in the United States. The good news, however, is that these standards are typically higher in the tourist areas of the Mexican Riviera and Baja. As such, this a pretty healthy area to visit, but some special precautions are worth mentioning.

You will often be tempted by the delectable appearance of food in local markets. One can never be sure about the freshness and safety of such things as fruit and produce, so I suggest avoiding it, unless you have been told by ship personnel that a particular location is known to be safe. Restaurants are usually alright if they are in major hotels that cater to American visitors. When patronizing other local restaurants a little caution should be exercised. Drinking water is supposedly safe in all the ports visited by cruise ships. But you should avoid it. Although it may be safe from a scientific standpoint, it is still *different* than what you are used to at home. As such, it has a higher chance of disagreeing with you. The famous food- and water-related illnesses that plague visitors to Mexico such as *Montezuma's Revenge* or the *Aztec Two-step* are

Practical Information

not really food poisoning per se in most cases but, rather, just your system's reaction to something that it hasn't encountered before. Always drink bottled water. Bottled or canned soft drinks are also alright.

Sunburn is always a possibility just about anytime of the year. Don't spend a long time on the beach (or even by the ship's pool) on your first or second day out. It is best to slowly increase the amount of exposure time each day. When touring it is a good idea to wear light-colored clothes that breathe. Exposing a lot of skin seems a natural way to keep cool, but that is not the way to protect yourself or even to keep cool. Covering up a bit and wearing a hat is always advisable.

Stinging and biting **insects** are, of course, quite numerous in these warm areas. If you are going to be hiking in the back-country, wear clothing that covers as much skin as possible. Use of an insect repellent is mandatory in such situations. For casual sightseeing or relaxing on the beach, you aren't going to encounter any dangerous insects unless you have an allergic predisposition. Again, an insect repellent is still a wise choice.

Poisonous plants and animals are not a big problem in this part of Mexico. In the desert regions of Baja you can encounter **rattlesnakes** and **scorpions** outside of urban areas. It isn't something you have to be particulary aware of unless you plan to get into the back-country on your own. Get medical assistance as quickly as possible if you are bitten. When swimming, be aware that there could be **jellyfish**, especially if your visit is between the months of May and October. **Sea urchins** that you step on are more of a possibility. Again, if you should be stung by any jellyfish or step on an urchin, do seek medical assistance right away. Don't wait to get back to the ship.

THOSE NASTY LITTLE VIRUSES

Beginning in the fall of 2002 the news media decided it was time to create a frenzy about a series of outbreaks of the so-called "Norwalk" virus that occurred on cruise ships. What was most sickening about this and subsequent similar stories was the reporting itself, since it was really much ado about nothing. You would have thought that people died or became seriously ill. These are mild viruses akin to what your mother used to call a "24-hour virus" when you were little because the worst of it was over in about that time. So let's put this picture into some meaningful perspective.

The Centers for Disease Control require that cruise lines report any contagious illness that affects more than 4% of the passengers and crew. Figuring an average of about 3,000 people per cruise, that means that anytime there are about 120 or more cases, it's reported. Then it becomes public information (meaning that the news media gets its hands on it). There are typically fewer than 50 cruises a year when this happens out of several thousand departures. Even when it does happen the outbreak is, more often than not, limited to under 200 people or about 7% of those onboard. Thus, your odds of coming down with it on a ship are not any higher than of getting it while on land. And that's the heart of the story – in reality, these viruses almost always originate on land. They are most common in winter (both on land and on ships). Anytime people are in close quarters they can spread. It doesn't make news when 5% of the kids in a school or people in an office have a

Practical Information

tummy ache, but let it happen on a cruise ship and.... well, you know the rest – it's headline time in the *National Enquirer*.

There isn't anything you can do to prevent this except to rely on the good scrubbings that cruise ship personnel give to their vessel after an outbreak. The ship's doctor is likely to confine infected passengers to quarters for a couple of days to prevent further spread. While I don't see the need to take any special precautions beyond what you would do when going anyplace where a lot of people are present, there are some who may be a bit more skittish about these things. If so, the best place for information on **sanitation conditions** for a particular cruise ship is the government's **Centers for Disease Control & Prevention**. Their website (www.cdc.gov/travel/cruise.htm) has the latest sanitation inspection report and rating for each ship. You can also call them at ☎ (888) 232-6789.

Passports, Customs & Other Considerations

You will have to present proper identification papers to the cruise line before you embark. It is your responsibility to make sure that everything is in order, not only for getting into each port but for returning home. Your embarkation will be delayed or possibly even denied if you can't show the cruise line that you have the documents necessary to satisfy government requirements both here and in Mexico. While documentation procedures for travel to

Mexico are fairly simple, they're even easier if you are taking a cruise that departs from and returns to a port in the United States. That is, the only time that you'll spend in Mexico are the daily port calls. If this is the case, which it will be with the majority of cruise visitors to Mexico, then all you have to do is present one of the following:

1. A valid **passport**. This is always the best form of identification for immigration and for just about any other purpose. You should begin the procedure for obtaining a passport at least 90 days prior to your departure. If you do not have a passport, then bring...

2. Either your original **birth certificate** (with raised seal) or a certified copy of it and a **photo identification** issued by a governmental agency. A driver's license is a good example. However, new regulations effective 12/31/06 will require all cruise ship passengers to have a passport.

If your cruise either begins or ends in Mexico (or you are otherwise going to be spending time in the country) then, in addition to one of the above, you'll have to get a Mexican **tourist card**. This is available from any Mexican consulate and from border stations. However, if you're flying into Mexico then the airline will supply the form during the course of your inbound flight. There is no charge for the tourist card itself. However, you'll have to pay a **tourist entry fee** that is roughly equivalent to $20. The fee will already have been included in the cost of your airline ticket if you are flying into Mexico.

What You Can Bring Into Mexico

You can bring into Mexico the equivalent of **$10,000** per person in cash, traveler's checks or the equivalent, although I can't imagine why anyone would want to do that unless they intend to engage in some illegal activity. You are also allowed a reasonable number of personal items. No **weapons** of any kind may be brought into Mexico. Illicit **drugs** are similarly prohibited. Don't even think about bringing in just a bit of marijuana or other "soft" drugs because Mexican laws are harsh concerning this and the local police would love to bust you.

When traveling in a foreign country it is always best to contact the nearest American embassy or consular office in the event of any legal difficulty such as a lost passport or infractions of local laws. On a cruise, however, you might first consider getting advice from the ship's purser. If they cannot resolve your problem then it is time to turn elsewhere. For areas covered in this book, American consular offices can be found in Acapulco, Ixtapa, Mazatlán and Puerto Vallarta.

Returning to the US

When you come back into the United States you'll again be required to show the documents mentioned above. Customs inspections for cruise passengers to places like Mexico are commonly very cursory even though they've tightened up since September 11, 2001. You'll be asked to complete a Customs declaration form and inspectors have the right to check your bags. Since you'll probably do at least some shopping while in Mexico you should have a general understanding of regulations concerning **Customs allowances and duties**. These can get rather complicated, so if you plan to bring back goods worth a lot of money it could be worth your while to contact the US Customs Service for one of their helpful publications on figuring Customs duties. The usual exemption is $400 per person. However, if you are on one of the short (three- or four-night) cruises that calls only on the Mexican port of Ensenada, your exemption will be only $200. There are also specific limitations on cigars, cigarettes and alcoholic beverages. Generally, you are allowed to bring back two liters of alcohol. Goods that you purchase in Mexico cannot be brought back into the United States if they were manufactured in Iran, Cuba or North Korea. Libya is also on this list but that might be changing soon. There are many regulations regarding importation of plants, vegetables and live animals. Again, if you have any intention of purchasing these items you should inquire with the Customs Bureau prior to your trip. There is a duty of 3% on the first $1,000 excess over the $400 or $200 exemption. Beyond that the rates get terribly confusing, but most people won't be affected by this.

Duty Free Shopping

Finally, you should be aware that the "duty free" shopping that may be advertised in some ports has absolutely nothing to do with American Customs duties. It simply refers to the fact that there is no local tax on the items you purchase. All of these are, however, subject to the foregoing regulations and limitations. True "duty free" shopping *does* apply to all purchases made onboard your ship. So you won't have to pay any duty on that $25,000 painting that you plan to buy!

Payments, Cancellations & Cruise Documents

Although payment procedures for your cruise and the process of issuing cruise documents do differ somewhat from one cruise line to another, there are so many similarities that some general guidelines are possible.

At the time you book your cruise you will be required to make a deposit. This is usually around $250 per person

Practical Information

for a week-long cruise. Shorter trips are less, while longer trips and some of the more expensive lines generally require more. Although the need for a second payment after the deposit isn't unknown, it is much more common that your second payment will be the final one for the balance of your fare. This will be due 60 and 90 days before your scheduled date of sailing. If you book after the full payment deadline you will, of course, have to pay the full amount at the time of booking. Options are available to pay for your cruise on a loan basis. But, like any loan, this does wind up costing a lot more.

All cruise lines have a schedule of refunds should you be unable to take the cruise. This also varies according to cruise length but a typical penalty schedule will look something like this:

If You Cancel...	You Will Forfeit...
Prior to full payment requirement date	nothing
30-60 days before sailing	your deposit
8-29 days before sailing	half of the total fare
a week or less before sailing	the entire fare

So, if you think there is any possibility that you may have to cancel, or you just don't like to take chances, consider purchasing **trip cancellation insurance**. This can be done through the cruise line but your travel agent or independent travel insurance companies can often give you the same or better coverage for less money.

Cruise documents is a fancy name for your tickets and other little bits and pieces of information that the cruise line will send to you (or to your travel agent). The date when documents are sent varies from one line to another but is, more often than not, anywhere from two weeks to a month prior to your scheduled sailing date. Some lines will, upon request, issue them earlier but this will always be at an additional cost, and a high one at that. There are also hefty fees for reissuing documents if you lose them or require a change.

The only time you need to consider having documents issued early is if you will be traveling for a week or more prior to your cruise. The cruise lines have been, for reasons I can't fathom, way behind the times when it comes to electronic ticketing and avoiding the entire hassle of sending documents. As of press time only Royal Caribbean had implemented a form of this, at least on a limited basis. However, if it should suddenly become a more common way of doing business, I'm sure your travel agent will be aware of it.

One of the things that will be included in your document package is **luggage tags**. These may have specific information identifying you and your stateroom number or they may simply be color-coded to the deck you're on and you have to write in your name and room number. In either case, be sure they're affixed to your luggage before you turn the bags over to dock personnel. It's a good idea to remove any airline tags before you put on the cruise tags.

The cruise lines also require that you fill out a **passenger information form** of some kind. This includes information needed by US immigration authorities. Every line now gives you the opportunity to complete these forms on-line or by faxing them back. If you can't avail yourself of either of these methods then ask your travel agent or cruise line personnel what procedure should be followed.

Practical Information

Safety on Shore

Because so many cruise passengers can't wait to get off the ship and start swimming, snorkeling, diving or otherwise partake in watersports, the issue of safety while doing so is of considerable importance. Be aware of your own skills and limitations. Take the time to find out about surf conditions at the various local beaches before selecting the one that is most appropriate for your level of ability. In general, Riviera and Baja beaches that face a sheltered bay are usually fairly calm, while those facing the Pacific Ocean are rougher. But there is a great deal of variation within this broad rule of thumb. Flags are posted at many major beaches when conditions are rough but this isn't always the case so you should find out the current conditions regardless of whether any warnings are up. Never go snorkeling or scuba diving alone, even if you are proficient at it. Novices should pay particular attention to local conditions. It is best to snorkel in protected waters. Guided snorkeling expeditions are a good idea if you are tackling more open waters. Always be aware that coral reefs are sharp! For even more adventurous activities such as parasailing and the like, it is again important to be aware of your skills. If you are new to it, you should always go with an experienced person. Shore excursions for these types of activities ensure that you are dealing with a reputable firm.

Crime

When it comes to crime, Mexico has a bad reputation. How true this is depends upon a lot of factors. Any discussion of safety from crime must be prefaced by the reminder that reasonable precautions have to be exercised no matter where you are traveling. Tourists are often confused and too often carrying far too much cash or valuables, making them good targets for savvy thieves. Don't attract attention to yourself by flashing large sums of cash or by wearing a lot of jewelry. Make sure that cameras and other valuables are firmly held when in use and out of sight when not in use. If you rent a car, do not leave anything of value visible on the back seat and always be sure to lock your car upon leaving it. Although traveling in a group as part of a shore excursion exposes you to less risk than individual travel, be advised that such nuisances as pickpockets are used to operating in groups and can even infiltrate your tour group. So the warning about leaving valuables onboard still applies. Take with you only what you need for the day, including money.

Most of your shore time will be during daylight hours. If, however, you are out at night, stick to the main tourist areas. Even during the day it isn't usually a good idea to go wandering around town away from the visitor attractions.

There is no doubt that both non-violent and violent crimes have always been a problem to some degree in Mexico and they have definitely gotten worse over the past few years. Some of this crime has been directed at tourists. The good news is that the worst crime problems have mainly been limited to three areas that are not part of a cruise ship visit to Mexico. These are Mexico City, areas of southern Mexico subject to political instability, and road crimes. The latter have been a particular problem in rural areas that Americans driving into Mexico have to pass through. The fact of the matter is that if you stick to the areas frequented by visitors in any of the ports in Baja or along the Mexican Riviera, the crime rate is not significantly different from that of an average American city. And, where it does exist in these areas, tourists have not been a target except for relatively minor crimes like pick-pocketing. This does not mean that you should throw caution to the winds. The general safety steps outlined above still apply.

Two situations have received quite a bit of media attention in the United States. These are the problem of **criminal taxi drivers** in Mexico, who deliberately rob American tourists, and visitors being **"shaken down" by police** for money in order to avoid being arrested on violations of local law, or worse – trumped up drug charges. The first situation is one that occurs primarily in Mexico City. However, you can assure yourself of a greater degree of safety by never getting into a car that isn't a clearly marked legitimate taxi. Avoid hustlers who wait outside the dock. Legitimate cabs will be allowed to pick up passengers in a designated area. If you are already in town and decide that a cab would be a good idea, look for taxi ranks by a major resort hotel. Again, the hotels will make sure that only legitimate taxis are operating from their property. Criminal behavior by police is an endemic problem in Mexico that won't be easily solved anytime soon. The best advice is to know the law and avoid situations that would put you in contact with the local police. Fortunately, the police in the port cities you're likely to visit have exhibited much better behavior and these cases are few and far between. It is worth noting that one of the disadvantages of driving in Mexico is that motorist visitors (especially once you drive away from the city and get into rural areas) are more likely to have encounters with the police. Be polite anytime you are stopped by a policeman but don't give in to paying a fine for something you didn't do. Never hand over original of documents such as passports. Carry copies with you.

Safety on the Ship

While it is impossible to be totally safe from crime in any environment, there is little doubt that cruise ships are one of the safest places to be. Few things are as rare as a person being mugged while on board a cruise ship. On the other hand, you never know who is traveling on the ship with you, so a few simple common sense precautions are still advisable. Women traveling alone or with another female friend should be especially wary (as they always should be) about the intentions of men. There are, no doubt, some men out there who figure that a woman on a cruise without a male companion is looking for some action. Behave as you would in your home city and you should not have any problems. When it comes to safeguarding your possessions, don't leave cash or other valuables on display in your room. Always use the in-room safe that most ships provide or check it with the purser's office for safekeeping. Also, always be sure that your room is locked upon leaving.

What more people are concerned with today in the aftermath of September 11, 2001 is the quality of ship security. Most of the cruise lines were paying more attention to this than the airlines were, even before that eventful day, but they have certainly been devoting more attention to it as of late. It is universal practice in the cruise industry to X-ray all baggage that is being checked in for delivery to your cabin. You will also have to go through metal detectors like those at an airport as you enter the cruise ship terminal and each time you get on board after a port call. Inspection of carry-on luggage may also be done. You will be required to show proper identification before being allowed to embark and, again, each time you return to the ship during the course of your cruise.

Practical Information

Today's cruise ships are technical marvels. They have the most modern and sophisticated navigational and collision avoidance systems. Officers are highly trained and all crew members receive extensive training in emergency procedures. It is very unlikely that you would ever be faced with an emergency situation requiring evacuation of the ship. However, all ships are required by law to conduct a lifeboat drill and all passengers are required to participate. Listen to the instructions carefully and familiarize yourself with safety procedures that are posted in your cabin.

Selecting the Right Stateroom

Not only is the stateroom the single biggest determining factor in the cost of your cruise, it might well determine how happy you are with the ship you select. The two major components of the price-determinant are whether the room is inside or outside and the location of the room (how high up, how far fore or aft). **Inside rooms**, obviously, have no window. However, on most ships (especially the newer ones) the size of the room is about the same as an outside room. So, unless you think you'll feel claustrophobic in an inside room or you just have to have that view or balcony, you can save a lot of money by going for an inside cabin.

Outside rooms have a greater variety. They can be with or without balcony, regular window or floor-to-ceiling window, and so on. All these things are very nice to have, but you must be willing to pay the extra price for them. The cruise lines make it seem as if you just have to have a balcony in order to enjoy your cruise. Nonsense! How much time are you going to spend on the balcony? With all of the activities on board, the answer is not much. One other item of caution. Although outside rooms with an obstructed or partially obstructed view (because of blockage by lifeboats) are less expensive than other outside rooms of the same type, they're not worth it. If you're going to get an obstructed view you might as well save some money and take an inside cabin.

Prices generally are higher within a specific cabin category if the room is toward the middle of the ship or if it is on a higher deck. The reason for this is that the further up you are from the water or the further away from the front and back, the more comfortable the ride. While this is technically true, the difference is slight and one has to wonder if the extra cost is worth it. On the other hand, cabins on the lowest deck or two sometimes have an isolated feel to them, especially on older ships where there may be only a few cabins of this type, so I suggest not taking these unless you must conserve your pennies.

There is a very important consideration in selecting a cabin that the cruise lines seem to pay little or no attention to and that is the **size** of the cabin. Excepting some of the most upgraded suites, which cost *mucho* bucks, ship cabins are considerably smaller than rooms at a land-based resort hotel. In fact, they're smaller than the rooms in a Motel 6! While many cruise line brochures don't give you a good picture of how big the cabin is (they'll tell you if you call and ask), you can count on a typical stateroom being anywhere between 150 and 185 square feet. This does not include the size of a balcony if the room has one. Some older ships may have a number of cabins that are even smaller, while a few can go up to around 200 square feet. Motel rooms typically start at around 250 square feet and luxury hotel rooms today are generally built in the 400- to 550-square-foot range or even larger. Ship cabins are well designed from a functionality standpoint but don't expect to have a lot of walking room. If you are going to be traveling with your children, you should try to select a ship where the cabins are bigger. I usually downgrade any vessel where the size of the standard cabins is less than 150 square feet. Once you get to about 165 square feet and up, I consider that a decent size, but 180 or higher is better for more than two people. Be aware that cabin square-footage can vary even within a single category, depending upon its location. Do not hesitate to ask the cruise line or your travel agent for the exact size of the cabin they plan to assign to you. Ask for a larger cabin if it seems too small to meet your needs.

Shopping

Unique Items

Rare is the traveler who isn't greeted by friends and relatives upon their return from a vacation with the question, "What did you buy?" That seems to be even more the case with cruising, perhaps because of the popularity of shopping in the Caribbean – the biggest cruise market. While every Mexican port isn't the shopping Mecca of the islands, there is no doubt that shopping south of the border is a fun experience where you can buy a variety of unusual items. A great part of Mexican shopping is regional in nature. For example, silver is especially popular in the silver-producing region of Taxco. None of Mexico's Pacific ports are well known for anything particularly special. However, there is a large variety of goods from all over Mexico in the biggest port cities. In addition, many Mexican handicrafts are produced throughout the country. Suggestions for specific places to shop and items to buy in each port of call will be detailed in the chapter on

Above: Bay in Baja California Sur (Bruce Herman)

Below: The Bay at night (Bruce Herman)

Above: Lands End Beach, Los Cabos (Bruce Herman)

Below: Aerial view of Los Cabos (Bruce Herman)

Above: El Arco, Baja (Pablo de Aguinaco)
Below: El Dorado golf course, near Cabo San Lucas (Bruce Herman)

Above: Paleolithic rock art, Cueva Pintada, Baja (Pablo de Aguinaco)
Below: Cabo San Lucas Marina (Bruce Herman)

port descriptions. Regardless of the port, however, among the most popular items are handicrafts that trace their origins back thousands of years. **Silver** and, to a lesser extent, **gold** jewelry are very popular. Other possibilities include **pottery**, **leather**, **baskets** and **woven textiles**, **gemstones** and **glass** products. Popular woven garments are the blanket-like poncho known as a *sarape* and the shawl-like *rebozo*. More elaborate are the heavily brocaded women's blouses called *huipiles* and men's pleated shirts called *guayaberas*.

It's usually not a question of whether or not you'll find something that you like and simply must bring home, but whether the price is good and the quality can be trusted. The answer to that is more complex and merits some further consideration. Quality goods at a fair price can certainly be found. Don't assume, however, that because a particular port is noted for a certain item that the prices will always be reasonable and that the quality is first-rate. This isn't so important if you're just buying a colorful tee shirt or little bauble to give to someone. If you like it, fine. That's enough reason to buy it. But, when it comes to jewelry or other expensive items, it is another question entirely. If you would not buy these items on your own at home because you can't tell the good stuff from the bad or because you don't know whether the price is reasonable, then the same rules should apply when you are on vacation. Don't buy it without advice. So, where do you turn to for that advice?

People who have cruised several times will tell you that the cruise staff knows all the best places to get a good buy on the highest quality merchandise. Furthermore, many cruise lines will guarantee an item if you buy it at an approved location. All of this is true, to a limited extent. Cruise-recommended shops can be relied on to sell authentic goods of high quality. But this doesn't always

Practical Information

mean that the prices are the best. And those cruise line guarantees at specified stores sound a lot better than they really are. There are a host of limitations (which vary from one cruise line to another) and getting a refund or adjustment can sometimes be a frustrating process. Read the fine print concerning any guarantee very carefully and be sure you understand it before buying something because you assume the cruise line will back it up. One thing is certain – none of the guarantees covers a change of heart. Once the ship leaves port and you decide that you don't like what you bought after all, you can definitely forget about getting your money back.

Authenticity and quality are more certain if you make your purchase at one of the **FONART** government-run handicraft stores that are found in all large ports and even some smaller ones. Prices for goods here and at other legitimate establishments depend upon the level of artistry used in making the item. The more elaborate the brocading on a *huipil*, for instance, the higher the price. If you purchase items in a market, then bargaining is an expected part of the system. Don't commit too quickly to a price. Start to walk away in disinterest when you hear a price that's too high. You might find that the price will suddenly come down. Comparison-shop among different vendors. This way you'll have a better idea as to what a reasonable price is.

Bargaining

Bargaining is not a universal practice in Mexico. While it's fine in the market, it isn't the way things are done in finer shops. You would be no more welcome bargaining in one of these places than you would if you tried that in an upscale establishment in your local mall. FONART store prices are also usually firm. When purchasing silver you should be sure that it is a fine grade. This can be ascertained by looking for the marking ".925." If it is in a repu-table establishment then you know you're getting the real thing. It is illegal to place such a marking if the item doesn't truly meet that degree of authentic silver but false marks are, of course, possible in markets, from street vendors and other unreputable dealers. I strongly recommend against buying jewelry and other supposed high-quality items off the street.

GOING ONCE...

Going twice.... Sold to the little lady in the front row with her hand over her mouth! Ah, the sounds of an auction. Nothing like it to raise the blood pressure a few notches. Yes, auctions at sea, specifically **art auctions**, have become a standard practice in the cruise industry. It probably started when cruise lines decided to make their vessels floating art galleries with wonderful works of art throughout. Someone got the idea, "hey, we can sell some of this stuff," and the rest, as they say, is history. Well, you can't buy what's used as decoration on the ship but art auctions at sea present a wide variety of paintings to choose from, often by well-known artists from all over the world. The auctions are conducted by professionals and the attraction is that you can buy yourself a nice piece to hang in your home or hold for investment purposes at prices that are said to be far lower than what you would pay in an art gallery. The cruise line will even crate and ship the purchase to your home. So, should you buy?

My advice is that, if you know anything about art and want to add to your personal collection, go right ahead. However, if you are a complete novice, you might wind up buying something that is far too expensive. On the other hand, if you see something you like and MUST HAVE, and you can afford it, there's nothing wrong with doing so, even if it might not be the wisest choice from an art investment standpoint. You also might want to attend one of these auctions just for the fun of it. Check out the art and watch people bid or see the auctioneer begin to sweat when no one is bidding. Best yet, many art auctions at sea provide free champagne to those attending, whether or not you ever make a bid or ante up a penny of your hard-earned money!

Sports & Recreation While in Port

The possibilities for outdoor recreation along the Mexican Riviera and in Baja are almost endless, although the most popular activities with cruise ship passengers are, naturally, connected with the sea. In most cases you will have the option of seeking out one or more of these activities on your own. However, many of the cruise lines' shore excursions are simply organized ways to take part in popular outdoor activities. This usually means providing transportation to a popular beach or a fully escorted adventure experience. Here's a very brief rundown on the more popular recreational activities. Specific port-related information will be provided in the chapter on the individual ports of call.

On Land

Golf and **tennis** are popular pastimes in all major resort areas. Unlike the United States, however, most of these locations do not have public courses (especially golf) although there are some exceptions. The resorts often limit facilities to their guests. Therefore, the best way to get "in" is to book a shore excursion especially for this purpose. The cruise lines have arranged for playing time for their guests at some of the local resorts. **Horseback riding** is another very common diversion and it can be done in a number of places. There are stables and ranches in just about every port city and in surrounding towns. Destinations for horseback riders often include the foothills of the mountains that form a backdrop to virtually every Mexican Pacific port. Easier riding is available on many beaches. The latter is obviously more convenient for cruise ship visitors. Although you can generally find a place to rent horses quite readily, again, doing it through your ship's shore excursion office is easier still.

On the Water

In addition to the obviously widespread availability of places to go **swimming,** there are many other watersports available, ranging from fairly tame to wet and wild. There's **waterskiing, windsurfing, sailing** and **parasailing**. **Surfing** has never been very popular among the Mexican populace but many visitors find that there are good places for this sport in both Baja and along the Riviera. The ever-popular sport of **snorkeling** is not nearly as good along the Pacific coast of Mexico as it is on the Caribbean side. Nonetheless, there are places where you can partake in this activity. Better suited to the waters of Pacific Mexico is **scuba diving**. Finally, enthusiasts of **fishing** will find that Mexico's Pacific coast is heaven, especially for deep-sea fishing. In fact, it is considered one of the best places in the world for serious sport fishing. Among the species found at various places along the coast are barracuda, bonito, marlin, pompano, red snapper, sailfish, shark, swordfish, and yellowtail. Fresh-water fishing opportunities also exist but not to any special extent. Again, most of these activities are best arranged through the shore excursion office. Doing so isn't likely to save you much, if any, money but it is considerably more convenient.

Spectator Sports

Both baseball and soccer are extremely popular in Mexico but few Americans go there to watch these sports. Visitors tend to opt for activities that are more uniquely Mexican such as **bullfighting** (*corrida de toros*) and **rodeos** (*charreadas*). Also of interest is the fast-paced game of **jai alai**. These sports are seasonal and will be found only in the larger ports such as Acapulco and Mazatlán.

Staying in Touch

Almost everyone likes to stay in touch with family or maybe even their place of work (for those unfortunate souls who can't separate themselves from their work). Being on a cruise doesn't prevent you from doing that. In the old days it was a complicated and very expensive procedure to contact someone on land. Today there are a number of ways to reach friends and family back home or for them to contact you. It's still rather expensive but not as bad as in the past. The expense isn't because of technology limitations but because the cruise lines make some extra money on the deal.

Telephones

Every stateroom on every ship of the major lines has its own direct-dial telephone that can be used to call anywhere in the world. Dialing procedures vary from ship to ship but are simple and well-documented in the information guide that will be provided in your room. If you have questions, just ask for assistance from the ship's operator. Prior to your sailing date (usually when you receive your documents) you will be given a toll-free telephone number that people in the United States can dial to reach your cruise line's overseas telephone operator. All they then have to do is inform the operator which ship you're on and then the call can be completed. Note that it is the recipient (you) who will be charged for all incoming calls and this may not be any less than if you made the call in the first place. In general, rates for either in- or outbound calls on the ship range from $7 to $10 per minute.

A less expensive alternative for calling home is to wait until you are in port. The Mexican telephone system, **Telmex**, has improved immeasurably over the last several years. Making a call from Mexico often used to be a real hassle but today it is much like using the phone right here in the States. International calls to the United States can be made in a number of ways. The first is to use an international calling card or credit card. Just make sure that Mexico is a valid country to originate a call from for the card you intend to use. Dial the international access code for the United States (001) and then the access number for your calling or credit card. Some calling cards or credit cards might have a local Mexican number for you to dial. If you are going to direct dial a number in the United States then dial 001 + area code + local number. If you need the assistance of an English-speaking operator, then dial 090.

The only public phones that can be used to make long-distance calls are ones that indicate they are part of the **Ladatel** system. These phones mainly accept Ladatel phone cards, although some will also take peso coins or major US calling cards. The cards are available in various peso denominations at pharmacies, mini-markets and at Ladatel vending machines. For local calls within Mexico, simply dial the phone number without any area codes. Should you be staying at a hotel in Mexico before or after your cruise, you should be aware that long-distance calls from your room will carry a hefty surcharge that is usually more than those charged by American hotels. So, your best bet is to go to the lobby or nearest public phone. Ladatel, or other similar phone cards that are readily available in all of the ports of call, are also the best way to go should you need to make a local call while you're in Mexico.

Another way to call home from Mexico is to make use of a **telephone call center**, which will almost invariably be available dockside in the major ports. Here you can place calls without having to get a local calling card. This may be the most convenient way to call home from Mexico. However, prices at these call centers do vary and usually are far from the cheapest way to place a call. As always, the consumer pays a price for the convenience and ease.

Finally, your **cell phone** might just work in some locations, depending on the distance from your cell company's nearest satellite link. If you are in a port of call (or even on the ship) and it is relatively close to the United States you should consider taking your cell phone along and see if it works. It could be a money saver.

Internet/E-Mail

Computer lovers – and who isn't addicted these days – who have never cruised before will be glad to hear that every ship sailing to Mexico has PCs available for passenger use. The negative is that the fees, which vary from one line to another, are generally high and in some cases might be termed exorbitant. You can do anything that you would do on your home computer including surfing the web and sending or receiving e-mail. Ship-board Internet facilities were originally always located in the ship's library. This is still the norm but there are some ships that now have separate Internet cafés. Prices will be posted and you will find that the more you use the computer the lower the per-minute rate. Various package plans are available and staff will be able to assist you in determining what best meets your needs and in resolving any problems that arise.

Time Zones

A cruise to the Mexican Riviera is likely to traverse three different time zones. Often, a time zone will be crossed overnight while you are cruising so that in most cases you simply set the time ahead or back one hour before retiring for the evening. You will always be advised via the daily information newsletter as to when to change the time. Note that although Daylight Savings Time is observed in Mexico, the dates are not the same as in the United States. Mexican DST runs from the first weekend in May through the last weekend in September.

The state of Baja California is on **Pacific Time**. The only port in this time zone is Ensenada. **Mountain Time** covers Baja California Sur and several mainland states in the northern portion of the Mexican Riviera. Ports on Mountain Time are Cabo San Lucas, La Paz, Loreto, Santa Rosalía and Mazatlán. **Central Time** is applicable to all ports on the Riviera in the state of Jalisco and points south. This includes Puerto Vallarta (right on the time zone border), Manzanillo, Acapulco and the Bahias de Huatulco. Because Puerto Vallarta is on the border it is the practice of some cruise lines not to change the time just for this port of call. Again, you will be kept informed of the proper time. It is important to know the correct

Practical Information

time on the ship because of the need to get back from port in time for the ship's sailing.

Traveling with Children

Although children are much more commonly seen on cruises these days than in the past, this is still the type of vacation that appeals more to adults than to the little ones. This is not meant to discourage you from bringing your children along. In fact, most of the mass market cruise lines actively encourage it so as not to lose the business of couples that won't travel without the kids. Yet, there is a difference in the child-friendliness among the cruise lines and that should be an important consideration in your planning. You know what your child's likes and dislikes are. Match those with what is available on the ship you're interested in taking to see if this will wind up being a positive experience for your child. In general, the more sophisticated the cruise line, the less child-oriented the ship. Several of the biggest lines do a great job in offering activities for children of all ages. **Carnival**, perhaps, comes to mind first, but **Royal Caribbean** and even **Princess** would be equally good choices.

Children, especially younger ones, may not particularly enjoy the shopping and sightseeing aspects of Mexico's Pacific ports of call, but they will almost certainly adore the swimming and other outdoor activities. They'll also be able to partake in a wide variety of special children's programs on most ships. It is common for cruise ships to have supervised activities all day long and into the evening so parents can enjoy some fun times by themselves. These are grouped by age so that teens won't be bored by activities that are geared to younger children. In fact, teens can almost always opt to join in special social programs and dances for their age group and usually find these a good way to meet new friends. Any specific questions that you have about facilities and activities on a particular ship should be directed to your intended cruise line before you book.

Zo, It's Your First Time Cruising...

So I stretched the A to Z promise a bit! I don't think I broke any laws in doing that. Getting more serious for a moment, newcomers to cruising will certainly have additional questions compared to experienced travelers, but being a rookie cruiser is no cause for concern. You've probably got the impression by now that vacationing on a cruise ship is really like staying at a full-service resort that's on the move. Most things are done for you, including the handling of your baggage to and from your stateroom upon embarkation and disembarkation. You'll find that cruises are well-organized and efficiently managed, especially given the large number of passengers on today's larger ships.

Frequently Asked Questions

If you have any questions or concerns, just ask a crew member – they're always happy to help. With that in mind, here a few things that first-time cruisers often ask about:

▸ **Documents:** It is the general policy of all cruise lines not to issue your documents (i.e., cruise tickets) until about three to four weeks prior to your embarkation. Consult the brochure of the line you select to be sure what the timetable is. If you don't receive them within a few days of the latest scheduled time, then contact your travel agent (if applicable) or the cruise line. Some lines will agree to send documents early but usually charge a hefty fee for doing so. Along with your tickets, you will receive lots of other goodies, including pre-coded tags for your luggage, more brochures to answer your questions, and information on shore excursions.

▶ **Seasickness:** Motion sickness is not usually a problem for most people. Although the Pacific coast of Mexico is not a particularly rough area, it can be prone to storms during the winter. Regardless, it is the open sea and it is not the same situation as is found in the almost always calm waters of Alaska's Inside Passage, for example. The contemporary cruise liner is stable enough to provide a comfortable ride even during unsettled weather. The captain will always select a route that avoids the roughest seas. However, if you have a history of motion sickness (and that is what seasickness is) then an ounce of prevention can be very useful, since it is far easier to prevent this malady than to treat it. Non-prescription drugs such as **Dramamine** and **Meclazine** (stronger forms require a prescription) are highly effective. They work best if you take them several hours before you set sail. If bad weather is anticipated, then you would be well advised to take them beforehand. You should consult your physician about these drugs if you are taking any other medications.

If you should get seasickness symptoms, these same drugs will provide some relief. How much seems to depend upon the degree of illness and the individual. Symptoms can be minimized by focusing on the horizon, which helps you regain your balance. Some people say that placing an ice cube behind the ear may also offer relief. The ship's doctor, in addition to having medications, will certainly have his or her own home remedies, which will probably work as well or better.

▶ **Time Schedules:** Although delays can occur for a variety of reasons, all cruise lines are known for their commitment to punctuality. The greatest possibility of delay is from your port of embarkation (because the ship might be waiting for late arrivals due to airline delays). At each port of call you will be provided with a time schedule that tells you when to be back on board. Comply with this schedule, as the ship will not wait long, if at all, for the tardy individual traveler.

▶ **Identification Card:** Every cruise line today operates with a sophisticated system for keeping track of who is on board and who is not. You will be issued a plastic credit card-like identification card that usually serves three purposes: as a room key, as your onboard charge card, and as a means of indicating your right to get back on board at each port of call. Be sure you have it with you before disembarking – not a problem since you won't be able to get off the ship without it – along with your other identification documents.

▶ **Safety:** This is of utmost importance to the ship's crew. Pertinent safety instructions are posted in each stateroom and you should familiarize yourself with all of them. Every cruise will have a lifeboat drill soon after embarkation (some might even have it before the ship

Practical Information

leaves its gateway port). You are required by law to attend. You should be fully aware of emergency procedures, as should your children. The drill (you don't actually get into the lifeboats) is actually kind of fun and colorful for the first-time cruiser. Your behavior onboard is of prime importance when it comes to safety. Although it looks romantic in the movies, don't sit on the ship's railing or lean over. You never know when you will slip or the ship might suddenly roll a bit because of the waves. It is also very important that your children be made to understand this. It is rare that people fall overboard, but it can and does happen, mainly because they had too much to drink and were feeling momentarily invincible! If you see someone fall overboard, try to toss a life preserver to them. After that, or in lieu of it if you are not near a preserver, notify the nearest crew member immediately. And as far as that romantic pose on the bow of the ship is concerned – forget that, too, if the ship is moving. They never tell you in the brochures or in the movies that you'll practically be blown away trying to stand there while underway. In fact, such areas of the ship are usually off-limits to passengers when the ship is moving for that very reason. Wait until you're in port to get that picture for your scrapbook!

Although I've tried to anticipate all of the areas where you might have questions, it isn't possible to cover everything. If there is something on your mind that hasn't been answered, the best course of action is to call or e-mail the cruise line and ask them. Your travel agent is also likely to know the answer.

ESPAÑOL 101

One of the nice things about foreign travel is the opportunity to experience other cultures. However, there are many people who feel somewhat uncomfortable in a strange environment. Cruising can be a plus to those people because, to a large degree, it shelters you from many things that are "different" – including the need to speak the local language. In fact, if you choose the guided shore excursion method of seeing the Mexican ports there is absolutely no need to speak any Spanish.

On the other hand, if you plan to explore on your own, it is always helpful to understand the language. Even a basic knowledge of a few key phrases can be expedient and even fun to try out. In the major Mexican tourist destinations almost everyone connected with the travel industry speaks at least a fair degree of English. Thus, while it isn't essential that you speak speak Spanish, the more you know, the better. Mexicans, like people all around the world, appreciate any attempt that you, as a visitor, make to speak their language. A few words in Spanish, even if mispronounced or grammatically incorrect, are likely to elicit a more favorable response than a question asked in English. So, for those who are going to be on their own while in port, I suggest that you visit your local bookstore or library and bring along a small Spanish phrase book. Even if you are on a guided shore excursion, greetings and thanks expressed in Spanish will be most appreciated by your hosts!

Practical Information

Ports of Call

*T*here are plenty of good reasons to take a cruise to the Mexican Riviera or Baja. A few of the better ones are the wonderful resort atmosphere, recreational opportunities, and the chance to see some interesting things in a country with a fascinating culture. While shopping may not be quite on a par with some of the Caribbean ports of call this, too, is a major activity. Almost all of these characteristics are present to at least some degree in every port in this chapter. The descriptions that follow will give you a better idea of what each is best suited for. In this way you will be better equipped to select an itinerary that interests you, as well as being better prepared to make full use of the time available to you in each port.

Gateways to the Cruise: Ports of Embarkation

Beyond the scope of this book and, therefore, not included are embarkation cities in the Caribbean or Florida for trans-Canal itineraries, which call on some Mexican Riviera or Baja ports.

Los Angeles

This is clearly the leading embarkation city for Mexican cruises. There are many reasons for this but among the most important are its relative proximity to Mexico; the wide choice of flights available from all over the United

States into the Los Angeles area; and the drawing power of the many sights in and around the city. The latter makes it possible to spend additional time here either before or after your cruise.

There are two different ports from which Mexican cruises depart and/or return to Los Angeles, although neither one is actually in Los Angeles itself. The **Port of Los Angeles World Cruise Center** in San Pedro is the larger of the two ports and holds the status as L.A.'s "official" port. San Pedro currently serves all lines leaving from Los Angeles except for Carnival and Princess. The cruise ship terminal facility covers Piers 91, 92, 93A and 93B. It can be reached via the Harbor Freeway (I-110) to the Terminal Island exit and then merging right to Harbor Blvd. The Harbor Freeway intersects both I-5 and I-10 in Los Angeles, along with most of the major east-to-west arterial highways in the greater Los Angeles area. The San Pedro port is 19 miles from Los Angeles International (LAX) airport, but allow at least 45 minutes for the transfer because of traffic.

Downtown L.A. is equally distant. If you don't have transfers arranged with the cruise line, this is one place where it might well pay to price what they'll charge because a taxi from the airport to cruise port will cost you approximately $65 each way. If arriving by your own or rental car, drop off your luggage at the designated lane prior to parking your vehicle, otherwise you may have to drag your luggage for a considerable distance. There are more than 3,200 parking spaces and they are protected by security. All parking facilities at the port are outdoors and the charge to leave your car is approximately $12 per day. If the spaces nearest to your ship are filled there is a separate lot a little farther away and free shuttle buses will take you to the terminal itself. If you are flying into Los Angeles on the day of your sailing and are making your own air arrangements, you should select a flight that is scheduled to arrive at least six hours before sailing time. Adjacent to the cruise ship terminal is the **Ports 'O Call Village**, an interesting complex of shops, restaurants and minor historic points of interest. You could easily spend some time here if you have a few hours to kill before embarkation begins.

The second Los Angeles area port is the **Long Beach Terminal**, which serves Carnival and Princess Cruises. It's located at the southern end of the Long Beach Freeway (I-710). Follow signs to the "Queen Mary," staying to the right and then following directional signs for parking and luggage drop-off. The I-710 freeway intersects I-10 and major east-to-west highways in the Los Angeles area. It is 23 miles from the Los Angeles International Airport so you should allow between 50 minutes and an hour for the transfer. Taxi service from the airport to the cruise ship terminal is slightly more outrageous than to San Pedro, running roughly $70. There is covered garage parking at this terminal and the cost per day is about $10. Allow the same amount of time between same-day flights and arrival at the dock as you would for San Pedro (six hours).

For early arriving passengers the area by the Long Beach Terminal has some things to see and do. There's a small shopping complex, but the major point of interest is the old Cunard liner, the *Queen Mary*. Although much of the ship has been converted into a hotel, other sections are available for touring, including the engine room. It's a bit expensive but lovers of ship history will find it worthwhile.

Note that Los Angeles has several airports. **LAX** is by far the largest and most passengers flying to their cruise will arrive there. However, keep in mind that if you can get service from your home city into either Long Beach Airport or the John Wayne-Orange County Airport, these two are closer and have less traffic. This is especially true for the Long Beach airport, which is very close to both cruise ship terminals. Taxi transfers will be far less expensive than from LAX. It is unlikely that cruise-line-arranged air will take you to either of these airports. Accordingly, you won't be able to use their bus transfer service.

San Diego

While the San Diego area has two major factors working to its benefit (it is even closer to Mexico than Los Angeles, and there are also a multitude of things to do in the area), the port facilities in aren't as extensive as those at its neighbor to the north. The cruise ship terminal is conveniently located at the edge of downtown San Diego on the Pacific Highway at the intersection of B Street (one block north of Broadway). This makes it easy to do some exploring in the city before you get on the ship. It is also quite convenient to the San Diego airport; a taxi ride to the cruise ship terminal will take only about 15 minutes and the fare should run less than $30, excluding a tip. There are two piers (the B Street Pier and the Broadway Pier). Drive-in passengers coming from I-5 should use the Washington Street exit and then proceed to Pacific Highway. Turn left and then right on Hawthorn and left on Harbor. It is about 2½ miles from the Interstate exit to the terminal. The terminal does not have any parking facilities for drive-in passengers. However, there are many private long-term garages within a short distance that allow cruise ship passengers to park. Rates range from $9 to $17 per day and free shuttle service to the terminal is often provided. Because of the relative proximity of the airport and the fact that there are usually fewer hassles getting out of it than in Los Angeles, you can schedule any arriving flight that arrives at least 4½ hours before the ship leaves. However, I remind you that, regardless of your port of embarkation, it is far more relaxing to arrive a day before your voyage, especially if you are flying in. You have several options to spend your time if you arrive at the terminal too early for boarding. Just north of the cruise ship terminal is San Diego's fine **Maritime Museum**. Less than a half-mile walk east on Broadway from the terminal is the heart of downtown, while about the same distance south from the piers will bring you to the **Seaport Village** shopping and entertainment complex.

San Francisco

Until recently the only cruises to or from Mexico from San Francisco were repositioning cruises at the beginning and end of the summer season when ships were making their way to or from Alaska. While this is still the case with the majority of cruise lines, there are a couple of major lines that now have regularly scheduled itineraries from San Francisco. This is probably somewhat overdue considering that San Francisco, in addition to being a major population center, is a natural for cruising with its location and own attractions.

The San Francisco cruise ship terminal is conveniently located near downtown along the famous Embarcadero at Pier 35 between the Fisherman's Wharf area and the foot of Market Street. If you are driving into San Francisco there is parking available at the cruise ship terminal. Costs run from about $15 per day. For those arriving at San Francisco International Airport without transfers arranged through the cruise line, a taxi ride to the ship will set you back between $35 and $40. If you are flying in on the same day you should book a flight scheduled to arrive in San Francisco at least five hours before sailing time. **Fisherman's Wharf** and its related attractions (**The Cannery**, the **National Maritime Museum of San Francisco**, and several restored historic ships) are all within walking distance, as is the ferry to **Alcatraz**. Downtown San Francisco is a bit farther, but local buses will take you there if you choose not to walk. Also relatively close by is **Telegraph Hill** and the famous **Coit Tower**.

Acapulco

More often than not, Acapulco will be a port of call during your cruise rather than an embarkation or disembarkation port. But some cruises either leave from or end in Acapulco. Information on Acapulco will, therefore, be covered later in this chapter in the alphabetic listing of ports. However, included here are some further details on arriving in Acapulco for those whose cruise commences or ends here. **Puerto Acapulco**, the city's cruise ship port, is just minutes away from the old downtown section of Acapulco opposite old Fort San Diego on the Costera Miguel Alemán. The airport is about 14 miles away and there is a special airport taxi service that runs to the hotels along the Costera. The ride takes approximately 30 minutes and costs only about $8 – a real bargain!

Because of the flight schedules from most cities in the United States to Acapulco, if you start your cruise here, you will almost always need to arrive the night before, even though cruises from Acapulco typically depart late in the evening. Even if you could make the ship in time, I strongly urge that you arrive the night before. If you haven't arranged a pre-cruise stay with the cruise line then you will also have to secure your own transportation to the cruise ship dock from your hotel. However, taxis are plentiful and if you stay in the main resort zone the trip is short and inexpensive.

Some cruises beginning or ending in Acapulco already include an overnight on board ship. which will allow you more time to explore the city and its many activities as well as avoiding an expensive hotel night.

Other Ports of Embarkation

There are a couple of other cities from which a smaller number of Baja and Mexican Riviera cruises embark. These are **Seattle** and **Vancouver** and both are solely for repositioning cruises toward Mexico after the summer Alaskan season ends. At the other end of the Mexican season they would often embark at Acapulco and wind up in either of those two northern cities. Because of the relatively few cruises of this type, port details for those cities won't be provided except to say that each location has an excellent cruise ship terminal in the heart of downtown.

Onboard Sightseeing

There is certainly no denying that standing on deck (or on your private balcony) and watching the brilliant blue waters of the Pacific is a beautiful sight. But, unless you're the extra-romantic type, the appeal of this kind of sightseeing will probably wear off rather quickly. The fact is that, unlike Alaska and some other places, you won't be doing a lot of what can be termed "scenic cruising" during your Mexican voyage. However, this isn't to say that there won't be times when you should try to be out on deck to see something of special interest. Most of the Mexican Riviera ports are, as you will soon read, situated along beautiful bays or particularly scenic stretches of the coast. Thus, your arrival or departure from the various ports can often provide stunning vistas – assuming that the ship gets there and leaves in the daylight. This is the case on most itineraries.

Among the best ports for this type of scenery are Acapulco and Cabo San Lucas. Acapulco is fantastic by day or night. It is the only Riviera port that merits seeing from the ship after dark. Your daily cruise program should point out those ports where the viewing will be especially good.

Tourism Information

In most of the major ports that are frequented by large numbers of Americans, the local tourist office will usually have someone who speaks good English. The location of these offices will be provided at the beginning of each section on a particular port of call. Offices are generally open weekdays (as well as weekends in the larger ports). They may close for an hour or two around lunch-time. However, if you want to do advance planning before your cruise, these offices are less useful because you may not be able to get someone on the telephone that understands English well enough to answer your questions. Thus, for the best general source of information on Mexico, contact the **Mexican Tourist Board**, toll-free in the United States ☎ (800) 446-3942, www.visitmexico.com. The MTB has offices in Chicago, Houston, Los Angeles, Miami and New York. If you live in or near those cities, you might want to consider dropping by for more in-depth service and information.

There are many websites on Mexico, including the areas covered in this book. However, most are geared more to individual travelers coming into the country via plane or car. They aren't that useful for cruise ship visitors. On the other hand, browsing the web is always an interesting way to come up with little bits of information that you might be looking for. Some of the Mexican state governments have or are developing websites in English. These presently include the state of **Baja California** (www.turismobc.gob.mx); **Baja California Sur** (www.bajacalifornia.gob.mx); and the city of **Acapulco** (www.visitacapulco.com.mex). The states of Sinaloa, Jalisco, Colima and Guerrero were all in the process of developing English-language sites that may be up and running by the time you read this.

Seeing the Ports

The remainder of this book is devoted to providing you with a detailed description of each port of call in Baja and along the Mexican Riviera. A short description of ports on trans-Panama Canal cruises will be found at the end of the main port listing. For each of the major ports there will be a brief introduction to the port followed by these informational sections:

▶ *Arrival*

▶ *Tourism Information Office*

▶ *Getting Around*

▶ *The One-Day Sightseeing Tour*

▶ *Shopping*

▶ *Sports & Recreation*

Shopping and recreation are, of course, important and will be dealt with at length. However, the real heart of the matter is **sightseeing**, so here's some clarification of how this topic will be handled. It is a description of what you should see in a full day tour of the port. Keep in mind the following important facts when planning your day. First, the number of hours you have is *not* equal to the hours of the port call. For instance, a typical port call as shown in the cruise line brochure might be from 8 am until 6 pm. But you often won't be able to get off the ship until about an hour after the scheduled arrival. You must also be back on board from a half-hour to an hour before departure, depending upon the ship. Thus, in this particular case your maximum available sightseeing time is from 9 am until 5 pm.

▶ A good rule of thumb to calculation the available port time by subtracting two hours from the ship itinerary hours to determine how much time you have.

Second, the tours described here assume you are not planning other types of activities. If you are like most people, however, and do plan on spending at least some time at the beach or shopping, then you will have to subtract that from the available sightseeing time. And, of course, most people will want to allocate some time for lunch. Then again, with all of the eating you'll likely be doing on board, skipping lunch or just having a quick snack will be a good idea for those who intend to do some serious sightseeing.

The sightseeing tours are based on your having about eight hours available in port. To help your planning process, a suggested amount of time will be given for some attractions, areas or segments of the tour as well as the travel time between attractions where appropriate. All attractions are open daily unless otherwise specified. Hours for attractions and points of interest are generally given (subject to the Mexican habit of constantly changing them, as well as the fact that hours in Mexico aren't always as rigidly adhered to as in the United States). If no hours are mentioned, you can count on that attraction being open during the time your cruise ship will be in port.

ADULT PRICE LEVELS	
$	Under $5
$$	$5-9
$$$	$10-20
$$$$	Over $20

Since prices for attractions (given in US dollars) seem to change rapidly, only a price range indicator will be shown. If there is no indicator, then the attraction is free.

Although I will frequently mention the availability of shore excursions, I have not included pricing information. The cost of an excursion depends upon the length of the trip, the types of activities, and whether or not it includes lunch. Rare, indeed, is the shore excursion that will cost less than $30 per adult. If it does, then it is probably only providing transportation to a place where you'll be on your own regarding everything, including admissions and costs of activities. Regular shore excursions that include these items run from $40 to $125, and sometimes even higher. Admissions to museums and other attractions that are part of the shore excursion itinerary are, however, included in the price.

Acapulco

Ah-kah-PULL-ko

(Mexican Riviera)

A brilliant gem along the Bahía de Acapulco, this destination resort city is world-famous and with good reason. Set around a crescent-shaped bay with beaches stretching for more than seven miles and backed by gorgeously verdant mountain slopes, Acapulco has the stuff that picture postcards are made of. But let's go back in time first and explore its history. The earliest Spanish settlement in what is now Acapulco dates from the 1530s. It

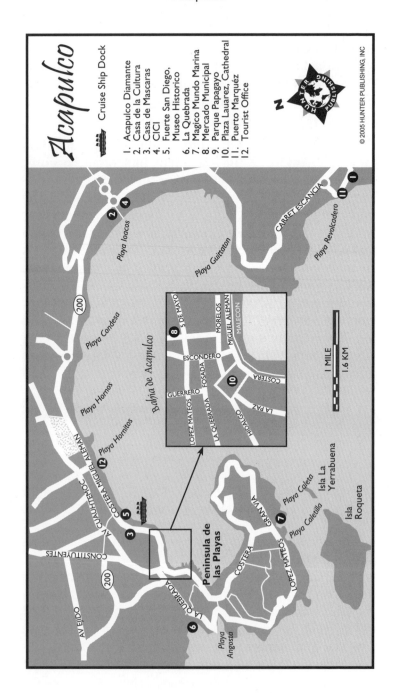

Acapulco

Cruise Ship Dock

1. Acapulco Diamante
2. Casa de la Cultura
3. Casa de Mascaras
4. CICI
5. Fuerte San Diego,
   Museo Historico
6. La Quebrada
7. Magico Mundo Marina
8. Mercado Municipal
9. Parque Papagayo
10. Plaza Lauarez, Cathedral
11. Puerto Marquéz
12. Tourist Office

© 2005 HUNTER PUBLISHING, INC

soon became the most important Pacific port for Spanish trade with the Orient. A series of forts were built in the 17th century to protect the settlement from the depredations of pirates. Although commercial port activities are still important, its dominant position had ended by 1815 due to wars of liberation against the Spanish colonial masters and other problems. Thus, for more than a century the city languished in relative obscurity. There had been some tourism development but nothing too much happened until after 1927 when a road was built from the interior and crossed the mountains to the sea.

The resort of Acapulco as we know it today began to grow in the mid-1950s. It was a prominent destination for Hollywood stars and the international jet-set. The city around the tourist haven also grew, but problems of urban decay beyond the resort zone and pollution in the bay itself were major blows to the city's image and by the mid-1970s its popularity had peaked. It might well have emerged from this storm without too much damage if it were not for the development of other Mexican resorts, such as the incredibly successful Cancún. Not willing to see their city sink any further, local officials and the Mexican government combined in the 1980s to spend more than a billion dollars on redevelopment. The city was spiffed up and the water pollution was gotten under control. Resort hotels spruced themselves up and the city of a million people took new pride in their home. While the number of competing places along both coasts of Mexico continues to grow, Acapulco certainly doesn't have to take a back seat to any of them. This Las Vegas of Mexico has a 24-hour vibrancy that few other places can match.

Arrival

Depending upon your ship's arrival time, you'll have a fabulous view of the Bahía de Acapulco as you come in to the dock, with Fort San Diego in the background. The cruise ship dock is an excellent facility that can handle up to three ships at one time, depending upon their size. The dock is well situated for touring the city and surrounding beach areas. It is located on Acapulco's main thoroughfare, the waterfront Costera Miguel Alemán, on the eastern edge of downtown Acapulco and just west of the Golden Zone (where the majority of resort hotels are). There are extensive facilities and services available at the dock.

Tourism Information Office

The Mexican state of Guerrero operates an information office (Procuraduriá del Turista). It is in the International Center (a convention facility) on Costera Miguel Alemán. Unfortunately, this is in the hotel area about two miles from the cruise ship dock. Unless you're going to be heading in that direction for sightseeing or other activities, the location is far from convenient for those who primarily intend to remain downtown. You can usually get most of the information you need by the cruise ship terminal.

Getting Around

Acapulco can, for visitor purposes, be divided into three main sections. These are (from west to east around the bay) the **old town**, **downtown** and the **main resort zone**. The old town comprises a small peninsula called the **Peninsula de las Playas** (Peninsula of Beaches). Downtown starts along the waterfront and heads inland, beginning just to the west of the peninsula, and extends to the cruise ship dock. Everything east and southeast of that point is the resort zone. The main thoroughfare that you need to be familiar with is the **Costera Miguel Alemán**, which runs from the peninsula into the hotel zone where it eventually changes name to **Carretera Escénica** (the Scenic Highway). Since Costera Miguel Alemán is such a long name everyone refers to it as *the Costera* and I will do the same from this point on except when giving "official" address locations. Almost all of the points of interest and activities for visitors are on or close to the Costera.

While Acapulco is large, it becomes quite manageable if you take in the three sections as described above. In fact, the first two are small enough to explore on foot. Only when you head into the resort zone or are traveling between areas do you have to consider motorized transportation. In that case, there are two options if you don't rent a car. The first is **taxi**. Finding a taxi in Acapulco never seems to present much of a problem. Taxis that station themselves at hotels are more comfortable and reliable but they can cost two to three times as much as cabs that cruise the streets. Although there are supposed to be set rates, negotiate a set price with the driver before you head out to your destination.

The local **bus** service is good (although often very crowded) and routes run along the entire length of the Costera all the way to the resort zone. Good maps showing routes and destinations are posted at the bus stops. The fare is inexpensive, being the US equivalent of less than 50¢. Do be aware that many of the older buses are not air conditioned, which can make things a bit uncomfortable. The Costera route, which stops directly in front of the cruise ship terminal, however, is mostly served by newer buses that are far more pleasant to ride.

Renting a **car** is an option since most of the major American companies are represented, including Avis, Budget, Dollar and Hertz. You can find their rental desks at various major hotels, some of which are fairly close to the cruise ship dock. However, unless you plan to travel much farther out from the city, it is a better idea to use a taxi or bus – or a combination of the two.

The One-Day Sightseeing Tour

There's little doubt that visitors to Acapulco are drawn more by the opportunity for fun in the sun than for traditional sightseeing. However, it would be a mistake not to see the city. There are plenty of interesting things to see and do, some of which can be combined with recreational pursuits. Certainly, a full day can be devoted to sightseeing and that is what this suggested itinerary will do. If you plan other activities, you will have to eliminate parts of this tour. Also, modifications may have to be made depending on how many hours your ship is in port (you'll need to be up and about from 9 am until 5 pm to include everything suggested here). Another factor to consider is what time your ship will be in port since certain attractions have limited hours or need to be seen at a specific time. There is little need to sign up for a shore excursion when it comes to sights within the city because you can easily get around on your own.

Let's begin in the downtown section because that is closest to the cruise ship dock. The active commercial wharves along the waterfront are traversed by an attractive promenade called the **malecón** that runs from opposite the cruise ship terminal to the Calle Escudero, somewhat past the downtown section of the city. The center of downtown is right where the Costera makes a large bend. Here you will find the *zócalo* or central plaza, whose full name is the **Plaza Alvarez**. It's a mildly attractive spot with plenty of shade trees and is best used for people watching.

On one side of the Plaza is the **Catedral Nuestra Señora de la Soledad** (Our Lady of Solitude Cathedral). Unlike the typical old Spanish colonial churches found in most

Mexican cities large and small, this cathedral is of modern construction and design. The most interesting feature is the exterior architecture, its colorful bulb-shaped spires contrasting with an all-white facade. A block west of the plaza turn to the left on Escudero and make your way to the **Mercado Municipal** at Avenidas Cuesta Hurtado de Mendoza and Constituyentes. This is the city's major marketplace and, even if you don't plan to shop, it's worth a brief look for the color, hustle and excitement that is found in its countless vendor stalls. Then retrace your steps back down to the Costera and head towards the fort. However, just before you get there turn onto Calle Morelos, where you'll find the **Casa de Mascaras**. This former house is now home to a wonderful collection of more than 500 ceremonial masks. Most date back to pre-Colombian times but some are the type still used in dances and ceremonies by Amerindian groups. This is both an educational experience and a glorious display of color that is fun for just about all ages. Very young children might be frightened by some of the masks. *Open daily except Sunday from 10 am until 6 pm and donations are suggested in lieu of an admission price.*

Opposite the Costera on a hillside is old **Fuerte San Diego**. The first structure on this site was built in 1616 to defend against marauding pirates, including the infamous Sir Francis Drake. However, the fort was destroyed by an earthquake in 1776 and the current larger and more elaborate structure dates from late in the 18th century. Lovers of ramparts, battlements and other such fort features will be mildly satisfied but the main attraction today is the excellent **Museo Historico de Acapulco**. Excellent exhibits of many types (all with English descriptions) explore more than 30 centuries of Mexican history. Much emphasis is on the Acapulco area. There is also a good collection of artifacts that shed more light on the cultural side of the nation's past. *Open daily except Monday from 10 am until 5 pm. It is also open on Saturday evening. ($)*

The downtown part of the tour should take about two hours. After leaving the fort you should head down the Costera in an easterly direction and you'll soon be in the resort area. Near the Acapulco Convention Center at Costera Miguel Alemán 4834 is the **Casa de la Cultura**, which has a small museum of archaeology and an art gallery. It isn't that great so skip it if you think you'll be running short of time. However, the museum store has a fabulous selection of Mexican handicrafts. *Open daily except Sunday from 9 am until 2 pm (and again from 5 to 8 pm on weekdays).*

The **Centro Internacional de Convivencia Infantil**, or CiCi to the locals, is on the Costera Miguel Alemán at Calle Colón. This is essentially a water-park for children, although it also has a small aquarium. If you don't have the kids in tow then you're better off skipping it altogether. On the other hand, for little ones it makes a great break. *Open daily from 10 am to 6 pm ($ but $$$$ for swimming with the dolphins).* **Parque Papagayo**, along the Costera between Playas Hornos and Hornitos, covers more than 50 acres and is a pleasant place that includes an aviary and a replica of a Spanish galleon. There are also numerous rides that children will adore although older kids might find them too tame (i.e., bumper boats and mini-racing). Grown-ups traveling without children can make quick work of the park but families could spend enough time here to require further itinerary alterations. *Open daily although rides generally begin operating after 4 pm. (Park is free but $ per ride or for a multi-ride package.)* This section of the tour can be done in about an hour unless you are going to let the kids go on rides, swim or whatever.

Once you get past Parque Papagayo, the resort hotels will start coming up with increasing frequency. You can take some time to tour the better ones (see further information under *Other Attractions* below) if that is your thing but if you do so it will not allow enough time to take in the rest of the highlight tour. Touring the resorts can take anywhere from an hour to much more, depending upon how much you're into hotel discovery. You also have to allow about an hour round-trip travel time if taking the bus. A taxi can do it much faster.

The final group of attractions is on the **Peninsula de las Playas** so hop in a taxi or take the bus. To get from downtown to the La Quebrada area by foot is also possible if you're somewhat more ambitious. It's a direct walk from the street called La Quebrada, which begins just north of the Cathedral. The total distance is just under a mile but it's hilly. Acapulco's most famous sight is probably **La Quebrada**, a tradition for 70 years. Here, divers known as *clavadistas* make a seemingly death-defying plunge from atop the nearly 135-foot cliff, which they have to scale by holding onto rock outcroppings, before landing in the pounding and treacherous surf of a narrow gorge. The best place to see this spectacle is from a nightclub in the La Perla hotel, but this will cost you a fortune for lousy service and bad drinks. Instead, spend the equivalent of about $2 and you'll be admitted to a viewing area adjacent to the hotel. There are other nearby vantage points, but the views aren't as good and you'll miss the chance to meet the divers in person when they make their way to the observation area. It is customary to give them a small tip. When to see the show depends upon your available time and ship schedule. The evening shows (hourly beginning at 7:30 pm) are the most dramatic. If you can't get there at night then the only daytime performance is at 1 pm. Unless you're on a guided tour that ensures there will be room for you to watch the divers, it is best to arrive early. While La Quebrada is at the beginning of the peninsula, the **Mágico Mundo Marino** is at the end. The Magical Marine World is an aquarium with performing sea lions. *Open daily from 9 am until 6 pm ($).* There is also the opportunity to make this a sports outing since you can rent equipment for use on Playa Caleta. Another reason to go to Playa Caleta is because from there you can take the 10- to 15-minute boat ride (*round-trip, $*) to **Isla de la Roqueta**. While the island is mainly known as a place of recreation, it can be a worthwhile destination just to walk around for awhile. Its location just outside the entrance to the Bay of Acapulco makes for some fine scenery.

Other Attractions

If you are on a cruise that embarks or disembarks in Acapulco it is likely that you will have another day to spend in the city, possibly on board the ship. Even if you don't have that built into your cruise itinerary you should consider adding on a day. The extra time can be devoted to shopping or recreational opportunities as discussed below, or you could add on some more sightseeing time. If you choose the latter then here are some more suggested places to see and things to do:

▶ *Calandrias* are colorfully decorated horse-drawn carriages that ply the Costera. This is a leisurely way to take in the scenery of Acapulco Bay.

▶ *Miradors:* Several lookout points provide some of the most dramatic views of Acapulco. Unfortunately, they are best reached if you have a car, although depending upon your itinerary it may be convenient for a taxi to stop and allow you to get a picture. Most can also be reached by bus, especially if you're heading out to some of the main resort hotels. One of the easiest to reach is located along Avenida Lopez Mateos, a 10-minute walk past La Quebrada. This one features a view of the ocean and coast rather than the bay. Another well known observation point is on the Carretera Escénica just past the Camino Real Acapulco Diamante Hotel. Regardless of whether you go to any of the Miradors, you should try to get a view of Acapulco's lights glittering on the bay at night. Hopefully, your ship will be in port late enough for you to do this.

▶ **Puerto Marques, Acapulco Diamante & the Resorts:** For those who like to see luxury this is a little excursion that can fill half a day. Although nice hotels are scattered in many parts of the city, the greatest concentration begins after the traffic circle at Playa Icacos, where the Costera becomes the Carretera Escénica. In addition to the resorts, the areas known as **Puerto Marqués** and **Acapulco Diamante** are upscale neighborhoods with fancy houses and great views of the bay. Puerto Marqués is a small inlet between the naval base and the airport. Although there are dozens of hotels, there are five that stand out in my mind as worth seeing. These are the **Fairmont Acapulco Princess** (the city's most famous hotel) and the smaller **Fairmont Pierre Marqués**. Both are in Acapulco Diamante and feature gorgeous grounds. Also in the general vicinity is the beautiful **Camino Real Acapulco Diamante**. Two Diamante hotels with gorgeous cliff-top locations are the **Hotel Las Brisas Ac-**

apulco and the **Quinta Real**. The latter is a small hotel with simply stunning vistas. You'll also have fabulous views along the way whether by bus or taxi. Of course, the latter will stop if you want to take a picture.

▶ **La Capilla de la Paz:** In the Las Brisas area (so it can be combined with a resort visit) this small but modern chapel provides an outstanding vista of the east side of the bay. A large white cross sits on top of the mountain. Landscaped grounds are another plus. The whole place is very peaceful – just as its name implies. Surprisingly, this is not a well-known spot and it never seems to get crowded.

▶ **Excursion to Taxco:** The round-trip journey to Taxco and time to see the famous silver town is an all-day affair. It can usually be arranged through your cruise line's excursion office. While this is a worthwhile place to see I would recommend it for those who have already been to Acapulco and want to see something new this time.

Shopping

Veteran cruisers and other travelers will give you a wide variety of opinions on where Acapulco ranks in the shopping hit parade, from near the top to near the bottom. Those who sing its praises will point to the abundance of stores that sell everything from A to Z. The detractors will point out that there is little in Acapulco that you can't buy in any major city and that little or nothing is unique. Both views are valid and so it all depends upon what you're looking for. Among the more commonly found items are apparel for both men and women and a wide variety of **folk craft items**. Because of its relative proximity to the silver center of Taxco, you can also easily find an excellent selection of authentic and high-quality Taxco **silver** products. Most of the shops, especially those in upscale malls and hotels, are reputable, but don't take a street vendor's word that something is authentic Taxco silver.

The Costera is loaded with boutiques and other shops throughout the resort zone and to a lesser extent elsewhere. There are many local family-owned businesses but you're more likely to encounter internationally recognized names on the storefronts here than at any other Mexican Riviera port. Among the many contemporary malls are the **Plaza Bahía** and the **Marbella Mall**, both on the Costera. Most of the larger hotels have several stores and many have shopping arcades. The biggest and best of these is at the **Acapulco Princess**. The city also has many department stores. One of the best-known is the **Artesanías Finas de Acapulco**. In fact, many cruise lines will have an excursion that goes here.

If you're looking for crafts than a good place to go is the government-run craft shop known as **FONART** on the Costera. More fun is the flea market-like **Mercado de Artesanías** (also known as the **Mercado Parazal**) in downtown near the main plaza at Calle Velázquez de León and Calle 5 de Mayo. Bargaining is expected here. The **Mercado Municipal**, previously mentioned in the sightseeing section, is also a good place to shop for just about everything. Locals shop here in droves but touristy souvenirs of all types and price categories can be found. Food is a major item here but, as is the case throughout Mexico, be wary of fresh fruit and vegetables.

Sports & Recreation

There is a wide variety of sports and recreational activities in Acapulco that you can do on your own. However, anything other than a day at the beach is probably most conveniently arranged as a shore excursion from your ship. It probably won't save you any money but it's easier because the transportation is provided for you.

Acapulco is synonymous with beaches so let's begin with the sun and sand scene. I've arranged the beaches from west to east. Keep in mind that if you intend to swim the ocean waters, undertows can be dangerous. You would be wiser to swim at beaches that face the bay rather than the open ocean, especially if you have children.

The first beach is away from the others about 10 miles northwest of Acapulco. It can be reached by bus or taxi. The **Pie de la Cuesta** is one of the more beautiful golden-sand beaches in the area. It is also less crowded than most. The negative is the rough water. Pie de la Cuesta is best known for its spectacular sunsets. In Acapulco on the Peninsula de las Playas are several beaches. **Playa La Angosta** is a small and usually uncrowded area near La Quebrada. There are nice views from this oceanfront beach. The twin **Playas Caleta** and **Caletilla** are popular with families. The surf is usually calm. Between the two beaches is the Mágico Mundo Marino, so this can be a good combined outing.

More centrally located in town are **Playas Hornos** and **Hornitos**, just off the Costera and very convenient to the cruise ship dock. That's the big plus of these beaches. The downside is that they are often very crowded and neither the beach nor the water are as clean here as other area beaches.

Somewhat farther west along the Costera is **Playa Condesa**, which has become the current "in" beach with the mostly younger crowd. This could be called "bikini" beach as it is where you'll find the most daring beach attire. Along the Carretera Escénica are **Playas Icacos** and **Guittarón**. The first is just north of the Icacos Naval Base, while the latter is just south. Both are clean, pretty and often relatively uncrowded.

Finally, down in the Puerto Marqués/Acapulco Diamante area are two excellent beaches. The calm and sheltered **Playa Puerto Marqués** is one of the most desirable of Acapulco's beaches. The same can probably be said for the beautiful **Playa Revolcadero**. This may also be the widest of Acapulco's beaches. Swimming with dolphins is an expensive diversion but children always love it. The most convenient way to do this is through ship-sponsored shore excursions.

With all those beaches (and I've listed only some of them) it shouldn't come as a surprise that every type of watersport beckons the Acapulco visitor. **Deep-sea game fishing** can mean catching barracuda, marlin, red snapper, sailfish and yellowtail, to name just a few. There is also **freshwater fishing** available in one of the lagoons by Pie de la Cuesta. If you don't want to arrange for a fishing trip with the cruise line, then go to the main dock near the main plaza where the **Pesca Deportiva** can put you in touch with the type of fishing tour operator you seek.

When it comes to boating there is no shortage of choices. They range from **canoes** and **kayaks** to **sailboats**, from **speedboats** to **yachts**. **Waterskiing** is popular, as is **wind-surfing**. Although **scuba diving** isn't one of Acapulco's main claims to fame, good diving conditions exist off of **Isla Roqueta**. Finally, for a different type of boat trip, you can try out one of Acapulco's newest attractions – the **Shotover Jet**. An offshoot of the river trip on New Zealand's Shotover River, this one will take you on a 35-minute ride (each way) to the Río Papagayo where you'll embark on a half-hour jet-boat tour. Although there is pleasant scenery on the river, most participants are there for the thrill of the ride, especially Shotover's famous

360-degree spin that's a real adrenaline rush. This tour is also available through most cruise lines.

Turning to land-based sports, **tennis** and **golf** are both popular and readily available at most of the major resorts. Of course, non-guests pay dearly for the privilege of playing. Golfers should check out the nine-hole public **Club de Golf Acapulco** adjacent to the Convention Center. The more expensive golf resorts aren't likely to let you in so if you want to sample their courses you'll have to book through the cruise line. They often arrange to play at the exclusive **Acapulco Fairmount Princess**.

Horseback riding on the beach is a pleasant diversion and the **Playas Revolcadero** and **Pie de la Cuesta** are the best places to do so.

Spectator sports in Acapulco include going to the **bull ring** (November through April) or **jai alai** (December to January and July and August). Both venues are conveniently located in the downtown section. However, the timing of the events (Sundays at 5:30 pm) means that most cruise ship visitors won't be able to do this.

A MALECÓN BY ANY OTHER NAME...

Even when we travel to another city, Americans are used to being able to find a destination because simple things like street signs are commonplace. Not so in Mexico, where such signs are likely to be absent. To make matters worse, many buildings do not have house numbers – they are listed in many publications as "s/n" for *sin número*, meaning "without a number. (By the way, when there is a house number, it will be listed at the end of the street name, such as Calle Alvarado 150.) Finally, just to make you throw up your hands in surrender, major streets often are known by more than one name! Which brings us to the name of this sidebar: the *malecón*.

Malecón refers to the waterfront promenade or street that is found in every Mexican seaport. Regardless of what the real name of the street is, locals are likely to refer to this thoroughfare as the malecón. In this book I'll always introduce such streets by their formal name but then will use the name and the term malecón interchangeably. As you travel from one Mexican port to another you will often find that important attractions, shopping and other services are on or near the malecón.

Cabo San Lucas
(Baja)

*C*abo goes by many names. Cabo or Los Cabos (The Capes) refers not to the town but to an area designated by Mexican tourism officials. It consists of the town of Cabo San Lucas and the larger nearby community of San Jose del Cabo as well as "the Corridor" between the two. The corridor is where most of the main resorts and golf courses are found. Cabo San Lucas itself (which I'll often refer to as Cabo for simplicity) is a small town that can trace its origins back to the 16th century when the area was a haven for pirates, including Sir Francis Drake. The pirates would seek out Spanish galleons loaded with treasure. By the 19th century it was a tiny fish canning community and, because of its isolation, remained largely unknown to most travelers until the 1970's when the trans-peninsula highway down the Baja Peninsula was completed. However, it had already been discovered

Cabo San Lucas

to The Corridor & San José del Cabo

OCAMPO

12 DE OCTOBRE

MATAMORES

CATTANZA

CABO SAN LUCAS

RAZARO CARDENAS

NINOS HEROES

❷

Playa Médano

Bahía de Cabo San Lucas

N

Harbor

❹

Playa del Amor

BLVD MARINA

❸ ❶

Playa Solmar

Pacific Ocean

© 2005 HUNTER PUBLISHING, INC

HUNTER PUBLISHING

1. El Arco
2. Faces of Mexico
3. Land's End
4. Marina: Tour & fishing boats

I MILE

Malecón ||||||||||||||||||||||

by the well-heeled traveler, including many Hollywood celebrities, for its sportfishing possibilities. Even today it is considered to be one of the great sportfishing destinations in all the world.

Beautifully located at the very southern end of the Baja Peninsula, Cabo marks the place where the waters of the Pacific Ocean meet the Sea of Cortés. Today's Cabo San Lucas is a thriving tourism destination that is so frequented by Americans that it may not have enough

"Mexican" atmosphere for some, especially if you confine your visit to the Marina area. Away from the main tourist paths Cabo has a laid-back small-town atmosphere that is a nice change of pace from some of the larger ports on the Mexican Riviera.

Arrival

The small marina and harbor at Cabo San Lucas cannot accommodate cruise ships, even the smallest ones. You will tender in (about a 10-minute ride) to the marina. From there you will be close to most of the activities and attractions. Taxis, which are located behind the flea market adjacent to the tender pier, are available if you do not wish to walk, but the center of town is only a five-minute walk from the tender pier.

Tourism Information Office

There are plenty of information kiosks in the marina area, but you should generally avoid taking advice from people on the street, who are mainly interested in having you listen to a time-share sales pitch. More reliable information is available from the Secretary of Tourism office on Avenida Madero at the town plaza (between Guerrero and Hidalgo). This is a very short walk from the marina. It is open weekdays from 9 am until 2 pm and on Saturday from 9 am till 1 pm. At other times you can try making inquiries at the front desk of the major hotels or get a copy of one of three English-language newspapers that are distributed free of charge all over town. These are the *Gringo Gazette*, the *Daily News Los Cabos Discover* or *Destination Los Cabos*. Although all of them are geared more to the resident American population or the visitor who is spending more time in Cabo, they each have some useful tidbits of information for the cruise ship passenger.

Getting Around

Many cruise ship visitors will spend all or almost all of their time in Cabo within the marina area. If this is the case then you don't have to worry about transportation because everything can be reached on foot. The pedestrian promenade that surrounds the large marina area is a safe place to walk and provides interesting views as well as access to the best shopping. It takes less than a half-hour to walk from the tender pier on the marina's west side all the way to the other end of the marina and the first of the beaches on the east side. That, of course, is without stopping to shop or browse.

The **Blvd. Marina** roughly parallels the pedestrian walk. **Blvd. Lázaro Cárdenas** is the main downtown street and is one block farther inland. The major streets heading farther into town from Lázaro Cárdenas are **Avenidas Hidalgo** (on the side of town near the tender pier) and **Morelos** (a few blocks past the town center).

There are **buses** that run from Cabo San Lucas to the beaches along the Corridor and all the way into San Jose del Cabo. The fares are inexpensive and, if you don't mind crowds, will do as well as a taxi. **Cabs** can also be found on the streets surrounding the marina but are expensive if you are going anywhere outside of town.

The One-Day Sightseeing Tour

The majority of cruise ships calling on Cabo San Lucas spend less than a full day in port. However, this shouldn't be a problem since the town is compact and it doesn't take long to see everything. Just keep in mind that you may not have enough time to wander out of town if you're going on your own.

While almost every Mexican Pacific port lies in a scenic setting, Cabo San Lucas is an especially worthy sight so you should make it your business to be out on deck (or on your balcony if you have one and you're facing in the right direction) to take in the view as you arrive outside the harbor and prepare to anchor in the **Bahía de Cabo San Lucas**.

Just where the ocean and the Sea of Cortés meet is called **Land's End** (*Finisterra* in Spanish). This rocky promontory is highlighted by the large natural arch created by the ceaseless pounding of the waves. **El Arco** (The Arch) is Cabo's most famous and most photographed point. You can generally get a good look from the ship but the best way to experience it is to take a boat ride that gets much closer. The easiest way to do this is to book an excursion from your ship. These tour boats provide a taped narrative that explains the history and ecology of the area. You'll be able to get excellent views of the Arch and numerous other rock formations, including the rocky pinnacles known as **Los Frailes** (The Friars). The water rushing in and out of narrow crevices and up against the rocks is a breathtaking sight. You'll also have an excellent chance of seeing one or more sea lions sunning themselves on the rocks near the shore. There is a permanent sea lion colony that makes this area their home. Many birds also inhabit the rocks. You can book rides to El Arco on small boats that depart from the marina. These have an advantage for those visitors who wish to spend some time on **Playa del Amor** (**Lover's Beach**), a small stretch of sand that is sandwiched between the rock formations and can be reached only by boat. You can come back on a later boat. The larger tour boats used by the cruise line excursions also offer an option of a bus ride into the surrounding area to see some more interesting rock formations as well as splendid views of the sea from higher elevations.

Ports of Call

Boat tours to El Arco take about 40 minutes to an hour, depending upon the operator, without time on the beach or any extensions into the countryside.

Except for Los Arcos, Cabo doesn't have a lot of what would be considered the usual kind of sightseeing. What it has is centered around the **Puerto Los Cabos**, the official name given to the **marina**. Since everyone calls it the marina, I'll do the same. In a sheltered harbor, the marina has 416 slips for boats of varying sizes. The marina is far more than a place to moor a boat. With restaurants, shops, hotels and more, the marina is the very heart of Cabo San Lucas. It is, in essence, a city within a town. A walk around the entire marina along the pedestrian-only promenade is a pleasant way to spend some time. The marina area is modern and features many different shopping and entertainment complexes with colorful buildings and architecture that is often reminiscent of the Spanish colonial era. The highlight is the **Puerto Paraíso Mall** with its interesting architecture (including a tower), waterfalls and sculptures. More about the mall will be found in the shopping section (page 186).

Also of interest is the small **Old Town**, with its town plaza, interesting shops and small museum. It's in the area around the intersection of Avenida Hidalgo and Blvd. Lázaro Cárdenas.

Faces of Mexico is primarily an art gallery but it also serves as a museum displaying religious masks from all over Mexico. Many of these beautiful works of art are several hundred years old. The gallery is at Lázaro Cárdenas and Matamoros and is a short walk from the center of Old Town.

If you want to venture a little farther away from town, then a pleasant journey is the three-mile trip to the **Faro Viejo**, a lighthouse that sits atop a high cliff known as

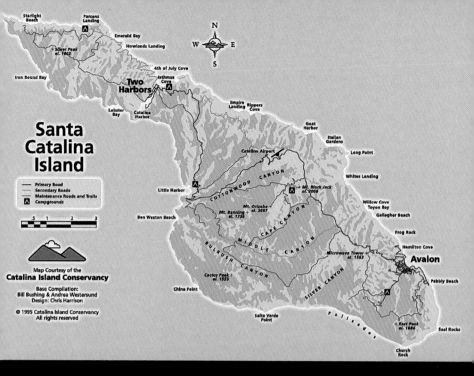

Above: Santa Catalina Island (Catalina Island Conservancy)
Below: Diamond Princess (bonj, photoblogs.org)

Above: *Zijuatanejo Bay* (www.amuleto.net)

Below: *Ixtapa* (Guillermo Aldana)

Aerial view of La Paz, Baja (www.findsiri.com)

Above: El Hongo rock formations in La Paz, Baja Sur (Bruce Herman)

Below: Marina in Loreto (Bruce Herman)

Cabo Falso. This translates as False Cape and is so named because at one time it was thought that it was the end of the Baja Peninsula. The lighthouse dates from 1890 (a newer one still in operation is nearby). There are wonderful views and the surrounding dunes are an interesting sight. You can get fairly near to Faro Viejo by taxi but to get closer requires four-wheel-drive, unless you walk. ATV tours to Faro Viejo are offered by several operators in town.

Cabo is known as a wonderful place to **whale-watch** and if you're here at the peak season (January through March), you're in for a special treat. You may see whales from your cruise ship, from the boat ride going to El Arco or even from the beach at Land's End. However, the best way to see the most is to sign up for a whale-watching cruise. Your shore excursion office will be sure to offer one during the season. Gray whales are the most commonly seen, but blue whales and humpbacks can also be spotted.

Finally, it isn't sightseeing, but Cabo has many restaurants of all types and is especially well known for fresh seafood. Many visitors decide to have lunch in town rather than tendering back to the ship for lunch. Not that doing so is a problem, especially given the beautiful views of bay, town and mountains on the way to and from the ship. If you do choose to eat in town you can rest assured that the food in any of the restaurants is safe to eat. An extra precaution is to drink only bottled water and ask for soft drinks without ice.

Shopping

Shopping opportunities in Cabo San Lucas are varied, especially considering that it isn't that big a place. There is a large **flea market** right by the tender pier and it's always jam-packed whenever cruise ships are in town. As you walk around the marina you'll encounter shops selling goods of all types. However, there's little doubt that the best place to shop in Cabo is at the **Puerto Paraíso Mall**, which has more than 80 stores. Goods range from inexpensive to very expensive and you can find clothing, crafts, art galleries and much more. If you're looking for jewelry, try **Diamonds International** (two locations, at the tender pier and Puerto Paraíso) or the **B&B Marketplace**, just off the marina (turn up the street by the "Lighthouse" restaurant). Other good choices for jewelry are the **Plaza del Sol** or **Ultrajewels** on Blvd. Marina.

Those seeking Mexican crafts can get them in the mall but you're better off heading to Old Town and all along Lázaro Cárdenas and Blvd. Marina. The **Galería El Dorado** is an especially good place to get authentic crafts. Art galleries are scattered all around town. Two of the best choices are the **Golden Cactus Gallery** at Guerrero and Madero; and the **Kristal Gallery** in the Puerto Paraíso Mall.

Party Town

Cabo has earned its deserved reputation as a famous party place. Of course, most of the action is in the evening after your cruise ship has left, but there are plenty of places to imbibe and have a good time during the daytime as well. Perhaps the best-known establishment in town is the wildly funky **Cabo Wabo Cantina** (they even have their own brand of tequila). It's just off Lázaro Cárdenas on Vicente Guerrero.

Sports & Recreation

There's a wide choice of beaches for those who want to soak up the sun. The aforementioned **Lovers' Beach** is the most interesting, but remember, it can be reached only by boat. On the Pacific side of the Land's End area is the beautiful **Playa Solmar**. This is a far less crowded beach, but it has dangerously high waves that can occur at any time. Therefore, it is better for sunning than for swimming. Back in town at the far end of the marina promenade in front of the Hacienda Beach Resort is where you'll find the closest beach. While not the most popular by any means, it is pleasant enough and even offers great views of the cruise ships anchored in the harbor.

Probably the most popular stretch of sand is **Médano Beach**, just up the coast a bit from Hacienda Beach, although this starts to become a long walk so you might want to take a bus or taxi. Beyond Médano are numerous other beaches that extend beyond town all the way through the Corridor and on into San Jose del Cabo.

With all these beaches you can be sure that there are numerous other **water-sports**. Diving, kayaking, sailing, surfing, parasailing, snorkeling, waterskiing and windsurfing are among the choices. You will often see the large and colorful sails of parasailers as your ship sails into or out of the harbor.

Snorkeling isn't as good here as it is in many other Mexican ports,, but it is still a possibility. If you do decide to snorkel, then the area by Lover's Beach or Chileno Bay are among the better choices. The top spot for surfing, without having to travel too far, is near the Sheraton Hotel by Monuments Beach. This is still several miles away and will require a taxi or bus to get to.

Cabo was put on the map by **sportfishing** and it is known especially for marlin, but there are many other catches, most of which run seasonally. Vessels for your fishing expedition range from small skiffs to more luxurious fishing cruisers. You can almost certainly arrange an excursion through your ship. Alternatively, contract with one of many operators found at the marina or use one of the boats from the fleets run by the larger resort hotels. All are reliable. Compare prices and be sure that the fishing trip will fit with the time you have in port.

The Cabo area has many excellent **golf courses**, most of which are open to the public. You can probably get a better deal by arranging a golf outing through your shore excursion desk, especially since most of the good courses are several miles out of town. Golf excursions will include transportation. Jack Nicklaus, Robert Trent Jones and Roy Dye are among the noted course architects who have built courses in Cabo. For those planning some individual golfing, the closest course is **The Raven**, which offers spectacular views of the ocean and Los Arcos. Other courses (listed in order of increasing distance from the tender pier) are **Cabo del Sol**, **El Dorado**, **Palmilla** and **Querencia**. Plan on a day of golfing costing more than $200 per person, including transportation.

Finally, your cruise ship excursion office will offer other types of recreational outings, including **mountain biking**, **ATV-riding** and **hiking** through ecological reserves. Many of these involve a great deal of physical exertion so know your limits. These activities can also be arranged through tour operators in Cabo, but we see little point in having to hunt them down when you can have everything taken care of by the time you arrive in port.

Catalina Island
(California)

*T*his is the one non-Mexican port of call where many typical Mexican itineraries stop. However, these calls are mostly limited to shorter Baja cruises that do not even go as far south as Cabo San Lucas. The primary current exception is the *Sapphire Princess*, which visits Catalina as part of its 10-day Mexican Riviera cruises from San Francisco. The mountainous island is 21 miles long and is under eight miles across at its widest point. It was inhabited by a small tribe of Native Americans upon its discovery by Europeans in 1542. After a period of time as a haven for smugglers, Catalina became the private property of wealthy families. The Wrigley family (of chewing gum fame) ultimately acquired it, with the intention of turning it into a vacation paradise. Members of the Wrigley family still have houses on Catalina. Most of Catalina was eventually turned over to the Santa Catalina Island Conservancy to protect the natural state of the island. Today, almost 90% of the land is owned by the conservancy. The primary town is **Avalon** and it has about 4,000 year-round residents.

Although Catalina Island (the full official name is Santa Catalina Island) is part of California, you would never know it by setting foot on this idyllic and expensive piece of real estate. It's separated from the sprawling coast of the Los Angeles area by a mere 22 miles, but it might as well be a world apart because Catalina is about as physically and culturally different from L.A. as any place could be. Protecting the fragile environment is the key element of life on Catalina. Cars are severely limited (there is a 15-year waiting list for residents to be issued a permit for a car), a sharp contrast to the motor-driven lifestyle of southern California. Tourism is the key industry. Day-trippers take the express boats that shuttle back and forth between various cities in southern California, while those with more time and money check into one of the island's many small and generally upscale hotels or bed and breakfasts. Cruise ship passengers represent a large proportion of visitors to Catalina.

Arrival

The port of Avalon (Catalina's only significant town) is set around an attractive crescent-shaped bay. However, the port facilities are designed to handle only the aforementioned daily ferry services, along with a myriad of small privately owned boats, many belonging to island residents. All cruise ships have to anchor outside the harbor and you will be transferred into Avalon via tender. You'll arrive either at Green Pier, which is only steps away from the heart of town, or at one of the piers next to the ferry docks. These are almost as close to town – the Green Pier being less than a five-minute walk away.

Tourism Information Office

The Catalina Island Chamber of Commerce operates a Visitor Center on Green Pier. The pier is not only the arrival spot for many tenders, but is central to the activities in and around the town of Avalon. Since Catalina is in California, this is one place where you can easily telephone in advance to request information and be sure to get your request understood. Their number is ☎ (310) 510-1520. You can also visit Catalina Island's website at www.catalina.com.

Getting Around

There are no **cars** available for rental, but they really aren't necessary. Every point of interest in the town of Avalon is within easy walking distance for most people. **Taxis** are available, but they don't come cheap. You can also rent gas-powered **golf carts** that hold up to four people. However, this is an even more expensive proposition because the rates are by the hour and they typically start at around $30. If there are four people in your party (couples on the ship who decide to explore Avalon together can share a cart), then it becomes a more reasonable alternative from a price standpoint. You'll see numerous places renting carts scattered on or just off of the main street running along the bay. It's important to note that the carts are allowed to be used only in and around the vicinity of Avalon, but not in the island's interior. So, they're only highly useful if you have a physical disability that prevents you from walking or are extremely lazy. **Bicycles** are also readily available for rental, but the mountainous terrain makes this difficult for most people once you get away from the immediate vicinity of the harbor. Should you plan on getting into the interior of the island – an absolute must in my opinion – then you should simply opt for one of the many excursions offered on the cruise ship.

The One-Day Sightseeing Tour

Given Avalon's small size and the fact that you can't explore the interior on your own, the best way to see Catalina is by a combination of foot power and shore excursions. Because most of the excursions take between two and four hours, cruise ship visitors who don't want to participate in any recreational activities should have enough time for two excursions (one in the morning and one in the afternoon) and still be able to explore Avalon on their own.

Before describing some of the better excursions, let's take a quick look at Avalon itself. Without allowing time for shopping, the entire walking tour of Avalon should take between an hour and 90 minutes. Your tour will actually begin on the five-minute tender ride from your ship as you will have a wonderful view of the entire bay and town fronting the hillsides. One point of interest that you'll see is the 1925 **Chimes Tower**, a gift to Avalon from Ada Wrigley. It looks like the belltower of a Spanish colonial church.

Crescent Avenue is the bay-fronting main street of Avalon. A small section of it in the center of town has been transformed into a pedestrian mall and is closed to traffic. However, the entire bay-front area in and around Avalon is traversed by a lovely pedestrian walkway. From Lover's Cove on one side of town to the famous Casino on the other, it covers a distance of about a mile. We'll begin our walking tour at the **Lover's Cove** end. Here you'll see several small, interesting rock formations that are home to hundreds of birds throughout the year. The cove itself is a popular dive spot, as is the **Casino Point Dive Park** at the Casino end of town. You'll also see the glass-bottom boats and semi-submersible submarine tours that take visitors to the clear waters of Lover's Cove. On a hillside at the edge of Avalon is the **Holy Hill House**. Now a bed and breakfast, this colorful structure with the large pointed cupola is an Avalon landmark perched on one of the town's many steep hillsides. The two blocks of Crescent Avenue on either side of the **Green Pleasure Pier** (as it's officially known) constitutes "downtown" Avalon. The pier was built privately in 1909, but was "sold" to the city of Avalon for five dollars in 1914. It has always been and is likely to remain one of the busiest places in Avalon. On the streets immediately nearest the pier is where you will find most of Catalina's shops, galleries and restaurants and it is the only place where you'll encounter crowds (especially on summer weekends).

As you continue on the waterfront promenade, you'll soon pass two prestigious clubs housed in historic structures. The first is the 1916 home of the **Tuna Club**. This is still a club for men only and many well-known dignitaries have belonged to it over the years. The second (the one with the lighthouse-like tower) is the **Catalina Yacht Club**. The rest of the promenade leading to the Casino and Casino Point Dive Park is a beautiful palm-lined walkway. The **Casino** is Avalon's most noted landmark. The large round structure with graceful columns all around never actually had a casino. Rather, it is an elaborate and beautiful ballroom that is used for private functions. It also contains a movie theater and, as such, is a focal point for residents. The interior can be seen only via guided tours available either as part of an excursion or on one of several daily tours offered at varying times. You'll see the 180-foot diameter ballroom that has no visible columns for support and many of the murals that grace different parts of the building. *$$.*

One part of the Casino building houses the small and mildly interesting **Catalina Island Museum**. Through documents and artifacts, it covers Catalina Island's past. It isn't necessary to be part of a tour to visit the museum. *Open daily except on Thursdays between January and March. $.*

There are a few other things to see and do in the area above and just beyond Avalon. The first is to get the best possible view of beautiful Avalon harbor from one of the "terrace" roads above town. Take Lower Terrace Road (off Crescent Avenue) to Wrigley Road and then follow it to either Middle or Upper Terrace Road. The climb is long and rather steep, so this is best done by golf cart unless you're an avid walker.

The **Wrigley Memorial and Botanical Garden** is two miles from town. From Green Pier, walk up Catalina Avenue to Tremont Street, turn right and then proceed left when you reach Avalon Canyon Road. This is also a difficult walk so you might want to consider doing it on your own only if you have rented a cart. You can also see it via a shore excursion. Either way, you'll see a large and elaborate memorial to the memory of William Wrigley Jr. surrounded by gardens containing plants that are native to Catalina Island. *Open daily. $.*

The choice of excellent excursions around Catalina is large. I'll deal only with the sightseeing variety. Recreational pursuits will be covered in the appropriate section. There are two companies (the Santa Catalina Island Company and Catalina Adventure Tours) providing the same basic trips and which one you'll be with depends on the one selected by your cruise line. However, it really doesn't matter. There are several variations of an Avalon "city" tour. Depending upon the itinerary you select you'll ride around town, see the Casino, and take a short trip to the Wrigley Memorial. Another highlight is the drive to the top of **Mt. Ada**, where the Wrigley family estate was built.

▶ Ada was the name of Mr. Wrigley's wife. What a romantic – naming the mountain after his wife!

If the beautiful scenery of Catalina Island is a lure for you, then the "Inside Adventure" tour is the number-one option I can recommend. This narrated bus tour will climb through the mountains and provide spectacular vistas of the coast (and your cruise ship), along with dramatic canyons. A large herd of wild bison (originally brought to the island for a movie) makes Catalina their home and it is almost certain that your driver-guide will point it out to you. The two-hour tour travels 10 miles to the Airport in the Sky – the name of Catalina's small private airport. After a brief stop here, the tour will return to town.

For those who are more interested in the sea than the land, there are two good water tours available, but it's only necessary to do one since they cover the same ground. The object of all Catalina water tours is to take advantage of the crystal-clear waters surrounding the island that are home to an incredible variety of fish and plant-life. One tour explores the water via a **glass-bottom boat** while the other takes you on the *Nautilus*, a semi-submersible vessel where the passenger compartment is beneath the water, while the top of the boat remains above the surface. The *Nautilus* generally provides a slightly better view, although the glass-bottom boat is preferable for those who are a bit claustrophobic. Both vessels have a feeding-tube system that allows passengers to eject fish into the water, thereby creating a feeding frenzy where you'll see the greatest number of fish. The local fish know the presence of the boats means food so they always hang around them. During the summer a boat ride to view the sea lions on their rocky home is another option.

Shopping

While Avalon doesn't have anything unique when it comes to shopping, there is an amazing number and variety of shops for such a small place. It seems that everyone who comes to Catalina Island by cruise ship just has to buy something to take home with them. Perhaps the reason is that you don't have to contend with overbearing street vendors or question quality and authenticity the way you sometimes should in Mexico. The compact shopping district runs along **Crescent Avenue** and also on **Catalina** and **Sumner Avenues**, which head inland from Crescent near Green Pier. All of the shops mentioned here can be found in this area. No one has any trouble locating a business in downtown Avalon.

One of the most attractive places to shop is at the **El Encanto plaza**, a small Spanish Colonial-style shopping center with several upscale shops and a fine restaurant. I might add that restaurants of all types can be found throughout downtown, although you can easily return to your ship for lunch. Another interesting shopping area is the **Metropole Market Place**, with 25 shops and restaurants. For men's casual clothing try **Lattitude 33**, which specializes in aloha shirts and tees, while the ladies can head on over to the **Avalon Bay Company**. Either place has a nice selection, but I prefer the co-ed shopping that can be done at the cutely named **Buoys & Gulls Sportswear**. **Steamer Trunk** offers a good selection of gifts and souvenirs, while more interesting hand-made items can be found at nearby **Catalina Crafters**. Those interested more in fine arts should visit either the **Perico Gallery** or the **Off White Gallery**. Those seeking fine-quality jewelry will find that the best place is the **Catalina Gold Company** shop, although **Bay of the Seven Moons** also has a good selection.

Sports & Recreation

When you think of Catalina Island you naturally first think of watersports. That's logical given that it *is* an island, but Catalina does offer a number of activities for the land-based sports enthusiast. Golf is the primary activity in this regard and the excellent **Catalina Island Golf Course** is a beautiful place to play. You can probably arrange a round through your ship's shore excursion office or you can arrange a tee time on your own by calling ☎ (310) 510-

0530. The other important land activity is **hiking** on the island's hills and mountains. Contact the visitor information center for details on trails and their relative difficulty.

Watersports are extremely varied. Catalina Island was first developed as a resort for sportfishermen. **Fishing** for a wide variety of game fish in the waters around the island is still an important part of the local tourist industry and you can arrange trips either through your excursion office or one of the many operators on or near Green Pier. The same goes for kayaking, scuba diving and snorkeling. The best places for **scuba and snorkeling** are the specially designated areas at either end of Avalon – **Lover's Cove** or the **Casino Point Dive Park**. Some operators will take you to less visited areas that are also excellent.

Catalina has several small beaches, but swimming seems to be a less popular activity here than at many of the other ports in this book. It's no doubt because the water can be quite chilly except during the summer.

SOME OTHER CALIFORNIA PORTS OF CALL

You will find some Mexico-bound cruises leaving from San Francisco that have among their ports of call **Monterey** and/or **Santa Barbara**. While I included detailed port information on Catalina because it is an integral part of a large number of sailings on several different lines, such is not the case with these two ports. At present, only two lines have regular itineraries that schedule port calls at other California destinations and these are relatively limited as to the number of ships and sailings. Consequently, I'll limit remarks on these ports to this brief sidebar.

Both Monterey and Santa Barbara make excellent port calls if you haven't seen them before. Monterey has a fine aquarium, several museums and a complex of buildings dating from the town's earliest days. There's also a Fisherman's Wharf that is smaller than the one in San Francisco, but perhaps even more charming. The surrounding Monterey Peninsula is a scenic delight, with the famous Seventeen-Mile Drive winding its way along the coast through golf courses and past such sights as the Lone Cypress Tree. Santa Barbara has a beautiful setting between the ocean and mountains. It, too, has numerous historic attractions, including one of the most impressive of the California Missions. Art galleries and museums, a zoo and gardens round out the long list of attractions.

Ensenada
Ehn-seh-NAH-dah
(Baja)

Bustling Ensenada has a population of 400,000, making it the third-largest city in Baja. There is a thriving business environment and oodles of visitors from southern California (especially on summer weekends) because it is only 70 miles south of the US border. It has become a favorite party destination, but, since your cruise ship visit will be during the daytime, you can easily avoid this aspect of Ensenada if you don't like that sort of thing. The Ensenada of today is a far cry from not very long ago. Although it was discovered by the Spaniards in the 17th century, no large permanent settlement developed for many years because of the lack of drinking water. There was some whaling and trading and privateers found it a useful place. Gold was discovered nearby in the late 19th century and it became the territorial capital in 1882. But when the mines gave out in the early 20th century, Ensenada became stagnant and the capital was moved to Mexicali. The city would remain isolated and in obscurity until American prohibition spurred some growth in tourism. The development of excellent port facilities and the opening of a paved highway from Tijuana were, however, the real precursors to explosive growth. Contemporary Ensenada's economic activity is dominated by port activities and tourism. Ensenada has a mild, southern California-like climate, with a pretty natural setting between the nearby mountains and Bahía Todos Santos (All Saints Bay).

Arrival

Ensenada's new Cruise Ship Village terminal is a thoroughly modern and large complex that can handle two of the largest mega-liners at one time. The final phase of the port's expansion from sleepy dock to a facility that can simultaneously accommodate three ships and will handle a half-million passengers a year was recently completed. It is within steps of the city's waterfront malecón and is within walking distance of all the downtown attractions. Shuttle service is also available at a modest cost (about $3 round-trip) for those who don't want to walk. The new terminal has a number of places to shop. This is a big improvement over the old docks, which were across the harbor in a rather unattractive industrial port area, requiring a shuttle to get into town.

Tourism Information Office

An office of the State Tourism department can be found on Blvd. Lázaro Cárdenas 1477 at the intersection of Calle

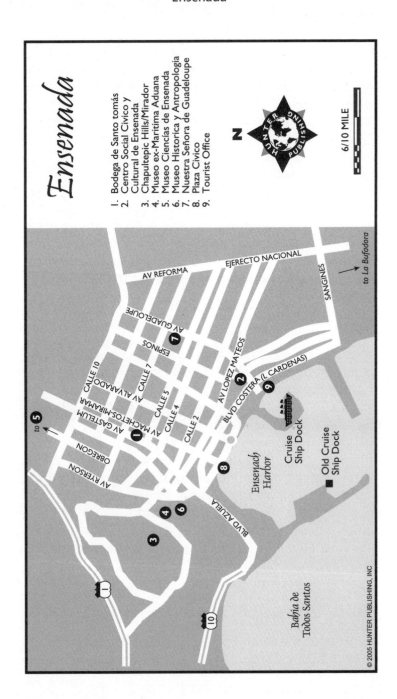

Ensenada

1. Bodega de Santo tomás
2. Centro Social Cívico y Cultural de Ensenada
3. Chapultepic Hills/Mirador
4. Museo ex-Marítima Aduana
5. Museo Ciencias de Ensenada
6. Museo Historica y Antropologia
7. Nuestra Señora de Guadeloupe
8. Plaza Civico
9. Tourist Office

6/10 MILE

Las Rocas. It is just a couple of blocks away from the cruise ship terminal. There is also a small information office north of the terminal along the malecón at Lázaro Cárdenas 540. You can find out anything you need to know at the cruise ship terminal itself.

Another way to get useful and current information is to pick up a copy of one of several English-language visitor newspapers just about anyplace downtown. These include the *Baja Sun, Ensenada Tour* and the *Gringo Gazette*. The latter is geared more toward American residents or people who stay for a long time, but is still my favorite because of its great sense of humor.

Getting Around

If you are going to be remaining in downtown Ensenada, then walking, either with or without the use of the shuttle from the pier, is the best way to get around. **Blvd. Lázaro Cárdenas** runs along the waterfront. Street signs will have the Lázaro Cárdenas name, but just about everyone in Ensenada refers to it as **"the Costero"** so I will do likewise from this point on. For most of its distance near the downtown area, the Costero is paralleled by the malecón or waterfront promenade. The compact downtown area is a block inland along **Avenida López Mateos**. This street is sometimes called Calle Primera (1st Street). Past Mateos, streets are mainly numbered, while those running inland from the waterfront are named. It's basically a grid pattern so getting around on foot shouldn't be too confusing, even for those who get lost easily. López Mateos contains the main shopping, dining and entertainment area and several other attractions are just off of this street. Various forms of motorized transportation, including cars and gas-powered carts, are available, but these aren't necessary for in-town activities and they involve considerable cost.

A great way to tour the downtown area and waterfront is by **horse-drawn carriage**. You can hire one near the cruise ship terminal. If you plan on heading out of town, a **car** can give you more flexibility, but the wide number of shore excursions available is a better option when in Ensenada. **Taxis** are relatively inexpensive within Ensenada, but are far too costly compared with shore excursions for any place outside of the city, except perhaps for some of the nearest beaches.

Ensenada is probably the only city of comparable size in Mexico without good public transportation so don't even think about local **buses** for getting around. If you don't want to heed my advice on buses, you will find the bus station at Calle 11 and Avenida Riveroll.

The One-Day Sightseeing Tour

There's enough to see and do within Ensenada to take up a complete day. But if you do that you'll miss some great attractions outside the city. So the first thing you have to do is decide on one of three options: (1) a full day in town, (2) a half-day in town, along with an excursion, or (3) a full day of excursions. The suggested tour that follows is for the first strategy. Then I'll review some of the best excursion options so you'll know if you have to cut down on the in-town sightseeing to accommodate other activities.

You'll be on the Costero as soon as you walk down the street leading away from the Cruise Ship Village. Right across the street at the intersection of Avenida Riviera is one of Ensenada's most beautiful and interesting attractions, and one that is passed up by far too many visitors. Covering several acres is the **Centro Social, Cívico y Cultural de Ensenada** (Social, Civic & Cultural Center of Ensenada). It's a mouthful of a name in either language so you can refer to it as the locals do – the **Riviera del**

Pacifico, the name it had as a casino and hotel when it was originally built. It was managed at one time by Jack Dempsey. Gambling was banned by the Mexican government in the 1930s and the building fell into a state of decay. Restored to its original splendor some 40 years later, the Riviera del Pacifico is an opulent display of gardens, statues and Moorish-style architecture. The main building is now used primarily for conventions and other events, but you can walk around and enjoy the intricate woodworking and other architectural details. Even more splendid is the outside, with its wonderful gardens and statues. The gardens feature plants native to Baja, including a large collection of incredible cacti. The statues honor the native Indian tribes, Spanish explorers and others important in the history of Mexico. Many of the statues sit on pedestals covered with colorful tiles that tell the story of what the statue depicts (in Spanish) through text and tile artwork. One cannot help but be impressed by the tranquillity and dignity of the surroundings.

At one end of the building is the **Museo de Historia**. It tells the history of Baja from indigenous groups through explorers and missionaries. Some of the displays are quite well done and they are in both English and Spanish. *The Riviera del Pacifico grounds and building are generally open from early in the morning until late, but the museum hours are from 9:30 am to 5 pm, though it closes between 2 and 3 pm; $ for museum only.*

Walk along the **Costero** and its adjacent pedestrian promenade (the **Malecón**). It has good views of the harbor and contains a couple of points of interest. The small park called **Plaza Civica** is more commonly known as the **Three Heads Park** because it contains monumental-sized busts of three important Mexican heroes. These are Miguel Hidalgo, the priest who led the struggle for Mexican independence; Benito Juárez, an Indian of humble or-

203

igins who was to become the country's greatest president; and revolutionary leader Venustiano Carranza. Each sits upon a large pedestal and is 12 feet high. With their gold color, the Three Heads makes for a great photo opportunity.

Speaking of monumental, that term can be applied to the **Mexican flag** that usually flies atop an equally huge pole in a plaza near Plaza Civica. (If you're still in port at sunset you can watch the Mexican Navy perform a flag-lowering ceremony.)

Now continue walking along the Costero and in a few blocks it will run into Calle Uribe. Three small but interesting museums are practically within a stone's throw of one another in this vicinity. At the corner of Gastelum make a right and you'll soon reach the first one – the **Museo Historico Regional**. The impressive castle-like façade of the building is due to the fact that the structure first served as a military barracks in 1886. It was then turned into a prison. You can still see some of the jail cells, the central courtyard, and the guard towers. One wing contains the regional history section and has displays in English. The material covers about the same ground as the museum at the Riviera del Pacifico so if you did that one then the historic nature of the property will be the main point of interest. *Open daily except Monday; $.*

Now go back to Uribe and turn right. At the intersection of Avenida Ryerson is the **Museo de Historia y Antropologia**. Housed in a building dating from 1887, it has seen many uses both public and private over the years. The Mexican government has been the owner and museum operator since the early 1990s and it has some good exhibits dealing with the early history of Baja California. Unfortunately, the explanations are only in Spanish. *Open Tuesday through Friday from 8 am until 3 pm and on Saturday and Sunday from 10 am till 5 pm; $.*

Upon leaving the museum, continue up Avenida Ryerson for a block and you'll reach the **Museo Ex-Aduana Maritima**, the former Customs house. Another museum devoted largely to area history, this one is a bit different because of its changing exhibits on Mexican culture. *Open Monday through Friday until 4 pm; $.*

Two more blocks north on Ryerson will bring you to the intersection of Calle 2. A left turn here will begin a trek up the **Chapultepec Hills**, the most desirable residential neighborhood in Ensenada and home to a significant American expatriate community. However, the reason to go up the hill is for the fine view of the city and Todos Santos Bay. Since the climb up to the best viewing areas is very steep, this part of the walk should be attempted only by those in good physical condition. Others might consider hiring a taxi. Regardless of how you decide to get there, it doesn't pay to make this detour if visibility isn't good because you'll get a disappointing view of what could have been.

On the way down take Calle 2 to Avenida Ruiz and turn right for one block to **Avenida López Mateos** (often called just Mateos), Ensenada's main tourist shopping district. There will be more about shopping later on but, even if you don't intend to shop, it is worthwhile exploring the short four-block distance that comprises the heart of downtown Ensenada for visitors. It is a busy area with a fine selection of shops.

Head up Calle Miramar to Calle 2 for the **Bodegas de Santo Tomas**. This winery can trace its origins to Dominican monks in the latter part of the 18th century. The facility was built in the 1920s. Tours trace the operations at the winery and conclude with wine tastings. Cheese is also offered. Although this isn't in the best section of town, you will notice several art galleries in the immediate surrounding area. *45-minute guided tours in English* *daily at 11 am, 1 and 3 pm; $. A small tip to the guide is also customary.* If you plan on less than a full-day walking tour of the city and are going to the wine country then, obviously, visiting this winery would be redundant.

Upon leaving the winery, head down Calle 6 (away from the Chapultepec Hills) until you reach Avenida Floresta. Ensenada's cathedral, the **Nuestra Señora de Guadalupe** (Our Lady of Guadalupe), is a famous landmark in town. Not only is it one of the tallest buildings, but its graceful twin spires are a wonderful example of Spanish colonial architecture at its best. The Avenida Floresta heading toward the waterfront will soon run into Avenida Riviera and return you to the Cruise Ship Village. By the way, you can get a good view of the cathedral's spires from your ship.

It's likely that, if you did the entire tour as suggested above, you will have run out of time. But some people are fast and others will not want to have seen everything on the tour. So, if you have a little extra time handy (especially if you have children), then you can consider a visit to the **Museo de Ciencias de Ensenada**, the city's science museum, at Avenida Obregón between Calles 14 and 15. The exhibits (labeled only in Spanish) concentrate on oceanography and the maritime aspects of Baja. Of special interest for children is the **Ark**, which is designed to be appreciated by smaller children. *Open daily at 9 am except on Saturday and Sunday when it opens at noon; $.*

When it comes to excursions outside of Ensenada you won't be lacking for good choices.

Most are about a half-day in length so you can schedule one for the morning and one for the afternoon during cruise visits. Some of the winery excursions are longer and would preclude doing multiple trips. One of the popular excursions from Ensenada is a trip to the rocky and pretty **Punta Banda** peninsula and its highlight, **La**

Bufadora. A comfortable bus ride of about an hour on good roads will take you to this unique sight. La Bufadora is a natural blow-hole, one of only three of its kind in the world (the others are in Hawaii and Australia). Waves are forced into a narrow gorge and finally into an underground cavern. Various physical factors, including the tides, force the water upward in a geyser. La Bufadora will always perform, but at differing levels of enjoyment depending upon natural conditions. If you're there at the right time you can expect to see spectacular water spouts up to 60 feet high. If it is quiet when you arrive, don't be impatient. Tours allow enough time to stay around awhile and La Bufadora tends to become active in sets of two or three water expulsions. Part of the fun of seeing La Bufadora is getting to it from where the bus parks. It is an easy walk of about a quarter-mile, but each side of the wide promenade is lined with vendors selling an unimaginable array of goods from clothing to jewelry and even food. This is, in effect, a flea market and bargaining is expected. In order to make sure you see La Bufadora the best strategy is to ignore the shops on the way down. Then, after you've had your fill of water spouts, you can shop to your heart's content. If driving on your own, take Mexico 1 south to the Punta Banda cut-off and follow signs for La Bufadora. The round-trip distance from downtown is about 23 miles, all on good roads.

To the north of Ensenada is the **Gold Coast**, a scenic stretch of coast with marvelous views of the pounding surf from atop rocky cliffs. There are several different excursions that cover various aspects of this region. They can easily be driven should you rent a car. Just take Mexico 1 north from the city. One of the most popular excursions visits the **wine country** that is close to Ensenada. These may take different names (such as Guadalupe Valley) depending upon the cruise line/tour operator and which wineries it visits. Many will make a stop at two different wineries. You'll also visit some quaint and pictur-esque typical Mexican villages and be given time to shop.

Another excursion that is to be highly recommended is a **whale-watching** trip. The coast off Ensenada attracts more gray whales than almost anywhere in the world. During the season you're almost guaranteed to see many of these magnificent beasts and the experience is sure to stay in your memory for a long time. However, these tours are only given from December through March. There are no whales to be seen at other times. Although there are many local operators offering whale-watching cruises, it is easiest to book one through your ship's shore excursion office. The remainder of the shore excursion options are mostly of a recreational nature and will be discussed under *Sports & Recreation* (page 212).

In the last couple of years the cruise lines have added a nearly full-day excursion north to the resort town of **Rosarito**. Besides the beach and recreational attractions, the main lure of this area is a visit to **Foxploration**, a Uni-versal-type theme-park adjacent to Fox Studios Baja. It in-cludes the usual "backstage" tour and visits to sets of movies filmed at the studios. Many recognizable films (in-cluding *Titanic*) were made here, at least in part. Excur-sions usually allow time for shopping in the resort area. If yours does, be sure to pay at least a brief visit to the wildly eclectic shopping area known as **Festival Plaza**. The colorful eight-story facility is designed to look like a roller-coaster and the interior is amazing. If you decide to rent a car in Ensenada and go on your own, take toll Highway 1-D north to the Puerto Nuevo exit and then Mexico 1 to the theme park and town. It will take about an hour or a bit longer if you decide to go one direction entirely by the more scenic old Highway 1. *Foxplorations is closed Monday and Tuesday, $$$.* Independent travelers should have enough time to incorporate much of the Gold Coast as well.

Shopping

Although Ensenada doesn't have much that is particularly unusual as compared to some other Mexican ports, it does have an excellent variety of shopping opportunities in a pleasant downtown atmosphere. The greatest concentration of businesses of all types is along Avenida López Mateos, just one block in from the Costero. The main shopping area runs for about four blocks. Among the items you will easily find are clothing, ceramics, pottery, glass, liquor, perfumes, wood carvings and leather. Jewelry, including both silver and gold, is hugely popular. The established shops along Mateos are all reputable so I would avoid street vendors in Ensenada. One other item that is popular with American visitors is **cigars**. Be careful when buying "Cuban" cigars, for two reasons. First, you cannot bring these back into the States (meaning you'll have to consume all that you purchase before the end of the cruise). Secondly, most are not authentic Cuban cigars. If you read carefully, they have Cuban tobacco, but are rolled in Mexico.

If you are interested primarily in jewelry, then I suggest that you shop at the **Artesanias Castillo** on Mateos or the **Centro Artesenal** near the cruise ship terminal along the Costero at number 1094. Both are marketplaces with local craftsmen and women. Other good places for jewelry, especially silver, are **Los Castillos**, **La Cucaracha** (on Blancarte just off Mateos) and **La Mina de Solomon** on Mateos.

For those seeking fine arts try **Pérez Meillón** in Centro Artesenal. They have (in addition to jewelry) native crafts of all types, including pottery and baskets. **Galería de la Ciudad** in the Riviera del Pacifico features works by local artists. Similarly, the **Taller de Artisinas Indigenas** is a native workshop representing the local Paipai and Kumiai tribes. It is at the Bodegas de Santo Tomas

A few other places are worth a special mention. **Uncle George's** is a good place to shop for general merchandise if you're on Avenida Mateos. Also on this street are **Gold Duck**, which has a fine selection of gifts. Many other shops also sell Gold Duck products, but you're better off getting them from the duck's mouth, so to speak. For clothing and other items try **Sara's** at the end of the Mateos shopping area closest to the cruise ship terminal. Those who want a flea market without having to go to La Bufadora will have to use the market patronized by Ensenada locals. This is the **Mercado Los Globos**, although it is a bit farther away from the main shopping district. It covers about eight square blocks, centered on Calle 9 at the intersection of Reforma. It is closed on Monday and Tuesday.

Although technically not "shopping," I should mention that Ensenada has many fine seafood restaurants on and around the Avenida López Mateos shopping district. Many cruise ship visitors decide not to go back to the ship for lunch. If your vessel is staying late, you might even want to consider dinner on shore.

ENSENADA IS PARTY CITY

Shopping for a good time? Well, as is the case with Tijuana, Ensenada has a reputation as a place where people go to let loose. For the most part Ensenada isn't as wild as Tijuana because the local population has a much more conservative social outlook than in its larger neighbor to the north. However, in the bars and cantinas (of which there are too many to even count), almost anything goes. This is especially true in establishments near the waterfront or near the main shopping street. Unlike places patronized by the locals, these spots cater to American tourists looking for a good time. Most of the action is, of course, during the evening hours after *you* have to be back on your cruise ship. But don't fret if you're limited to a daytime visit because many of the bars open early and there's enough going on, especially during the summer or on weekends to give you an idea of what party city has to offer.

Perhaps the best-known of all of Ensenada's party places is **Hussong's Cantina** on Calle Ruiz just off Avenida López Mateos. It dates back to 1892 and looks its age. In fact, most people who go there find it rather ugly. But that doesn't seem to matter, especially after you've had a few drinks! It can get extremely wild and rowdy, but is far less so during the day. Opening at 10 in the morning, Hussong's is more than just a bar. It has become a noted tourist attraction based on its reputation.

For another type of partying, try to time your visit to Ensenada during one of its many local celebrations. In addition to much *fiesta* activity on national holidays such as Independence Day and the Day of the Dead, Ensenada has celebrations that are unique. These include the *Carnaval* in mid-February and the **Wine Harvest Festival** in mid-August. Many festivals are connected with yacht racing and Baja's famous road races. The latter include the Baja 500 in June and the Baja 1000 in November.

Sports & Recreation

As in most Mexican ports when it comes to sports and recreation, the name of the game in Ensenada is the water. This isn't to say, however, that there are no land-based activities. Golf and tennis are largely limited to people who are staying in area hotels, but your cruise ship might offer excursions that include these sports. More popular with visitors is **horseback riding**, usually along the beautifully scenic Gold Coast. While there are numerous tour operators who will take you on guided or hosted horseback rides, it is much more convenient to arrange this through the ship's tour desk – it's an activity that will always be offered.

Let's now turn our attention to the water. There aren't any beaches within Ensenada itself. The best beach that's reasonably close by is called **Estero**, about seven miles south of downtown. If you don't rent a car, you can get there by taxi, although the price won't be cheap. **San Miguel** beach is another nice spot. This one is north of Ensenada and is more popular with **surfers** because of the wilder wave conditions. However, it's also a great place if you just want to soak up the sun and sand. There are numerous ways to get out on the water, including everything from calm kayak rides to adventurous jet skiing and everything in-between. Either sign up for a shore excursion or head out along the waterfront and connect with one of the many operators. All of those that are based in a storefront or other structure are legitimate businesses. Be wary of street hawkers who direct you to private boat operators. Although many are reputable, you may wind up getting less than you paid for. **Scuba** lovers will find that the best place to head for is Punta Banda near La Bufadora.

In many ways Ensenada first appeared on the tourism map as a place to go **sportfishing**. Although it has diversified over the years, fishing remains one of the most popular activities. Ensenada has long billed itself as the "yellowtail capital" of the world. Other big game species include barracuda, bonito and rockfish. There is also the possibility of landing sea bass, cod, halibut and whitefish. There are many fishing charter boats at the **Sport Fishing Pier** on the Costero just north of the Plaza Cívica. It's also almost a sure thing that one or more fishing excursions will be offered through your cruise line.

Ixtapa & Zihuatanejo
Eeks-TAH-pa & See-wah-tah-NAY-ho
(Mexican Riviera)

*A*lmost every Mexican travel guide you can pick up will combine Ixtapa and Zihuatanejo into a single entity as far as a heading is concerned, separating them with a slash. I won't entirely buck the trend except to use an ampersand instead of a slash. There is a good reason for this. First of all, they are only about four miles from one another. Just as important is the fact that almost everyone who visits one will spend some time in the other. Yet, despite this joint treatment and some similarities, in most aspects the two ports are about as different as two places can be.

Ixtapa is a planned community whose history dates back only to the 1970s when the government tourism development office (FONATUR) decided to help reduce the economic impoverishment of this part of the state of Guerrero by creating a new resort destination à la

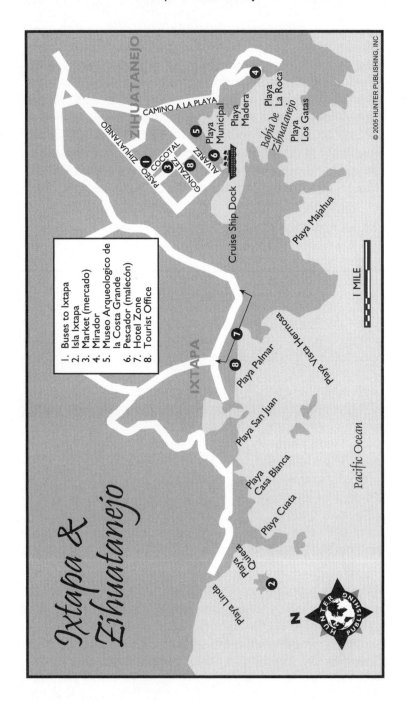

Ixtapa & Zihuatanejo

ZIHUATANEJO

CAMINO A LA PLAYA

PASEO ZIHUATANEJO

COCOTAL

GONZÁLEZ

ÁLVAREZ

Playa Municipal

Playa Madera

Bahía de Zihuatanejo

Playa La Roca

Playa Los Gatas

Cruise Ship Dock

Playa Majahua

1. Buses to Ixtapa
2. Isla Ixtapa
3. Market (mercado)
4. Mirador
5. Museo Arqueologico de la Costa Grande
6. Pescador (malecón)
7. Hotel Zone
8. Tourist Office

IXTAPA

Playa Palmar

Playa Vista Hermosa

Playa San Juan

Playa Casa Blanca

Playa Cuata

Playa Quieta

Playa Linda

Pacific Ocean

1 MILE

N

© 2005 HUNTER PUBLISHING, INC

Cancún. While Ixtapa has not grown nearly as big, it is dominated by a stretch of mostly expensive high-rise hotels along a two-mile stretch of beautiful bay-front and caters to those seeking the luxury resort life.

On the other hand, Zihuatanejo is rich in history. There is archaeological evidence that the indigenous Indians occupied the site as early as 1500 BC. In later centuries the nobility of various tribes used it as a vacation destination. FONATUR wasn't very original when it decided how this portion of the coast should be used now. The conquistadors arrived early and by 1527 had established a settlement here that would play a major role in the maritime trade for many years to come.

▶ The name Zihuatanejo is a Spanish corruption of an Amerindian term meaning "place of women." Now, guys, don't get any ideas from this – it only reflects the fact that the indigenous society was organized in a matriarchal fashion.

The port activities slowly gave way to other ports up and down the coast and the town languished into a sleepy fishing village. With the beginning of development in Ixtapa, however, things also looked up in Zihuatanejo. Development of resorts in Zihuatanejo has been far less aggressive than in Ixtapa and it caters less to well-heeled travelers. Moreover, the town retains its traditional Mexican pace and style so it is a striking contrast to Ixtapa. That is, in many ways what makes a visit to these twin ports so interesting.

Geographically the two resorts and the area between them cover a 16-mile stretch of beaches with many small offshore islands, numerous pretty coves and lagoons, all with the magical Sierra Madre del Sur mountain range as a backdrop. Zihuatanejo loops around a bay of the same name, while more spread out Ixtapa directly faces the Pacific. Bahía de Zihuatanejo is, in the opinion of many seasoned travelers, one of the prettiest bays on the Mexican Riviera. The hotels in Zihuatanejo are set mainly atop cliffs that fringe the bay.

Arrival

Cruise ships will generally tie up to the **Muelle Pier** at the western end of downtown Zihuatanejo. Some of the larger ships might have to anchor in the harbor and use tenders. Either way, you will still reach land at the same location.

Tourism Information Office

There are several places to get information in Ixtapa. The only one that is really convenient for cruise ship visitors is the small information booth in downtown Zihautanejo at the main square on J.N. Alvarez. There are other offices in Ixtapa's hotel zone along Blvd. Ixtapa. The Guerrero State Tourism Office is in La Puerta Shopping Center on Blvd. Ixtapa. However, if you happen to be on foot in the hotel zone you can get just as much information at any of the major hotels.

Getting Around

Downtown Zihuatanejo is compact and you can explore the entire area on foot. The **Paseo del Pescador** parallels the waterfront and is the main street that visitors need to be aware of. Ixtapa is much more spread out, but most everything is found along **Blvd. Ixtapa**, which runs virtually the entire length of the resort zone – so a taxi or bus comes in handy. Both are inexpensive. There is a **bus** line that runs along Blvd. Ixtapa and goes all the way into Zihuatanejo where the terminal is at Avenido Morelos and Blvd. Juárez, about a 10-minute walk from the pier.

While the bus costs the equivalent of less than 50¢ and is convenient because it runs every 20 minutes, a **taxi** between the two towns usually costs under $6, making it quite affordable even if you have to use it a few times. It's also faster and less crowded. Since the road connecting the two towns is very good and traffic in either place isn't that bad, a **car rental** does present some advantages, especially if you're planning to spend more time in Ixtapa. **Budget** is in Ixtapa, but you can save the time traveling there by bus or taxi to pick up your car if you go to the **Hertz** agency in Zihuatanejo.

The One-Day Sightseeing Tour

Given the size of the two towns and the number of things to see, a full day in port is just about perfect for seeing everything of interest. On the other hand, if you plan to shop or take part in recreational activities, something will have to give on the sightseeing side. There are ways that you can combine a little of both as you will soon see.

Since you'll be arriving in Zihuatanejo we'll begin our little tour there. The **Paseo del Pescador** has been turned into an informal malecón. It's rather simple compared to some of its counterparts in larger ports, but it has an excellent view of the bay. It lies alongside an in-town beach called the **Playa Municipal**. A block inland from Paseo del Pescador is the main business street, J. N. Alvarez. Head east and the street will run into the Paseo de la Boquita. At the Kioto Plaza, turn right onto Camino a la Playa Ropa and you will soon reach a *mirador* (lookout) that has an absolutely stunning view of the **Bahía de Zihuatanejo** and its narrow opening between two small peninsulas that jut out from the mainland. This is also the route to some of the area beaches. Because this is not the shortest of walks and it does rise in altitude, those of you who don't enjoy a vigorous walk will be better off taking a taxi. The return is downhill and somewhat easier if you want to go one way on foot.

Back in town along the malecón at the intersection of Calle Vincente Guerrero is the **Museó Arqueológico de la Costa Grande** (Archaeological Museum of the Grand Coast). The Costa Grande refers to the area between Acapulco and Ixtapa/Zihuatanejo and the museum's exhibits cover its history, from the pre-Colombian era through the end of the colonial period. It relates local history to the larger Mexican picture by tracing the history of the extensive trade that existed between the coastal peoples and such groups as the Aztecs. While it isn't a huge or impressive museum, it is interesting and will help give you a better appreciation of the native cultures. *Open daily except Monday ($).*

Now you can make your way to Ixtapa. Buses make stops at just about all of the hotels so you can pick and choose how many you might want to see. However, more important than the hotels is the sightseeing highlight of the entire area – **Isla Ixtapa**. This is a small island off the coast of the western edge of Ixtapa. On a map it almost looks like an octopus, with its many small peninsulas extending out into the sea like tentacles. The boat ride to reach it takes only 10 minutes and on the way you'll see many interesting and unusual rock formations. Once on the island, you can explore on your own and see the exotic flora and fauna. This is also a popular spot for swimming and snorkeling, so you can sightsee and have some recreation at the same time.

There are numerous ways to arrange your trip to Isla Ixtapa. Boats depart at 10- to 20-minute intervals and are inexpensive *($)*. The first one departs at 11:30 am and the last one returns to the Ixtapa mainland at 5 pm. There are many tour operators in Zihuatanejo who will arrange an outing that includes transportation from town to the boat. But it's easiest to reserve a spot with an excursion from your cruise ship. This is certain to be one of the more popular excursions in Ixtapa/Zihuatanejo. A ship's shore excursion to Isla Ixtapa is about four hours. On your own you could spend anywhere from a couple of hours to a full day, depending upon your interests.

Other popular shore excursions include trips into the nearby jungle for some hiking, and sailing trips on Zihuatanejo Bay that include a stop at a beach where you can snorkel. Other trips can take you into the surrounding countryside and some of its quaint towns. Most of the available shore excursions last between three and four hours so, depending upon the length of time you're spending in port, you may have sufficient time to do one of them plus most of the sightseeing options.

Shopping

In downtown Zihuatanejo you'll find much to choose from, including apparel, jewelry and handicrafts such as woven goods, pottery, glass, ceramics and even paper-maché. Prices range from moderate to high, as does the quality. In addition to the better stuff, you'll find lots of inexpensive souvenir shops selling things of all kinds, including the ubiquitous T-shirts. Most of the stores are clustered along the Paseo del Pescador and nearby streets. **La Zapoteca** sells woven goods, and this is among the most popular places because you can watch weaving demonstrations.

The local **artisan market** is on Calle 5 de Mayo about four blocks from the waterfront. The Central Market on Avenida Benito Juárez is known mainly for food, but you can also find good buys on quality leather goods. Hammocks and woven baskets are also in plentiful supply.

In general, the shopping isn't as good in Ixtapa and the prices are mostly higher. Small shopping complexes along Blvd. Ixtapa near the largest hotels often consist of collections of boutiques. However, one interesting place to check out is the **Mercado de Artesanía Turístico** on Blvd. Ixtapa. Like the artisan market in Zihuatanejo, this place has everything from cheap souvenirs to finely made handicrafts in a festive bazaar-like atmosphere with many vendor stands.

Sports & Recreation

Numerous fine beaches are the main outdoor attraction. In Zihuatanejo itself is the **Playa Municipal**, which runs along the malecón. It's a lively and colorful spot, but far from the best of the beaches. **Playa Madera**, just east, is better. Zihuatanejo's biggest beach and one of the best in either town is **Playa La Ropa**. It provides a scenic spot with fine sand and excellent swimming conditions. Yet, none can compare with **Playa Las Gatas**, which sits just across the bay from Playa La Ropa. There is a coral reef offshore, which makes Las Gatas as popular with the snorkeling set as with those who come just to sun and swim. Getting to Las Gatas is half the fun since it can be reached only by boat. A 10-minute ride on a small launch from the municipal pier will get you there. Somewhat farther out of town along the coastal road from Zihuatanejo is beautiful **Playa Larga**. It's among the least crowded of all the area beaches.

Checking out the sand scene in Ixtapa begins at the main beach called **Playa Palmar**. This is a beautiful curving stretch of sand with many offshore rock formations adding to the enjoyment of just gazing out to sea. However, be forewarned that the water is much rougher here (and at virtually all Ixtapa beaches) than at any of the more sheltered playgrounds of Zihuatanejo. Red flags will be displayed when swimming conditions become unsafe. The warning should be strictly heeded.

Although there are several beaches between Ixtapa and Zihuatanajeo most of the best ones in the Ixtapa area are farther west from Playa Palmar. These include **Playa Casa Blanca**, **Playa Cuata** (nicely situated on a small peninsula), and **Playas Linda** and **Quieta**. The latter two have great views of Isla Ixtapa and are lovely places that are frequented by guests from nearby hotels.

Watersports of all kinds can be found throughout the Ixtapa/Zihuatanejo area. These range from **fishing** expeditions to **windsurfing**, **sailing** and **scuba diving**. Game fishing is mostly for sailfish and is good, but less so than in other ports. There is even good surfing; the best place is at **Playa Petacalco**, which is somewhat farther afield and requires an expensive taxi trip or a car. Most of these activities are best arranged through your ship's shore excursion office, although if you make your way to Ixtapa you can arrange any type of water activity at the **Marina Ixtapa**. When it comes to fishing expeditions, however, your best bet is to go to the municipal pier in Zihuatanejo and look for the **Cooperativa de Lanchas de Recreo** (known simply as the Boat Cooperative).

A good place for water recreation if you have children is at **Magic World**, a part of the Ixtapa Palace Resort complex. You don't have to be a hotel guest to use the park, which contains wave pools, water slides, a lake for boating and a not-very-authentic-looking pirate ship that will, nonetheless, amuse small children. There is a fee for entry into the park *($)*.

Turning away from water-based recreational opportunities, **golf** is the number one sport on *terra firma*. Many courses are open to the general public, including **Club de Golf Ixtapa Palma Real**, the **Marina Ixtapa Golf Course** and the **Dorado Pacífico**, part of a resort hotel. All have rather expensive greens fees. The first two courses mentioned also have tennis facilities. **Horseback riding** can be arranged through **Rancho Playa Linda** near the beach of the same name. Rides last approximately 1½ hours.

La Paz
(Baja)

*C*apital and largest city of the state of Baja California Sur, La Paz dates back as far as 1533, when a party of Spanish explorers under Cortés landed here in search of pearls. They didn't find them, although later settlers would. The city lies on a wide cove of the Báhia de la Paz, the largest such bay along the entire eastern coastline of Baja. Known for its magnificent sunsets, the name of the city means "Peace" and, despite a wild history, one can agree with the name when sitting on a beach watching the sun go down. There is even a large sculpture known as the **Dove of Peace** on Highway 1 at the entrance to the city. Since it isn't worth a special trip, you're unlikely to see it unless you rent a car and explore on your own.

Despite its population of about 250,000 people, La Paz maintains a laid-back, almost small-town atmosphere in many respects. After Cortés' expedition failed, the area lacked a permanent settlement for more than 300 years. The bay was a popular refuge for pirates. Actually, they came to seek the valuable black pearls as much as to hide from the authorities. There was a 30-year attempt by the Jesuits to colonize the area, beginning in 1720, but this also was doomed to eventual failure, largely because of the isolated nature of the area. It was not until 1811 that a permanent settlement of La Paz was founded. Mining

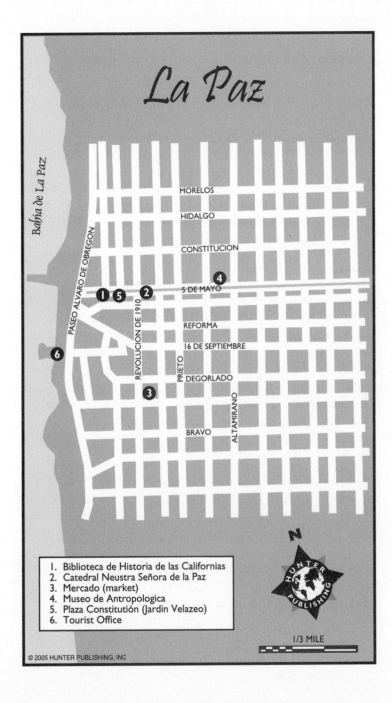

La Paz

Bahía de La Paz

MORELOS

HIDALGO

CONSTITUCION

PASEO ALVARO DE OBREGON

5 DE MAYO

REVOLUCION DE 1910

REFORMA

16 DE SEPTIEMBRE

PRIETO

DEGORLADO

ALTAMIRANO

BRAVO

1. Biblioteca de Historia de las Californias
2. Catedral Neustra Señora de la Paz
3. Mercado (market)
4. Museo de Antropologica
5. Plaza Constitutión (Jardin Velazeo)
6. Tourist Office

N

HUNTER PUBLISHING

1/3 MILE

was added to pearl diving. The latter died out in the 1930s due to a mysterious disease in the oyster beds.

The first real impetus for sustained growth came in 1829 when La Paz was made the capital of Baja Territory, which then included both the northern and southern regions of Baja. (Baja California Sur was made a separate state in 1974 and La Paz retained the status of capital.) It was the scene of some fighting during the Mexican-American War. Today's modern city has been fueled by an important tourism industry, mostly of a drive-in nature since the number of cruises calling here is limited. La Paz is also home to a substantial number of Americans.

Arrival

The deep-water port for La Paz is in **Pichilingue**, approximately 11 miles from downtown La Paz. Generally, the cruise line will arrange for transportation between the two. There are also buses and taxis, should you find that more convenient at the time you plan to shuttle between them. **Buses** are very inexpensive and quite reliable. **Taxis** will run you about $20 for the trip, which isn't too bad on a per-mile basis by American standards.

Tourism Information Office

The La Paz Hotel Association staffs an information center on the waterfront by the Bahía de La Paz at Paseo Alvaro Obregón and Calle 16 de Septiembre. Although they have a fairly good amount of general information, their purpose is mainly to provide visitors with lodging. So, a better choice is the Baja California Sur State Tourist Office. This is very near the former on Calle Mariano Abasolo, one block inland from the malecón.

Getting Around

Once you arrive in downtown La Paz almost all of the important points of interest are very close and you should have no trouble getting around on foot. Much of the city is laid out in a neat grid pattern, although some streets near the historic waterfront are somewhat irregular. For visitors the important streets to know are the waterfront malecón (**Paseo Alvaro Obregón**) and **Calle 5 de Mayo**. The latter intersects the malecón and soon passes by the central square of La Paz.

You can get around the rest of the city by local **buses**. You'll find the main terminal at Avenidas Revolución de 1910 and Degollado, a few blocks from the plaza. It is helpful to know some Spanish or have precise instructions since bus drivers are unlikely to speak English. Buses between the city and Pichilingue leave from the Paseo Alvaro Obregón 125. For exploring out of town, it is more convenient to have a car if you will not be going on organized tours. There are many reasonably priced local **car rental agencies** along the malecón, but you're better off using one of the major American companies. Represented in La Paz are **Alamo**, **Avis**, **Budget**, **Dollar**, **Hertz** and **Thrifty**. Most have in-town locations so you don't have to wait for them to pick you up and go to the airport.

The One-Day Sightseeing Tour

If you do the entire tour as suggested here, it will take three to four hours, so you will still have time to fit in a guided shore excursion or head out to the beaches. The best place to begin is the **malecón**, which is in many ways the tourism heart of the city. The promenade is attractive and offers splendid views of the bay. At the southern end is a large marina. At the center you'll find a plaza with a large white gazebo. Musicians sometimes play there, but this is usually in the evening rather than during your shore call time.

After strolling along the malecón and perhaps exploring the many shops along it, head inland via Calle 5 de Mayo for a few blocks until you reach **Plaza Constitución**, the historical center of the city. Also known as **Jardín Velazco**, the plaza is nicely landscaped and tree-shaded. Pretty tile pathways wind through it. It's a good place to people-watch and to take a break if your feet start to tire. Along one side of the plaza, on Calle Juarez, is the **Nuestra Señora de la Paz**. Originally a Jesuit mission that dates from 1860, the structure now serves as the city's cathedral. It is quite attractive, but may be of more interest to visitors because of its collection of material on La Paz' history. Another corner of the plaza (intersection of Avenida Madero and Calle 5 de Mayo) is the **Biblioteca de Historia de las Californias**, which houses a large number of vivid paintings that tell the story of Baja. There is also a good library collection, all in Spanish. *Open daily except Sunday and may sometimes be closed on Saturday as well.*

Two blocks inland from the cathedral is the **Museo de Antropologia y Historia de Baja California Sur** at Calles Ignacio Altamirano and 5 de Mayo. This is an excellent museum that deserves a fair amount of your time. A wide range of exhibits portray the geology and geography of Baja, as well as its wildlife and human history. *Open daily except Sunday. Closes at 2 pm on Saturday. Donations are requested.*

There are a few attractions of some interest away from the main downtown core. The **Teatro de la Ciudad** is La Paz' cultural complex and theater. Of interest in the large rotunda is a monument commemorating men who fought off the raid of American soldier of fortune William

226

Walker in 1853 and the French in 1861. There is a small museum about the whales of Baja on the square opposite the theater. This is a new facility and the hours of operation are always in a state of flux. The theater is at the intersection of Gómez Farias and Navarto.

A few blocks away at 5 de Febrero between Revolución and Serdán is the extravagant monument to Guadalupe, the city's patron saint. It is known as the **Santuario de la Virgen de Guadalupe**.

In addition to the above suggested tour, many visitors will find that it is worth spending a few hours exploring the off-shore **Islas Espirtú Santo** and **Los Isolotes**. These islands, in addition to being good places to spend time on the beach or go snorkeling, are known for their large colony of sea lions. Not to be outdone by the wildlife, however, beautiful and strange rock formations cover the islands. See the *Sports & Recreation* section below for information on operators that can take you there from town. At last check, I wasn't able to find any cruise line-sponsored shore excursions to the islands.

Shopping

In addition to the usual touristy junk that can be found in numerous shops along the malecón and around the plaza, La Paz does have a good amount of interesting quality goods on sale. These include locally made **coral jewelry** and all sorts of things made from colorful **seashells**. Other popular items are **leather goods** and woven **baskets**. These items are best found along the malecón. Some particularly noteworthy places to shop include **Curios La Carretera** (Avenidas Morelos and Revolución de 1910) and the **Artesanías la Antiqua California** on the malecón. Both have authentic native folk arts and crafts items. For well-made hand-woven goods, try the **Artesanías Cuauhtémoc**, also on the malecón.

The public market, the **Mercado** (Avenida Revolucion 1910 and Degollado) is a colorful place to visit. It sells produce and foods of all types. I suggest that you look, but don't sample. If you want to bite into one of the delectable fruits, be sure to wash it thoroughly with bottled water.

Sports & Recreation

La Paz and its surrounding area, especially the peninsula to the north of the city, is an outdoor enthusiast's paradise. Swimming, diving, and just about every other form of watersport is available in abundance.

First, let's take a look at the **beach** scene. There is a beach in town along a portion of the malecón, but the water is far less clean here than in outlying areas and so it isn't frequented that much, even by the locals. Generally speaking, the farther north you go from the city, the better the beach, although some that are closer by are deservedly popular. Closest to La Paz, in the order they would be reached if driving up the coast from the city, are **Playas Palmira** and **El Coromuel**, followed by **Playa El Caimancito**. Midway up the peninsula are the beautiful **Playa El Tesoro** (one of the most popular) and **Playas El Pichlingue** and **de Balandra**. These three are the closest stretches of sand to the port of Pichlingue, so if you plan to spend your entire shore time in La Paz soaking up the sun I would suggest one of these, preferably El Tesoro. Still a little farther north at the top of the peninsula are **Playas El Tecolote** and **El Coyote**. These are absolutely beautiful beaches and somewhat less crowded than those in the Pichlingue area. All of the beaches can be reached by buses that travel up and down the coast from La Paz.

Snorkeling, **scuba diving** and even **waterskiing** are popular along the entire coastal area, but the best places for the first two activities are by the coral banks that line several islands off of the coast. The best way to reach these (if you can't arrange it through your ship's shore excursion office) is by going to the marina and looking for charter boats. A good choice is **Baja Diving & Service**. Besides the opportunity to partake in watersports, this outfit can take you to the interesting off-shore islands, mentioned in the sightseeing section. **Sportfishing** is a major reason why a lot of people come to La Paz and these visitors often spend a week or more doing so. Large game fish such as blue marlin (up to a thousand pounds) and sailfish are among the draws. But there is a wide variety of species to be found and the catching always seems to be good. Fishing expeditions of a few hours to a full day are available at the marina.

Because the waters around La Paz are unusually calm (except during the occasional winter storm), kayaking has become extremely popular. Some of these trips can last overnight, but much shorter versions are available for the day-visitor. Finally, between January and May is the **whale-watching** season. Just about every whale-watching excursion travels far up the coast to the **Bay of Magdelana**. Unfortunately, this is a 12-hour excursion that will almost definitely exceed your available time in port. However, you can check to see if your cruise line conducts a shorter excursion or if shorter trips are leaving from the marina. While these may not be as good as those going all the way to Magdelana, they're still worthwhile and certainly better than nothing.

FONATUR... MEANS FUN FOR TOURISTS!

Known by its acronym, FONATUR stands for the Fondo Nacional de Fomento al Turismo (the National Clearinghouse for Promotion of Tourism). In plainer English, FONATUR is a Mexican government agency that has worked wonders in transforming formerly wilderness areas of coastline into beautiful master-planned resort communities. It has been so successful that they have expanded the concept to include developing resort complexes in existing towns and cities. Cancún was FONATUR's first and perhaps still most notable achievement. The new Costa Maya resort area, also on the Caribbean side of Mexico, is another. In Baja and along the Mexican Riviera, Ixtapa was created from nothing to become a major resort destination. The same thing is now slowly taking place along the Bahías de Hualulco. Considerable development is done or is being planned for Los Cabos and Loreto in Baja. Los Cabos has already seen much change over the past few years.

Loreto

Loh-RAY-toh

(Baja)

L oreto has a beautiful setting, sandwiched between the Sea of Cortés and Baja's backbone mountains It has the distinction of being the oldest permanent settlement in all of Baja. It was founded as a Jesuit mission in 1697. At one time both Baja California Norte and Baja California Sur were one territory and Loreto served as the capital. This lasted until 1829 when a devastating hurricane reduced the town to near ruins. For more than a century it never recovered and could have vanished from the map if it were not for the fact that American sportfishermen began visiting the area and brought back tales of the big catch as well as the location's beautiful spot. While still not a big tourist destination, Loreto, with a population of around 13,000, is on the planning board for major development. Some even see it as a future rival to Cancún. That doesn't seem likely, although it could become another Cabo San Lucas. For some people that would be a negative because one of its biggest charms is the quiet small-town atmosphere that prevails.

Arrival

Although Puerto Escondido, nine miles south of Loreto, has docks that can accommodate cruise ships, the only major cruise line currently serving the town (Holland America) has chosen to anchor in the small harbor of Loreto itself and tender passengers directly into town. Once you've arrived in Loreto all the points of interest are within a short distance; foot power is the only transportation you need.

Tourism Information Office

The Loreto Tourist Information Office is in the municipal building (known as the Palacio de Gobierno) on the Plaza Principal, the town's main square. There's also a small information office at the marina on the north end of the malecón.

Getting Around

The town is small enough to be explored on **foot**. There are things to be seen away from town, but these are best explored either by a guided shore excursion or with local tour operators. **Rental cars** are scarce and expensive and the roads to some of the outlying areas aren't recommended for timid drivers. However, if you don't heed this advice and want to explore on your own, both **Budget** and **Thrifty** car rentals have offices in Loreto.

The One-Day Sightseeing Tour

It won't take more than a couple of hours to tour Loreto town so you should also plan on doing at least one shore excursion or other guided tour. More about those possibilities in a moment. The town's major point of interest is the **Mission Nuestra Señora de Loreto** (Our Lady of Loreto) at the Plaza Principal, intersection of Calles Salvatierra and Misioneros. This is the second mission church on the site. Dating from 1752, it is noted for its fine Baroque interior. Some of the more notable decorative features include numerous gilded altar paintings. Adjacent to the church is the **Museo de las Misiones**, which houses an interesting collection of historic and religious artifacts, mostly relating to Baja. *Open daily except Monday ($)*. The other attraction in town is the Calle de la Playa, the newly rebuilt **malecón**, where you can stroll and admire the colonial architecture of the town and the pretty setting.

If you intend to spend the entire day sightseeing then you will definitely have time to take at least one of the following three tours outside of Loreto. The first is the popular shore excursion to **San Javier Mission**. This 6½-hour trip travels 22 miles through beautifully rugged canyons and the Cerro de la Giganta mountains to the isolated mission. Built of dark volcanic rock, the 1699 mission seems strangely out of place with its Moorish-style architecture. The town that surrounds the mission has only about 300 residents, who greet visitors with enthusiasm.

The second possibility is to visit the islands offshore from Loreto. There are five islands, now all part of the **Parque Maritímo Nacional Bahía de Loreto** (National Maritime Park of the Bay of Loreto). The two most interesting islands are the **Isla Coronado** and **Isla Danzante**. The former is uninhabited except for the colony of playful sea

Santa Rosalia Marina (Bruce Herman)

Beach hotel, Huatulco (Carlos Sanchez)

lions that visitors come to see. Coronado is only 1½ miles from the Baja shore. Danzante, while pretty, is mainly a recreational area, described below. Tours to the islands are available at the Loreto waterfront.

The final tour opportunity is a seasonal one. From January through March the waters off Baja are prime territory for migrating **gray whales**. These awesome creatures can be seen in all their glory from small skiffs, which leave from nearby Bahía Magdalena. Loreto-based **Las Parras Tours** can take you there (☎ 52-613-135-1010, lasparras@prodigy.net.mx, www.lasparrastours.com).

Shopping

Of all the ports in Mexico, Loreto is one that won't much interest you if your idea of a good time is a day of shopping. There are numerous small shops along the malecón and in and around the few hotels. Locally made handicrafts as well as mass-manufactured tacky souvenirs are the order of the day. The good news is that prices are fairly reasonable and you won't get much in the way of high-pressure sales tactics.

Sports & Recreation

A sports complex has been developed at **Nopoló Bay**, about five miles south of Loreto. This includes the excellent **Loreto Tennis Center**, along with a fine 18-hole **golf** course. Beaches in the immediate vicinity of Loreto aren't good places for sunning. The nearest good beach is about an hour north of town at **Bahía Concepción**. **Snorkeling** and **scuba** are popular in the previously mentioned Maritime Park. This can be done both at Isla Coronado and Isla Danzante. Loreto's original claim to tourism fame, if you can call it that, was its abundant year-round **sportfishing**. That's still the case and experienced anglers still prefer the waters off Loreto to many others around Baja. If your cruise ship doesn't sponsor a fishing excursion, you can simply walk along the malecón and take your choice of charter fishing operators. **Alfredo's Sport Fishing** (☎ 52-613-135-0165) has been around for awhile and has a good reputation.

Manzanillo
Mahn-sah-NEE-yoh
(Mexican Riviera)

*W*ell before Manzanillo became one of more than a half-dozen major Mexican Riviera fly-in, drive-in and cruise-in vacation destinations, it was an important commercial port. A Spanish settlement and shipbuilding facility was established as early as 1522. Over the next five centuries Manzanillo was to be sustained by the maritime industry and international trade. Today it is still a major port for the export and import of goods. The city has a population of more than 130,000.

While Manzanillo is still primarily a commercial center, tourism is increasingly important. In some ways it is the center of the Mexican Riviera because, of the five biggest ports, two are to the north (Puerto Vallarta and Mazátlan) and two are to the south (Ixtapa/Zihuatanejo and Acapulco). Yet, despite its central location, Manzanillo sees less cruise ship traffic from the typical week-long cruise originating out of Southern California. This is because, while Manzanillo has a lot to offer in the way of recreation, there is less to see and do here than in either Puerto Vallarta or Mazátlan. The fact that it hasn't quite captured the "imagination" of Riviera visitors also affects cruise line schedules. The resorts to the south, on the other hand, are also visited less than PV and Mazátlan because of their distance from California. Manzanillo is, however, a big-time resort. The arrival of this status dates from the opening of the Las Brisas Hotel in 1974 (more about this in the sightseeing section).

▶ Manzanillo is where the movie *10*, with Bo Derek prancing on the beach, was filmed in 1979.

Manzanillo sits around two large bays, the Bahías de Santiago and Manzanillo, which are separated by a small but valuable piece of real estate known as the Peninsula de Santiago. Mountains and a jungle serve as a backyard to the city. The resort areas lie along the shores of the two bays, while the downtown area is on a narrow isthmus at the southeastern edge of Manzanillo Bay.

Arrival

Cruise ships dock at the downtown piers, which are only a few blocks from the city's main square. Unfortunately, most of the activities and points of interest are not downtown so you will have to make your way along the bayfront (see *Getting Around*).

Tourism Information Office

The best choice for arriving cruise ship passengers is to go to the small tourism office at Avenida Juárez 100, about a block inland from the cruise ship dock. There is also a large tourism office operated by the Mexican state of Colima. It can be found at Costera Miguel de la Madrid 1294-B. This is on a peninsula reached by causeway from north of downtown and is between Playa las Brisas and Playa Azul. In the beginning of the resort zone, it is not convenient for cruise ship arrivals unless you're going to be headed in that direction to begin with. However, as in

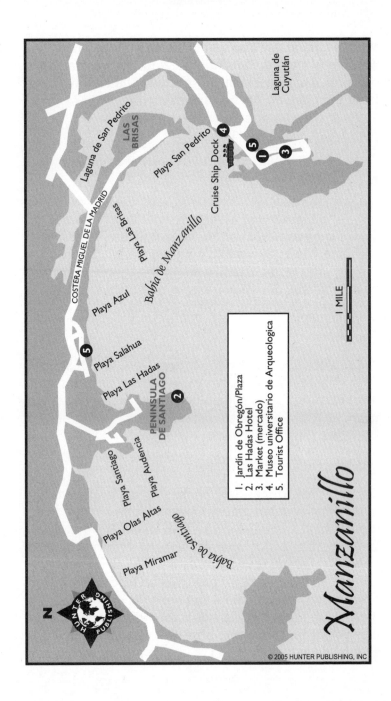

1. Jardín de Obregón/Plaza
2. Las Hadas Hotel
3. Market (mercado)
4. Museo universitario de Arqueologica
5. Tourist Office

I MILE

Manzanillo

© 2005 HUNTER PUBLISHING, INC

many Riviera resort ports, you can also get a lot of information at any of the major hotels. This means that if you go to the resort zone you don't even have to hunt down the tourist office.

Getting Around

In downtown Manzanillo everything is within a short walk from the cruise ship terminal and no transportation is needed. Furthermore, most of downtown is either a grid pattern or close to one, so navigation shouldn't present any unusual problems. Visitors can get to the resort areas by one of three methods. The first and least expensive is to use the city's public **bus** system, which offers frequent and reliable service. Routes run from downtown along the bay-front highway connecting all the major hotels. Destinations are clearly marked in the front window of the bus.

Another method is to use one of the many **taxis** that seem to be available just about anywhere. This is, of course, more expensive than bus travel, but is faster, more convenient and also avoids the possibility of being crushed like a sardine.

Finally, you can **rent a car**. Many American companies have offices in Manzanillo. Other than high rates, the major drawback is that they are not downtown by the cruise ship terminal, but are scattered among the resort hotels. This can waste a lot of time until you get your car and also when you return it. I do not suggest renting a car unless you plan to head way out of town on your own.

The One-Day Sightseeing Tour

Of the five most popular Mexican Riviera destinations, Manzanillo has the least to offer in traditional sightseeing and perhaps even less in recreational opportunities. A self-guided tour of the major sights will take only about a half-day and part of that is attributable to the fact that things are rather spread out. Let's start with the city center, which is not particularly attractive. From the cruise ship dock walk to your right on Avenida Morelos for four blocks to Morelos. This area has been recently refurbished to be a sort of malecón, although it doesn't compare well to those in other ports. The highlight is a huge statue of a leaping sailfish because Manzanillo, along with several other places, calls itself the "sailfish capital of the world."

The reason for redevelopment in this area is to attract more cruise ship traffic. There's little doubt that this will be accomplished within a few years. At Morelos you will have reached the main plaza known as the **Jardín de Obregón**. There are fine views of the bay from this pretty plaza.

Leading south from the opposite side of the plaza is Avenida Mexico, where most of the city's shopping is located. In the opposite direction from the cruise ship terminal, by the northern edge of downtown on Blvd. Miguel de la Madrid at the San Pedrito traffic circle, is the University of Colima campus. Here you will find the **Museo Universitario de Arqueologia** (University Museum of Archaeology). This is a large facility whose collection includes more than 18,000 artifacts that help trace the cultural history of Mesoamerica. *Open daily except Monday from 10 am until 2 pm, 1 pm on Sunday. ($).*

Now you'll have to make your way farther up Miguel de la Madrid and across the causeway into the resort zone. As you go over the causeway you'll notice two large lagoons. The larger one is the **Laguna de San Pedro**. This is a good spot for those who like bird-watching. In fact, several lagoons in this area provide a decent birding experience.

The Costera Miguel de la Madrid runs the entire length of the bay-front resort section. The most significant attraction here (other than the beach and watersports) is the fabulously beautiful and architecturally stunning **Las Hadas Hotel**. On the Santiago Peninsula, Las Hadas is a snow-white structure complete with countless minarets, cupolas and turrets – all done in Moorish style. Besides the architecture, the meticulously landscaped grounds of the resort are definitely worth seeing. The only problem is that Las Hadas is a private resort and sometimes the guards at the gate won't let you in if you aren't a guest or don't have restaurant reservations. Therefore, you might consider making reservations for lunch. You could splurge and actually eat there (probably busting your budget for the entire port) or be a little dishonest and cancel out once you get inside, returning to the ship for lunch or dining where the prices aren't so high. The Santiago Peninsula, although small, is home to about half of Manzanillo's best resort hotels. One other resort on the peninsula that's worth visiting is the new **Kármina Palace,** with its Mayan motif and splendid landscaped grounds.

The rest of your day can be spent on the beach or engaging in some sporting activity. Because most interesting destinations are too far for day-trips from Manzanillo, the choices aren't numerous. I strongly recommend a side-trip to **Colima**, the capital city of the state of the same name. Guided excursions to Colima (an available option on almost every cruise visiting Manzanillo) take about seven hours; you can do it in the same amount of time on your own if you rent a car. There is also bus service from Manzanillo for those squeamish about driving. The round-trip over good roads takes about 2½ hours so, depending upon how long you'll be in port, you can judge how much time you have to explore this well-preserved colonial city. You'll need to have the equivalent of about $15 in pesos to pay the tolls in each direction on the Manzanillo-Colima Highway.

Among the points of interest in this small city of about 125,000 people are the huge **King Colima Monument**, the **Plaza Principal**, **Jardín Libertad** (Garden of Liberty) and the **Palacio de Gobierno**. There are also some good art museums. Perhaps the most alluring feature of Colima isn't any one point of interest, but the overall Spanish colonial atmosphere.

The area around Colima also has some worthy points of interest. **La Campana**, just north of the city, is a recently excavated archaeological zone that is believed to date back to 1500 BC *($)*. There are several volcanic mountain national parks near Colima, but most are too far to include in a day-trip from Manzanillo. Depending upon your schedule you might be able to work in a visit to **Volcán de Fuego**, the 13,068-foot-high active volcano, only 15 miles north of Colima.

Regardless of your day itinerary, you will get some good views of several volcanoes as you travel near the city. Other possible day-trips are to the enchanting town of **Comala** (an hour from Manzanillo) and the village of **Cyutlán**. The latter has an interesting salt museum, old haciendas and a turtle sanctuary.

Shopping

For those who live to shop, Manzanillo will most likely be something of a disappointment compared to the other larger ports. There are lots of stores on **Avenida Mexico** selling just about everything. Quality can sometimes be a problem (especially if you're purchasing from the numerous beach vendors) so your best bet is to look for Mexican crafts from relatively nearby Guadalajara, which is known as one of the country's major craft centers. There is upscale shopping in the bigger hotels in the resort zone, but you will pay dearly for whatever it is you buy. The Santiago Peninsula is home to a decent **flea market** where you can bargain for just about anything. Bo Derek may no longer be a household name, but the braided hair style she introduced in *10* is still popular and some women and plenty of young girls might want to try it. There are many braiding specialists (called *trensistas* in Spanish) along Playa Audencia who will do the job in practically no time for about $5.

Sports & Recreation

Manzanillo is well known for its fine **beaches**. In all, beaches extend for about seven miles along the twin bays that span the resort area. The sand is often a golden color sometimes tinged with spots of black from natural debris in the rivers that run into the bay. The color and texture of the sand make Manzanillo's beaches something special. **Playa Las Brisas** is the first beach you will come to when arriving in the resort area from downtown. This is an older section and isn't as visually appealing as others, but the beach is pleasant and swimming conditions are very good.

Playa Azul, which extends for almost five miles from near downtown all the way to the Santiago Peninsula, is the next beach and is quite a bit nicer and offers good swimming. Other nice beaches are near the Santiago Peninsula. From a visual standpoint they are superior to the previous two selections, but the water gets rougher as you approach the peninsula, which makes them more suited to sunning than swimming. The two best beaches in this section are **Playa Salahua** and **Playa Las Hadas**. The latter is the closest beach to the Las Hadas Hotel. Remember that *all* beaches in Mexico are public, so even though it may touch on the hotel's property, access to it for all cannot be denied. The same is true, of course, for all other "hotel" beaches. Once you get to the west side of the peninsula and into Santiago Bay, the water is even cleaner and clearer – not that it's bad at all on the Las Hadas side of the peninsula. **Playas la Audencia**, **Santiago**, **Olas Altas** and **Miramar** are the main beaches in this section.

The last beach at the eastern end of Santiago Bay is **Playa la Boquita**, which is popular with the locals on weekends. Olas Altas is the best beach for surfing, while windsurfing enthusiasts flock to Playa Miramar.

Snorkeling and **diving** are available, but not to the extent found in most other port resorts. The best diving locations are near **Playa Audencia**, the **Elephant Rock** and **El Arrecife**. Beginning divers will find the area near Las Hadas to be a good spot to hone their skills. **Fishing**, especially big-catch sportfishing, is king here. In addition to the famously huge sailfish you'll be able to catch marlin, dorado and tuna among others. If you don't like the selection of water-related activities offered by your ship's shore excursion office, then try looking into **Pacific Watersports** at Las Hadas. This is a good place to go if you want to get in on the fishing action or most other water activities for that matter.

Land-based recreational activities are also numerous – everything from tennis to horseback riding. Most of these pursuits are run by various resort hotels, but they often allow non-guests to sign up. **Golf** is a big activity in and around Manzanillo. The nine-hole **Club Santiago** and the 18-hole **La Mantarraya** at Las Hadas are the most convenient. However, the latter is very expensive. The Manzanillo area's most opulent golf facility is definitely the 27-hole **Grand Bay Hotel**. Unfortunately, it is much farther away. Taxi would be the best method of getting there. Both Grand Bay and La Mantarraya are considered to be among the best golf courses in Mexico.

Mazatlán

Mah-saht-LAHN

(Mexican Riviera)

This growing city of nearly 400,000 people isn't, upon first sight, what comes to mind when you think of the Mexican Riviera. That's because it is a major commercial port where business is conducted and people live and, yes, work. The beautiful resort areas are several miles away. However, as you'll soon learn, you shouldn't immediately run to the resort zone because downtown has quite a bit to offer, as does neighboring Old Mazátlan with its unique charms. In fact, the two together probably have more to see than just about any port of call on the Mexican Riviera. The city occupies a peninsula that juts out into the Pacific Ocean. Between the peninsula and the mainland are several islands in the Bahía Dársena (Darsena Bay), which provides a sheltered harbor for the commercial port and your cruise ship.

Mazátlan was founded in 1531. It grew very slowly at first, with no permanent settlement of any significance taking hold until the early part of the 19th century. Its development as a port soon after that led to a period of growth that was interrupted by military sieges (by the Americans during the Mexican War and by the French in 1864 during their occupation of Mexico). Although there were some who knew about its potential as a vacation destination because of its warm, sunny climate and the abundance of fishing opportunities, Mazátlan didn't become a major tourist destination overnight, as have many other Mexican vacation hot spots. Today, however,

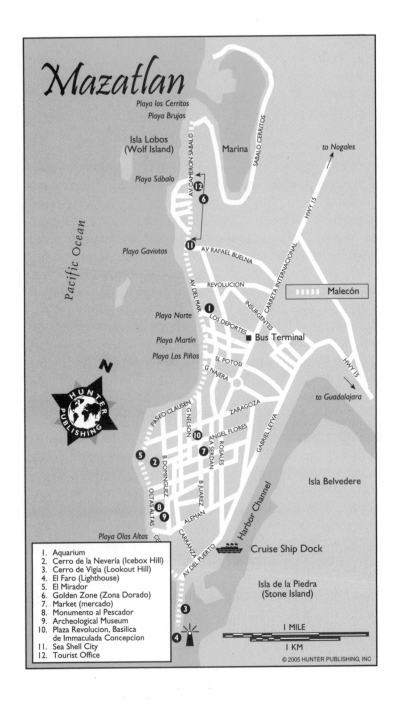

1. Aquarium
2. Cerro de la Nevería (Icebox Hill)
3. Cerro de Vigía (Lookout Hill)
4. El Faro (Lighthouse)
5. El Mirador
6. Golden Zone (Zona Dorado)
7. Market (mercado)
8. Monumento al Pescador
9. Archeological Museum
10. Plaza Revolucion, Basilica de Immaculada Concepcion
11. Sea Shell City
12. Tourist Office

Mazátlan rightfully asserts its place among the most popular Mexican Riviera getaways.

Arrival

The cruise ship docks are on the **Bahía Dársena** in the middle of the vast commercial shipping operations. Several large cruise ships can tie up here at one time, so there will be no need for tendering. You will be shuttled a short distance by a free tram from your ship to the port terminal. There you'll find some shopping and transportation to the city and other points. There are good information and other facilities at the pier and many downtown attractions are within walking distance (about 20 minutes). If you decide not to hoof it, you can easily get a taxi by the port. City buses also circulate along the street that runs by the port.

Tourism Information Office

An excellent combined city and state of Sinoloa tourism office is on Avenida Camarón Sábalo (corner of Tiburón) in the Banrural Building. Unfortunately, this is in the Zona Dorada, which is not close to where cruise ships dock. However, many visitors will be heading up in this direction because the Zona Dorada and points north is where much of the recreation (as opposed to city sightseeing) is located. And, as stated, there is a reasonable amount of information available at the cruise ship terminal.

Getting Around

Although it is within walking distance of downtown, many people will find the trek a bit long for their liking. The street layout near the port can also be confusing. Should you want to stroll into the city center, turn left when you get out of the cruise ship terminal and walk down Avenida del Puerto. In short order you'll reach

Avenida Miguel Alemán. Take a right onto this street and continue until you reach Avenida Sérdan. Take another right and follow this street until you come to the main plaza downtown. Alternatively, a **taxi** will cost you about $5. There are also city **buses**.

Downtown can be negotiated on foot, but you will need transportation for other parts of the city. There is an extensive network of **buses** that cost only about 5 pesos a person (50¢). The most important route to know is the one marked "Saballo-Centro," which connects downtown with the Golden Zone resort area. While most of Mazátlan's buses are older, crowded and rather uncomfortable, many of the vehicles on this route are modern and have air conditioning. The only other way to get around town is by **taxi**, which can be expensive (for example, $10 to the Golden Zone). In addition to regular taxis you will see golf-cart-like vehicles whizzing around town. These covered but open VW-chassis affairs are called *pulmonías* and cost the same as a taxi. They're a fun way to zip along from one section of the malecón to another and are never difficult to find.

The One-Day Sightseeing Tour

There's enough to fill an entire day sightseeing and shopping in the city. Trips to the beach or other recreational activities will require some trimming of the suggested sights on this itinerary. Also, if you plan to stay within the city, there is no need to sign up for a shore excursion; you can see more in the same period of time on your own. Use the excursion route if you plan to spend time outside the city.

You should begin your tour of Mazátlan in the heart of downtown at the main square. It's not uncommon in Mexico to find a place that goes under two different names, but this one actually has three commonly used names – **Plaza Revolución, Plaza Principal** and **Plaza República**. Situated at the intersection of Avenidas Juárez and 21 de Marzo, this is a lovely tree-shaded area with a pretty wrought-iron bandstand and benches where you can sit and ponder.

On the north side of the plaza is the **Basilica of the Immaculate Conception**, which was built in the late 19th century. It is one of the city's most recognizable landmarks because of the gold-colored twin spires. Despite the spires and some colorful painting on the top, the basilica's main interest lies within, where there is a beautiful gilded altar as well as many notable statues. Another side of the plaza has the city hall or **Palacio Municipal**.

Two blocks north from the Plaza on Juárez is the main **Mercado**. This cavernous indoor market covers a square block and is where Mazatlanos come to buy their fresh meat, seafood and produce. It's quite a place and worth a look around, but think twice before purchasing anything to eat.

A few blocks from the Plaza area is the part of town known as **Old Mazátlan**. To get there, walk west to Avenida 5 de Mayo and then south. As you enter Old Mazátlan the name of the street changes to Carnaval. This area of narrow streets is being carefully restored to its mid-19th-century appearance. The atmosphere is not particularly Mexican or Spanish because much of the architecture dates from the French occupation period. Thus, there are wrought-iron balconies and a New Orleans feel to the area. Of special interest is the **Teatro Angela Peralta**, Avenida Carnaval and Calle Libertad, a late 19th-century theater named for a Mexican opera star who, unfortunately, died of cholera upon her arrival in Mazátlan to perform. The European-style interior has rich woods and is highly ornate. It is still used for performances of all kinds. On the second floor is an interesting little museum with pictures of the theater before its careful restoration. *Open daily from 9 am to 6 pm. $.*

The theater is one block south of **Plaza Machado**, one of the city's most delightful squares. From Old Mazátlan it is just a few short blocks to the waterfront and the wonderful **malecón**, where there is much to see. On the way, if you wish, you can stop into the small but interesting **Mazátlan Archaeological Museum**, Calle Osuna, a few blocks southwest of Plaza Machado via Constitución Venus to Osuna. *Open daily except Monday from 10 am until 1 pm and from 4 to 7 pm. $.* The downtown and Old Mazátlan portion of this tour should take two to three hours.

Mazátlan's **malecón** extends for 11 miles, so you obviously can't walk the entire stretch. It's easiest to do it in sections and perhaps take a *pulmonaría* to connect the dots. The pedestrian promenade is flanked all the way by a major boulevard, which constantly changes names. In the southern section nearest to downtown it is called **Paseo Olas Altas**. This becomes the **Paseo Claussen** farther north, then **Avenida del Mar**, before finally becoming **Camarón Sábalo** (known simply as Sábalo to most residents) in the Golden Zone. Wherever you are along the malecón there are fantastic views of the sea, the many islands that lie near the shore and are dotted with birds, and the fabulous monuments on the promenade itself.

Beginning along Olas Altas, near the archaeological museum, is the **Escudo de Sinaloa y Mazátlan**, a stone monument with the shield of the city and state colorfully emblazoned on it. Also along this section of Olas Altas is **El Mirador**. In keeping with the well-known Mexican tradition of giving more than one name to mostly everything, this area is also called the **Punta de las Clavadistas**. The latter is more descriptive since it means "point of the cliff divers." Whatever name you use, it is where brave young men dive 45 feet off a tower into the rough and rocky water below. This is generally done on the hour but, if you see a tour bus arriving, hurry up because it will certainly be done for the bus passengers. While not as famous or quite as dramatic as the dive in Acapulco, it makes for an interesting sight. It is customary to tip the divers.

In the vicinity of El Mirador are several statues and sculpture groups. These include monumental works that feature people, dolphins and a women with her arms spread outward and her hair and gown blowing in the "wind." More traditional historical monuments, such as one dedicated to national hero Benito Juárez, are also here, along with the compulsory gigantic Mexican flag. Next to the Juárez statue, sitting on a rock by the water, is a tiny figure reminiscent of Copenhagen's "Little Mermaid."

Near all of this wonderful scene, but on the land side is **Icebox Hill (Cerro de la Neveria)**, one of several high vantage points along the waterfront. There is a road that goes to the top, but it's a rather strenuous climb so you might want to consider taking a taxi. Even easier, and providing just as good a view of the coast and the city, you can go into the nearby waterfront Best Western Posada Freeman Hotel and take the elevator to the top floor. From there, climb a few flights of stairs to their observation deck.

Before heading farther north on the malecón, it's worth noting that you can add a little detour to the south. Both **Lookout Hill (Cerro del Vigía)** and the lighthouse known as **El Faro** are south of the malecón and each offers more great vistas. But the view is not that different from what you have already seen. If you do decide to see one or both of these, keep in mind that the route to them is even steeper than at Icebox Hill, so a taxi is well advised.

Continuing from the vicinity of Icebox Hill north along on the malecón, on the Paseo Claussen section is **El Fuerte Carranza**, the small remains of some old fortifications. Then on Avenida del Mar is the famous **Monumento al Pescadero** (Monument to the Fisherman), which depicts a fisherman dragging his net, watched by his wife (both without clothes). Other monuments in this area, and all along the malecón, show everything from deer to life itself. How long it takes to tour the malecón and its adjacent hills depends upon several factors, including the amount of walking you do versus riding, how many of the high viewpoints you go up to, and the detail with which you examine the various monuments. You should allow a minimum of 90 minutes (two hours, including time to get to the Golden Zone), but some people will no doubt easily be able to spend double that time.

The **Golden Zone** (or **Zona Dorada**) begins where Avenida del Mar becomes Sábalo. At **Shrimp Point** a well-known local nightspot called **Valentino's Disco** is perched on the rocky outcropping. The bright white building is built in Moorish style and seems strangely out of place. Still, it's beautiful and makes a good vantage point. Although the malecón ends here, the streets will be teeming with people wandering around the many shops and restaurants of the Golden Zone. Here is where most of the city's bigger hotels and best beaches are located. You can thread your way through any of the pedestrian passages that lead to the beach to get a great view of the sea along with three offshore islands that are almost always teeming with bird life. Two of the bigger islands are **Isla de los Venados** and **Isla de los Parajos**.

Aside from myriad shopping and recreational opportunities, the Golden Zone has two places of special interest. The first is the **Mazátlan Arts & Crafts Center** on Avenida Rodolfo Loiaza at the very beginning of the

Golden Zone. Besides being a place to look at the best in Mexican crafts (whether or not you want to purchase), the center is the Mazátlan home of the famous **Papantla Flyers** and their **Flying Pole Dance**. An open-air theater is the venue for this exciting performance where men in native garb are suspended from atop a 50-foot pole and slowly wind their way down to the bottom. It is an ancient tradition connected with the harvest. Times vary (find out by checking at the front desk of a hotel or at the tourist office). Often, they are timed to excursions from the cruise ship so that is a way of being sure to see it if you're interested.

Farther north on Loiaza is **Sea Shell City**. This is a large gift shop, but the entire second floor is a wonderful exhibit comprised of countless shells of all shapes, colors and sizes. The extravagant fountain is made entirely of shells and is amid a pool with sea turtles. This free exhibit is open whenever the craft shop is open and that will cover all the time when your ship is in port. Finally, walking around the Golden Zone and browsing the shops, sampling the food at restaurants and cantinas, and people-watching are all good ways to spend some time.

On the way back from the Golden Zone to your ship you can make one last stop. The **Acuario**, on Avenida de los Deportes just off Avenida del Mar, is a good aquarium with hundreds of species displayed in about 50 different tanks. Several shows are given throughout the day, including sea lions and trained colorful birds. This is probably the best place to take children in all of Mazátlan. Give yourself at least an hour for this attraction. *Open daily 9:30 am to 5:30 pm. $$.*

Alternative sightseeing options outside Mazátlan are best done by shore excursion. Although you can rent a car in town, getting around in the surrounding countryside isn't all that easy, given the way many Mexicans drive, the poor roads and even worse signage. Among the many popular half- and full-day excursions that get away from the city are tours to ranches, tequila factories and/or breweries, small villages of Spanish colonial style, and excursions into the nearby Sierra Madres. The scenery on the latter trips is quite good, but this isn't the most scenic stretch of mountains along the Pacific coast.

▶ If you can time your cruise to be in Mazátlan during *Carnaval* (equivalent to Mardi Gras and taking place either in late February or early March), you will be in for a special treat. Although most of the major activities occur in the evening after your ship has departed, there are also daytime festivities and the whole city takes on a party atmosphere.

Shopping

The **central market** has some non-food items such as leather goods (apparently more for the benefit of visitors than residents) and there are many shops in the downtown area. **Midart** is a high-quality art and native craft gallery adjacent to the Angela Peralta Theater. This part of town also has several other galleries. However, there's no doubt that the biggest opportunity to spend some money is in the **Golden Zone**, both along Sábalo and Loaiza. Popular items run the gamut from clothing (especial casual and resort wear) to leather, jewelry and craft items. Don't limit yourself to the two main streets of Sábalo and Loaiza. There are "mini"-pedestrian malls leading off these streets, where you'll find even more shops. Don't forget to try the **Mazátlan Arts & Crafts Center** if you're interested in Mexican-made crafts. **Sea Shell City** also has a good selection of gifts in addition to shell work.

Sports & Recreation

Let's first look at the **beach** scene. Mazátlan's long stretch of coast means that you'll find lots of beaches. Working our way from south to north, the first important beach is **Playa Olas Altas**. The Spanish meaning of the name is "high waves" and that should give you an idea of what you'll find here. The water is, in fact, better for surfing than for swimming, but it's a pleasant setting if you just want to laze away a few hours on the sand. Farther north are **Playa Norte** and **Playa Martín**. These are both good beaches that are especially popular with local residents. After those two beaches you'll have reached the Golden Zone, which is considered to have the best beaches. **Playa Las Gaviotas** is very popular with visitors as it juts out into the ocean. The main beach in the Golden Zone is the always popular and, therefore, usually crowded **Playa Sábalo**. There are several other less-crowded beaches north of the Golden Zone, but they're getting farther away from ship, thus increasing the time spent traveling rather than relaxing on the sand.

Sportfishing is big in Mazátlan and this is considered one of the top places in Mexico for sailfish and striped marlin during the season – which runs from fall through spring. How convenient, since that's the time when the cruise ships come here! Also in good supply are blue marlin, bonito, dolphin and yellowfin tuna. Other watersports include kayaking, parasailing, windsurfing and jet skiing. Many of these activities are conducted through various resort hotels, so anyone wishing to partake is likely to be better off booking through their ship's excursion office. However, if you want to venture out on a fishing boat, the fishing fleets are centered on the south end of Darsena Bay between El Faro and Lookout Hill. Full-day fishing excursions will cost more than $250. It's a short taxi ride from the cruise ship terminal to the boat docks.

When it comes to spectator sports, **bullfights** are the big attraction. They take place on Sundays at 4 pm from December through April. The only way you can see them (or at least a good part of the program) and get back to your ship in time is if departure is scheduled after 7 pm, not commonly seen in Mazátlan port calls.

Puerto Vallarta

PWER-toh Vah-YAHR-ta

(Mexican Riviera)

S tretching for miles along the beautiful **Bay of Banderas** (**Bahía de Banderas**), Puerto Vallarta is sandwiched between the water and the abruptly rising mountains of the Sierra Madre range. As a result, the city is only a few blocks wide in many places. With an official estimated population of about 175,000 (probably considerably more in reality), it's hard to imagine all those people fitting in. Despite tremendous growth, Puerto Vallarta maintains the atmosphere of a much smaller community and has a special charm. It wasn't always such a busy place. The site was discovered by Spanish seamen in the early 16th century. Despite rave reviews about its bountiful location and the shelter its harbor provided both from the sea and pirates, it stayed a backwater for centuries, serving only as a small shipbuilding facility. The first permanent civilian settlement did not take hold until 1851, when it was called Las Peñas. It was only 37 years later when more than half the town was destroyed by a fire.

The name was changed in 1918 to Puerto Vallarta to honor Don Ignacio Vallarta, a state governor and drafter of the Mexican constitution. The economy in the first half of the 20th century was largely agricultural and banana plantations provided for significant growth. Tourism began in the 1930s and continues today as Puerto Vallarta sees more than two million visitors a year. In many ways Puerto Vallarta is Mexico's premier Pacific coast resort destination.

Arrival

Puerto Vallarta's **Terminal Marítima** (Maritime Terminal) is a modern facility that can handle several large ships at one time. The terminal is on the Bay of Banderas at the beginning of an inlet leading into the Marina Vallarta. The Marina area is worthy of some exploration (as you will read about later), but most of the important sights are farther down the coast in central Puerto Vallarta. Downtown is approximately three miles from the terminal. Taxis and buses can easily be found at the port. A cab to the main plaza will cost about $6 one-way.

Tourism Information Office

Puerto Vallarta's municipal tourism office is downtown in the city hall (Presidencia Municipal) at Avenida Independencia 123 on the main square. It's open weekdays from 9 am until 8 pm and from 9 am to 1 pm on Saturday. There is also a Jalisco State Tourism office at the Plaza Marina Shopping Center in the Marina Vallarta. While the latter is a logical first choice because it's closest to the cruise ship terminal, most visitors will be right near the municipal office as well because it is close to the city's main attractions.

A good source of information is the daily English-language *Vallarta Today* or one of several other smaller newspapers available just about everywhere free of charge.

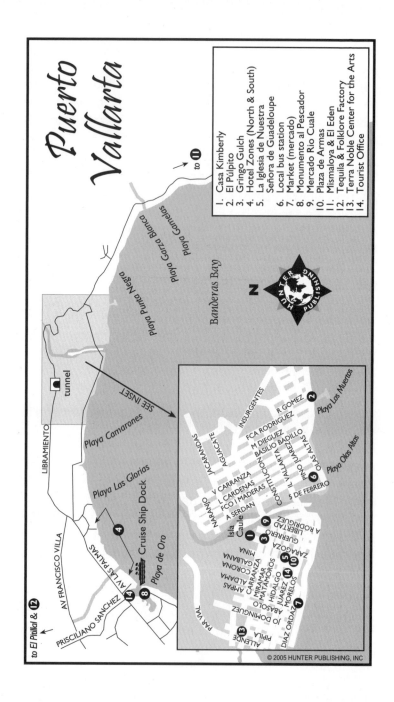

Puerto Vallarta

1. Casa Kimberly
2. El Púlpito
3. Gringo Gulch
4. Hotel Zones (North & South)
5. La Iglesia de Nuestra Señora de Guadeloupe
6. Local bus station
7. Market (mercado)
8. Monumento al Pescador
9. Mercado Río Cuale
10. Plaza de Armas
11. Mismaloya & El Eden
12. Tequila & Folklore Factory
13. Terra Noble Center for the Arts
14. Tourist Office

Banderas Bay

HUNTER PUBLISHING

Playa Garza Blanca
Playa Gonvalos
Playa Punta Negra
Playa Camarones
Playa Las Glorias
Cruise Ship Dock
Playa de Oro

tunnel

LIBRAMIENTO

SEE INSET

AV FRANCISCO VILLA
AV LAS PALMAS
PRISCILIANO SANCHEZ

to El Pitillal & 12

PAR VIAL
JO DOMINGUEZ
ABASOLO
CARRANZA
MIRAMAR
MATAMOROS
ALDAMA
CORONA
GALBANA
MINA
ZARAGOZA
GUERRERO
LIBERTAD
A RODRIGUEZ
5 DE FEBRERO
Isla Caule
A SERDAN
FCO I MADERAS
L CARDENAS
V CARRANZA
CONSTITUCION
IL VALLARTA BADILLO
PINO JUAREZ
OLAS ALTAS
BASILIO BADILLO
M DIEGUEZ
FCA RODRIGUEZ
R GOMEZ
INSURGENTES
AGUACATE
JACARANDAS
NARANJO
PIPILA
ALLENDE
DIAZ ORDAZ
MORELOS
JUAREZ
HIDALGO

Playa Las Muertas
Playa Olas Altas

© 2005 HUNTER PUBLISHING, INC

Getting Around

If you're not going to take the guided shore excursion route for at least part of your day in Puerto Vallarta, you'll be glad to know that getting around is rather easy. Only a block from the cruise ship terminal is the stop for **buses** that will take you straight into downtown. The ride is about 15 minutes and costs only a few pesos. Buses have their destinations painted onto the window or other prominent place, but the easiest way to know which bus to take is by its color. The blue and white buses are the most important ones for visitors; they go to El Centro (downtown) from Marina Vallarta. Once downtown, these buses ply the main streets only a few blocks inland from the waterfront. It's hard to get lost downtown as there are only a few streets and all of the important ones parallel the water, so you can always get yourself oriented.

The Isla del Río Cuale separates the downtown into two sections and is another good point of orientation. Buses do go to many attractions both north and south of the city, but these are more easily reached by taxi or guided shore excursion. **Taxis** are expensive if you're traveling any distance. **Car rentals** are available both at Marina Vallarta and downtown if you want to venture off on your own. However, the same general reasons for not renting in other Mexican Riviera locations also apply here.

The One-Day Sightseeing Tour

Puerto Vallarta doesn't have a wealth of the usual tourist attractions as compared to most large cities. Mazátlan, for one, has more. This doesn't mean that PV (as Puerto Vallarta is often called) isn't worthwhile. It just may not take much more than a half-day, so you can consider recreational pursuits or a half-day excursion along with the standard sightseeing.

The logical place for beginning a city tour is in the heart of **El Centro**. PV's "downtown" is a rather charming place with its cobblestoned streets, whitewashed buildings with red tile roofs, and the small-town atmosphere of the shops and eateries along the waterfront malecón. The main plaza is **Plaza de Armas**, although you'll also hear it referred to as **Plaza Principal**. Situated across the street from the waterfront, the plaza has a statue of Señor Vallarta and a bandstand. It is the venue for free concerts on weekends. The **city hall** is on one side of the plaza. It contains the tourist office, but you should also walk in to see the pretty courtyard and the mural painted on one wall.

PV's most famous building is on another side of the plaza. **La Iglesia de Nuestra Señora de Guadalupe** (Church of Our Lady of Guadalupe) is a distinguished looking structure. The interior doesn't have much to offer, but the crown on top of the church is something else. An oversized version of the crown worn by Carlota, wife of the Archduke Maximilian who ruled Mexico for a time in the 1860s, it is one of the symbols of the city. This is a fiberglass copy of the original crown, which was toppled by an earthquake in 1995.

The **malecón** extends for a mile, from the Isla del Río Cuale on the southern end to past the main shopping district on the north. The **shopping area** is about eight blocks long and extends north from the area of the Plaza. Besides being the main shopping district, this section also has many of the city's restaurants and nightspots. But back to the malecón, beginning at the southern end. **Los Arcos**, immediately opposite the plaza, is a three-arched monument that is also frequently used as a symbol of the city and marks the spot of an open-air amphitheater.

Within a short distance of Los Arcos are three famous monuments. The best-known (and *the* undisputed main symbol of PV) is the relatively small but pretty statue of a **boy riding a sea horse**. The other monuments are the **Fountain of the Dolphins** and **Neptune and Mermaid**. There are also some less well-known sculptures, including a few that defy description. They aren't labeled so you can't even know exactly what the artists were thinking!

On the north side of the river a few blocks inland from the waterfront is **Gringo Gulch**. In a hilly area, Gringo Gulch was so named because of the large number of Americans who settled here in the 1950s and '60s. Many still live here to this day. Some of the residents were famous, but none more so than Elizabeth Taylor and Richard Burton. Ms. Taylor bought a house here that today is a bed & breakfast. It isn't that much to look at from the outside, although the interior is more interesting. Since it is an operating inn, **Casa Kimberly** is open to non-guests only via what I consider to be overpriced guided tours. *Open daily. $$$.* Getting back to our story, Burton wanted very much to be near Liz so he bought a house across the street and connected the two homes with a pink bridge that today is known as the **Bridge of Love**. It's all so romantic I could just cry! Despite my sarcasm there is little doubt that American visitors flock to see this area. A statue of the famous couple is nearby on Avenida Miramar close to the municipal market. The market, by the way, is worth seeing briefly as well. The lively and colorful atmosphere gives you the true flavor of Mexico. This part of the downtown tour can be completed in two hours, or less if you don't go into Casa Kimberly.

Isla del Río Cuale is a narrow (only a couple of hundred feet), but comparatively long (the equivalent of about six blocks), island that literally cuts El Centro in two. It's a fun place to visit for an hour or so. The vegetation is lush and there are many trees and benches so you can find a shaded spot to cool off. Don't swim in the river, however, since the water is polluted. On the island are restaurants, a small archeological museum and dozens of stalls and stands with vendors that sell just about anything you could imagine. Near the north end of the island is a seated statue of noted actor and director John Huston. Huston lived in Puerto Vallarta and directed the motion picture *Night of the Iguana*, which was filmed in the vicinity.

At the southern end of the island, where the walkway meets the sea, is an especially attractive area. The island is reached by a number of sturdy stone bridges or by swinging bridges for the slightly more adventurous. At the western end of the island (nearest the bay) there's a small museum devoted to handicrafts of the ancient native groups. The collection isn't very big, but the quality of the displays is high. *Open daily except Sunday and Monday*.

Although two major streets cross over it, the island itself is pedestrian-only. From the bay side of the island there is another pedestrian walkway that is a short extension of the malecón. You can be back at the main square from here in under five minutes. However, one last near-downtown attraction you might want to see is **El Púlpito**, a rock formation by the pier several blocks south of the river on the waterfront off Olas Altas.

There are a couple of more time-consuming attractions that aren't within walking distance of El Centro, but you might want to consider them if they're not included in a guided tour and they fit into your schedule. These are the **Terra Noble Center for the Arts** and the **Tequila & Folklore Gallery**, both on the north side of town. The former pretty much reduces the opportunity to do anything else in PV. It's a four-hour hands-on experience where visitors learn about making clay pottery and other craft arts from skilled local artisans. As such, you would really have to be into this kind of thing to partake. *The program is given daily at 10 am; $$.* The Tequila sojourn involves an actual production plant and the usual tour combined with a museum-like exhibit that relates tequila to a broader cultural and economic context. It's fairly interesting. Hours vary but should be available whenever your cruise ship is in town. The trip is also available through excursions from most ships. *$$.*

When it comes to longer excursions, PV isn't lacking. They range from coastal drives to trips into the countryside and beautiful mountains. Some are easy and some are only for the truly adventurous. Always popular is a tour that gives participants the chance to **swim with dolphins**. The more adventurous and recreation-oriented tours, especially those centered around the nearby community of Mismaloya, are more appropriately addressed under the heading of *Sports & Recreation*.

Shopping

If there is a shopping capital of the Mexican Riviera, Puerto Vallarta may well be it. From the visitor's standpoint it offers a great deal of variety in a compact area so you won't tire yourself out just getting from place to place. However, let it be said at the outset that you generally won't find any great bargains. There are goods from all over Mexico, but they are often less costly in other places, especially if you buy them in the part of the country where they were produced. Of course, that isn't possible on a week-long Mexican Riviera cruise so, if you're willing to spend the money, you'll probably be able to find it here. Popular items include ceramics, clothing, glassware, jewelry (especially silver), leather goods and pottery. There's a wide selection of handicrafts and the noted work of the Nayarit and Michacán Indians (the latter from Central America) is especially prized.

Shopping is concentrated in El Centro along the waterfront **Paseo Díaz Ordáz** and in the Municipal Market (**Mercado**) at the **Avenida Insurgentes Bridge** on the north side of the river. The malecón is home to many chic boutiques as well as art galleries. Among the latter are the **Galería Uno** (all fine arts); the **Galería Pacífico** (Mexican artists); **Galería Manuel Lepe** (painting); and **Galería de Ollas** (pottery). For hand-blown glass, try **La Rosa de Cristal**, while native baskets, wood carvings and other handicrafts are in evidence at the **Alfarería Tlaquepaque**. All of these establishments usually have fixed prices, but you can bargain at the *mercado*.

The downtown area also has one art form that is unique to the Puerto Vallarta area. The Huichol are an Amerindian tribe said to be directly descended from the Aztecs. They live mainly in the mountains near Puerto Vallarta. You will find Huichol peddling their wares along the malecón. If you feel more comfortable purchasing from a regular retail establishment, try the **Huichol Collection**, also on the malecón just a few steps from the main plaza.

There's no lack of shopping in the **Hotel Zone** and at **Marina Vallarta**. The shops here are almost all upscale with the exception of the flea market next to the cruise ship terminal. Wandering around in the resort atmosphere of Marina Vallarta is a good way to spend a few hours if you like to mix a pleasant walk with your shopping. Unless you spend the day in the Marina area it is unlikely that it will be convenient to return to your ship when lunch time comes around. No need to worry. PV has lots of great places to eat and fresh seafood is a specialty. However, it seems that many American visitors prefer the funky atmosphere offered at a lot of touristy restaurants to fine dining, especially for lunch. If that's the case with you then one of the popular chains such as **Carlos O'Brian's** or **Señor Frog's** will be to your liking. There's plenty of drinking and even decent Mexican-American food. These places can be found in many of the Mexican Riviera resort ports but seem to be especially numerous in Puerto Vallarta, with Sr. Frog's being the most common. Both have branches in El Centro. Along with eating they offer large gift shops where you can purchase plenty of tacky souvenirs.

Sports & Recreation

With about 27 miles of beautiful beaches, Puerto Vallarta should have one just right for you. If you plan to spend most of your day on the beach than it makes sense to go to a beach that is convenient to Marina Vallarta. Luckily, some of the best beaches fall into this category. **Playa las Glorias** and **Playa de Oro** are two of the best. **Playa Camarones** is about half-way between Marina Vallarta and downtown. Beaches near El Centro aren't as good for swimming because the water isn't as clean as at the northern beaches. However, they're great for sunning. In this group are **Playa Olas Altas** and **Playa los Muertos**. The latter is near the pier and El Púlpito. Once you get south of the city then the water is again clean enough for swimming. **Playa Gamelas**, **Playa Garza Blanca** and **Playa Mismaloya** fall into this group. Mismaloya is in a sheltered cove and may be the best, although it is the farthest of the three. However, Mismaloya has other charms as you'll read about in a moment.

In addition to swimming there's a great variety of other recreational opportunities. **Sportfishing**, of course, is a staple and there are charters at the north end of the malecón, at Marina Vallarta and through your excursion office. **Boating** is also popular and the departure venues are much the same as for fishing trips. **Diving** and snorkeling are better in Puerto Vallarta than many other Mexican Riviera ports. **Snorkeling** is especially good in the vicinity of Mismaloya. **Surfing** is best off **Punta Mita**. Then, of course, you can also choose from **parasailing**, **kayaking** and all the other known methods of enjoying yourself on the water.

Mismaloya, about seven miles south of the city, is where *Night of the Iguana* was filmed and since that time it has become almost a pilgrimage site. Besides the beautiful aforementioned beach, there is much more recreational activity in this area, which is often known as **El Edén**. Several miles inland (you can get here either by taxi or shore excursion) is **Chico's Paradise**. This is a great soft adventure. You'll take a hike through the jungle and on the way back you'll have to take your shoes off so you can cross a stream. Having worked up an appetite you'll be served an authentic Mexican lunch at the restaurant, which consists of *palapa* huts. Then you can swim by a lovely waterfall before heading back to town.

Some other popular active shore excursions offered by all of the lines calling on Puerto Vallarta include **horseback riding** in the Sierra Madres, **mountain** and **off-road biking**, **scuba diving**, **ecological discovery tours** and various **hiking** trips. One of the most unusual is an adventure through the jungle canopy. This doesn't use an aerial tram as in some places. Rather, you'll be taught how to move your body over a guide rope and how to rappel back down to the ground. This, and many other excursions, do require a degree of physical fitness in addition to a spirit of adventure. Know your own limits and feel free to ask questions of the shore excursion office to determine if it's right for you. This, of course, applies to similar excursions in *all* of the ports.

Finally, if **golf** is your bag, PV is known for having some of the best links in Mexico. Many of the most popular courses have restricted playing privileges so it is best to use your ship's excursion office as a means of gaining access. If you want to play on your own, then a wise choice is the 18-hole **Marina Vallarta Golf Club**. It's just a short distance from the cruise ship terminal and the taxi fare won't put a big dent in your budget.

Santa Rosalía
(Baja)

*B*y Mexican standards Santa Rosalía is a young community. Its origins go back to the 1880s when a French mining company began operations. Although the copper mine and smelting operations shut down in the 1950s, the mining legacy is evident almost everywhere, including the rather unattractive copper smelter on the edge of town that sits eerily quiet. Because it was the French who built the town from scratch you will not see much evidence of Spanish colonial architecture in Santa Rosalía. What is all around you are buildings (especially private homes) constructed of wood in French colonial style. Such a colorful array of clapboard houses in a dazzling variety of pastel shades is seldom seen anywhere in Latin America. The entire town has been declared a national historic landmark by the Mexican government.

Arrival

Despite the fact that Santa Rosalía is a small town (population 15,000), it is a significant port and its harbor can handle large ships. A new facility was recently completed that can accommodate cruise ships, thereby eliminating the need for tendering that existed just a few years ago. Once on the dock you're only a short distance from the historic part of town.

Tourism Information Office

There is no official tourism office. Information in verbal form as well as maps and a few brochures can usually be obtained at the cruise ship dock.

Getting Around

Because it is a small town, Santa Rosalía is best explored **on foot**. There is no public transportation in the form of buses, although you can get a **taxi**. However, this shouldn't be necessary unless you have difficulty walking. All of the points of interest outside of town are difficult to reach except by guided tour (and even then some require effort). There are no car rentals readily available so plan on a self-guided walking tour of the town and a guided tour of anything away from town.

The One-Day Sightseeing Tour

As with some of the other small ports of call in Baja, it will not require more than a couple of hours to see the sights in town. So you should have more than enough time to take an excursion, especially since Santa Rosalía has little to offer in the way of recreational facilities compared to other Baja ports. Start your little tour at the city's primary square, **Plaza Benito Juárez**. On one side of the square is the city hall, a classic example of the best in French colonial architecture. Nearby at Avenida Obregón and Calle 1 is the **Iglesia Santa Barbara**, one of the more unusual churches in Mexico. Designed by Alexandre Gustav Eifel (the same Eifel of Eifel Tower fame), the church is built entirely of iron. It was designed in 1884 and built for the 1898 Paris World's Fair. Disassembled afterwards, it was shipped to Santa Rosalía in 1897 and has been a noted landmark ever since. Although the iron exterior has a cold or even somber appearance, the interior is graced by beautiful stained glass.

Mining isn't the only thing Santa Rosalía is known for. Curiously, it is home to some of Mexico's finest bakery products – especially bread. So, after visiting the Iglesia, continue on Avenida Obregón to Calle 4 and the **El Bolero Bakery**. Some people say their bread alone is worth the trip to Santa Rosalía. That's a bit too strong, but there is no denying that it is sooo good!

The **Museo Histórico Minero** (sometimes known as the Biblioteca Mahatma Gandhi), at Calle Playa and Avenida Constitución, has some mildly interesting exhibits related to the town's former mining operations. *Open daily except Sunday from 8:30 am until 2 pm ($).*

There are three choices for excursions (two are easy and one requires a spirit of adventure and no physical disabilities). They can last anywhere from a half-day to a full day. Depending upon how long you have in port you might even be able to take both of the first two.

A cruise line shore excursion to the **Mulega Mission** lasts about three hours. You will travel by bus for 40 miles south of Santa Rosalía to the pretty town of Mulega, passing through the Giganta Mountains en route. The panoramic drive itself might be the highlight, but the oasis-like setting of the mission is also of great interest. A second excursion lasts six hours and goes to the resort of **Punto Chivato**. Although the scenery on the 1½-hour drive (each way) ranges from pleasant to beautiful, the time spent at the resort's pool and other recreational areas hardly seems worth the trip, especially since most of the facilities at Punto Chivato are available onboard your ship. The final possibility is the most interesting for those that can handle it. Out in the mountains are the **Caves of San Borjita**, which contains paintings by indigenous Indians. It is believed that these are the oldest such cave paintings in all of Baja. The caves and the scenery getting there are excellent, but the method of getting there is what makes this trip special – you have to go via pack mule! It's a bouncy and uncomfortable ride, with quite a lot of strenuous walking and climbing, but if you are up to the challenge you will be rewarded with a day to remember. You can arrange this trip on your own by hiring a guide in town. Go to the city hall and they will put you in touch with a reputable guide.

Shopping

Santa Rosalía has a lot of shopping, but little is authentic Mexican. The reason for all the shops is that the town is the primary commercial port of entry for manufactured goods coming into Baja. Among the most readily found items are **electronics** and **apparel**. Both can be had at decent prices. The majority of stores are concentrated around the harbor, with a secondary batch scattered in the neighborhood surrounding the town square.

Sports & Recreation

Without a doubt Santa Rosalía is at the very bottom of the list of Mexican ports when it comes to sports and recreation. You simply do not come here for those kinds of activities. There aren't any good beaches in the vicinity (the nearest one is an hour's drive to the north) and even the fishing isn't that terrific. For any sort of comprehensive recreational activities you have to take the aforementioned excursion to Punto Chivato.

Other Ports

*I*t was previously noted that there are many reposition-ing and other cruises with itineraries through the Panama Canal that also include some ports in Baja and along the Mexican Riviera. Some more detail will be provided on the one additional Mexican port that these cruises might call on. For the others only a brief description will be given because these itineraries are beyond the scope of this book.

Mexico

Bahías de Huatulco: Selected in 1988 by FONATUR as one of its resort development projects, the nine Bays of Huatulco (pronounced wah-TOOL-co) stretch along 22 miles of wild, twisting and still mostly pristine beaches – one of the more beautifully rugged portions of Mexico's long Pacific coast. Development of previously untouched areas is always a two-edged sword. From an economic standpoint it is much needed in Huatulco because this has been one of Mexico's most impoverished areas, in-habited largely by Amerindians. The entire area covers some 52,000 acres, but a large portion has already been set aside as an ecological preserve where no develop-ment will take place. Although some luxury hotels have been built, there is yet to be a high level of development and the largely unspoiled natural beauty of the area is a prime attraction, along with watersports. The beaches – of which there are at least three dozen – are backed by mountains and dense jungle. There are three major areas of development, each named for one of the bigger towns. These are **Santa Cruz**, the original settlement in the area; **Crucecita**, a modern planned community built in traditional Mexican style; and **Tangolunda**, the most developed of the resort areas on a bay of the same name.

Cruise ships dock in the harbor at Santa Cruz where, at least for a few years, you'll have to tender in. Getting around on shore is either by guided excursion or local tour, by minibus between towns or by taxi. There is little in the way of traditional sightseeing, but several offshore islands have such features as blowholes and jagged boulders popping out of the water. The islands are filled with wildlife, especially birds. But most people who come to Huatulco do so to relax on the beach or take part in recreational ecotourism. There is **river rafting** and **kayaking** into the jungles or seeing the jungle via trails or **four-wheel-drive** vehicles. On the water you can go **snorkeling**, **diving** or **sailing**. Boat rides on the bay that explore various hidden coves are a most popular diversion. There are also more traditional recreational pursuits, such as **golf** and **tennis**.

Topolobampo: This picturesque small town on the mainland coast side of the Sea of Cortes is now visited by a select few itineraries of Holland America. While the town itself doesn't have all that much to offer (there's whale-watching and lots of water-based recreation, just as in nearby ports both on the mainland and on the Baja Peninsula), a single shore excursion possibility makes any trip to Topolobampo worth strong consideration. The town is only a few miles from Los Mochis, the gateway for the exciting ride on the **Chichuaha-al-Pacifico Railway** that makes its way to the fabulous **Copper Canyon**, truly one of the world's most beautiful places. The train ride is thrilling and the construction of the line, with its numerous bridges and tunnels, is an engineering marvel. Port calls at Topolobampo range up to 16 hours because that is about how long the excursion takes. It's worth the time and the high cost. It still comes out as one of the least expensive ways you could ever get to the remote Copper Canyon.

Costa Rica

Puntarenas/Puerto Caldera: These two can be considered as the same port from a practical standpoint. Puerto Caldera is a specially-built facility for cruise ships visiting Costa Rica's Pacific coast. It is a few miles south of the city of Puntarenas. There is nothing to see in Puerto Caldera, although an excellent shopping arcade is in the cruise terminal. Most cruise ships, especially the larger ones, will dock at Puerto Caldera, although some go directly to Puntarenas. Within the city there is little to see, except for a good marine park with an aquarium. The real attraction for Puntarenas visitors is the opportunity to take one of several outstanding shore excursions. Almost any excursion will involve a significant amount of travel time via motorcoach.

The first of the two most popular all-day trips is highlighted by a visit to the fabulous **Rain Forest Aerial Tramway**. On a private reserve adjacent to a national park, the tramway allows you to do something that few people can – explore the biological ecosystem of a forest canopy. Open-air cars suspended from a cable carry small groups on a 90-minute journey that begins near the top of the canopy. From this vantage point you'll be able to see countless types of birds and flora. The return portion of the trip takes you above the canopy for a bird's-eye view of the rain forest. There is no easier way to explore the rain forest than this. This excursion typically includes some other stops for shopping or quick views of some of Costa Rica's incredible volcanic mountain peaks.

The second trip takes you to the capital of **San Jose**. The city is the cultural capital of the country and has several fine museums, including the outstanding **National Museum** with its exhibits of pre-Colombian native art. Also of interest are the **Opera House, National Library, National Archives**, a **cathedral** dating from the 18th century and the **National Theater**. The trip also stops at a small village (usually the quaint **Moravia**) for shopping.

The other available excursions are generally recreational, although you may be able to find one that devotes most of its time to one or more of Costa Rica's volcanic national parks.

Guatemala

Puerto Quetzal: This is one port that you generally won't see on the itineraries of the mass market lines. At the current time only some of the more upscale lines with smaller ships are calling on Puerto Quetzal and, even then, infrequently enough so that it's hard to find an itinerary with this port of call. As in Costa Rica, the overwhelming majority of visitors will find it much more convenient to go the shore excursion route. The most popular sightseeing activity is a day trip to the capital of **Guatemala City**, which has a very scenic mountain valley location and several interesting historic attractions. Otherwise the shore excursions will run the gamut of the usual sports and recreation found in tropical places – heavy on water-related activities.

Panama

Transiting the Panama Canal: For many people the highlight of their cruise may not be the ports of call, but the fascinating passage through the Panama Canal itself. It doesn't matter if you're on a fast ship or a slow one since the time for passage is the same either way – about 10 hours. That gives you lots of time to watch the sights as the ship slowly glides past them and anytime you get hungry or bored (unlikely) you can run inside for something to eat or even take a dip in the pool.

Talk of constructing in a canal across the isthmus of Panama began in the early 16th century. There were stops and starts, but in the 19th century several companies were organized to build a canal. They all went bankrupt. The last, a French concern, sold its assets to the United States. A deal with the newly independent Panamanian government in 1903 gave a strip of land to the US. Construction on the canal took from 1906 through 1914 and it was (and remains) one of the great engineering marvels of the world. The Panama Canal Zone was given back to Panama in 1979 and control of the canal itself was turned over to the Panamanians in 2000.

The canal is 40 miles long with an additional combined nine miles of dredged canal at the two ends. The minimum width is 300 feet. The Atlantic (or Caribbean) side is actually north of the Pacific entrance so, contrary to popular belief, you aren't traveling from east-to-west while in the canal. Traveling from the Atlantic to the Pacific this is what you'll encounter: After passing through a seven-mile stretch of canal the ship will reach the **Gatun Locks**, a series of three locks that lift the ship 85 feet. All locks at Gatun and throughout the canal are double locks – that is one ship will be raised at the same time that another vessel is being lowered. Each lock is 1,000 feet long and 110 feet wide. Not all of the mega-liners cruising the seas today will fit in the locks and that restricts which ships can be utilized on Panama Canal itineraries.

At the end of the Gatun Locks is **Gatun Lake**, the dammed waters of the Chagres River. The **Gaillard Cut** follows, bringing vessels to the 31-foot elevation change in the **Pedro Miguel Lock**. After passing through **Miraflores Lake**, the final locks – the double **Miraflores Locks** – bring ships 55 feet down to the level of the Pacific Ocean. In addition to watching the works of the locks, staying out on deck during most of the journey will bring splendid views of the lakes and the jungle-like terrain of Panama, with an impressive mountainous background from one end of the canal to another.

The majority of cruise ships that transit the Panama Canal do not have any shore time in Panama as part of their itineraries. A few do stop for anywhere from a couple of hours to nearly a full day in the port city of Colón on the Atlantic side of the canal. No one comes to visit Colón itself, which is a drab and crime-ridden city, but interesting shore excursions let passengers explore other aspects of the canal and surrounding areas. However, most visits to Colón are done on southern Caribbean cruises that visit this port for a full day rather than traversing the canal itself so you may not easily find a trans-Canal itinerary with this feature.

Index

Index

sports & recreation, 233-234; time zone, 145; tourism information, 231
Los Angeles: accommodations on land, 88; air arrangements, 117; as port of embarkation, 153-156
Los Cabos, 230
Los Mochis, 270
Low season, 92
Luggage, 129, 133, 148

Malecón: defined, 178-179; in La Paz, 225-226; in Loreto, 232; in Mazatlán, 248; in Puerto Vallarta, 258-259, 262
Manzanillo: about, 234-235; arrival, 235; getting around, 237; itineraries including, 76; map of, 236; one-day sightseeing tour, 237-240; sports & recreation, 241-243; time zone, 145
Maximillian, Emperor, 10
Maya people, 9
Mazatlán: about, 243-245; arrival, 245; getting around, 245-246; map of, 244; one-day sightseeing tour, 246-252; shopping, 252-253; sports & recreation, 253-254; time zone, 145; tourism information, 245
Meclazine, 148
Medications, 110, 148
Mercury (Celebrity), 30-31
Mestizos, 12-14
Mexican Riviera: Acapulco, 163-179; geography, 7-8; itineraries, 75-76; Ixtapa & Zihuatanejo, 213-222; Manzanillo, 234-243; Mazatlán, 243-254; Puerto Vallarta, 254-265
Mexican Tourist Board, 160
Mexican War (1846-1848), 10
Mexico: crime in, 130-132; facts about, 3-4; gambling in, 203; health matters and, 121-122; history, 9-12; language of, 4, 13, 151; peoples of, 12; permanent residents of, 14; ports of embarkation, 158-159; religion of, 13; social classes of, 13-14
Mexico City, 117, 131-132
Midnight buffet, 103
Mirador, 217
Mismaloya, 264
Monarch of the Seas (Royal Caribbean), 57, 62-63
Money matters: ATM cards, 115-116; credit cards, 115, 143; crime and safety, 115, 126, 131; foreign currency exchange, 115; guidelines, 114-116; onboard expenses, 93-94
Monterey, 197-198
Montezuma's Revenge, 121
Moravia, 272
Mountain time zone, 145
Mt. Ada (Catalina Island), 194-195
Mulega, 267
Museums: in Acapulco, 169-170; on Catalina Island, 193; in Costa Rica, 272;

in Ensenada, 203-206; in Ixtapa & Zihuatanejo, 218; in La Paz, 226; in Manzanillo, 238, 240; in Mazatlán, 248; in Puerto Vallarta, 260; in San Diego, 157; in San Francisco, 158; in Santa Rosalía, 267

National Action Party (PAN), 11
National Association of Cruise Oriented Agencies (NACOA), 95
Nautical mile, 85
NCL America, 42-43
Night of the Iguana (film), 260, 264
Norwalk virus, 123-124
Norwegian Cruise Line: costs, 91; Norwegian Star, 43-45; Norwegian Sun, 45-46; Norwegian Wind, 46-47; overview, 40-43, 70
Norwegian Star (NCL), 43-45
Norwegian Sun (NCL), 45-46
Norwegian Wind (NCL), 46-47

Oceania Cruises, 67-68
Onboard considerations: health matters, 121, 123-124; onboard expenses, 93-94
One-day sightseeing tours: in Acapulco, 168-172; in Cabo San Lucas, 183-185; on Catalina Island, 191-195; in Ensenada, 202-209; in Ixtapa & Zihuatanejo, 217-219; in La Paz, 225-227; in Loreto, 232-233; in Manzanillo, 237-240; in Mazatlán, 246-252; in Puerto Vallarta, 257-261; in Santa Rosalía, 266-268
Oosterdam (Holland America), 34-37
Outside rooms, 134-135
Oxygen, 104-105

Pacific storms, 90
Pacific time zone, 145
Package deals, 96
Packing, 109-110
Panama Canal: Celebrity Cruises, 29; cruise lines, 17; Holland America Line, 37, 39; Norwegian Cruise Line, 45-46; Princess Cruises, 49; Royal Caribbean International, 57-58; transiting, 273-274
Paradise (Carnival), 25-26
Parasailing in Puerto Vallarta, 264
Partying. See Entertainment; Watering holes
Passenger information form, 129
Passports, 124-127, 132
Payments, 127-129
People & culture, 12-14
Personal Choice cruising (Princess), 48
Personal expenditures, 94
Peso, 115
Phone cards, 143-144
Photo identification, 125
Plants, 5, 122, 127